Phenomenology of Human Understanding

Brian Cronin

PICKWICK *Publications* · Eugene, Oregon

PHENOMENOLOGY OF HUMAN UNDERSTANDING

Pickwick Publications
An Imprint of Wipf and Stock Publishers
199 W. 8th Ave., Suite 3
Eugene, OR 97401

www.wipfandstock.com

PAPERBACK ISBN: 978-1-4982-9282-5
HARDCOVER ISBN: 978-1-4982-9284-9
EBOOK ISBN: 978-1-4982-9283-2

Cataloguing-in-Publication data:

Names: Cronin, Brian.

Title: Phenomenology of human understanding / Brian Cronin.

Description: Eugene, OR: Pickwick Publications, 2017 | Includes bibliographical references and index.

Identifiers: ISBN 978-1-4982-9282-5 (paperback) | ISBN 978-1-4982-9284-9 (hardcover) | ISBN 978-1-4982-9283-2 (ebook)

Subjects: LCSH: Phenomenology | Knowledge, Theory of.

Classification: LCC BD161 C69 2017 (print) | LCC BD161 C69 2017 (ebook)

Manufactured in the U.S.A.   MAY 4, 2017

Contents

Preface

In the *Confessions,* Augustine remarks about how much more interesting it is to explore the hidden reaches of the memory than it is to travel abroad to see the wonders of the world. He describes how we can search the vast caverns of memory and retrieve half hidden images of long ago. He considers how some images are retrieved easily and others have to be dragged into the light of day, and how some bring happiness and laughter, while others bring sadness or fear or dread. He notes how entertaining these memories can be. He wonders how these memories are retrieved, how they are preserved, and how they can change over time.

His focus was on memory; my focus is on the mind. How much more interesting again is it to explore the ideas of the mind than the images of the memory! In the mind we find a vast storehouse of ideas, principles, and laws operating beneath the surface, and we did not even know they were there. We find a variety of activities like thinking, criticizing, classifying, comparing and contrasting, dividing and defining. They appear and disappear, overlap, jump ahead, and crash into one another in a never ending stream of thoughts and possibilities. We find feelings of encouragement and discouragement, joy and frustration, determination and surrender, excitement and boredom. How do we sort out this buzzing, chaotic confusion of thoughts and feelings? Where did they all come from? How are they remembered? Where are they leading us to? We can ask so many questions with so many possible answers. What unlimited power we have to ask any question under the sun; how fragile are our tentative answers leading to yet more questions. In our mind we can visit Mars, travel at the speed of light, understand black holes, go back in time to the beginning of the universe—or go forward in time to the big crunch. How much more interesting are these explorations of the mind compared to visiting the Grand Canyon or seeing the Taj Mahal.

This book is an exploration of the human mind as it attempts to sort out the buzzing confusion of our mental activities to which we normally pay such little attention. The human mind is not a chaos of competing forces but a structured sequence of mental activities heading in the direction of truth and value. I am proposing this text as a map to guide the explorer through the labyrinth of possibilities. A map or GPS is very helpful if one is on a journey through unknown territory. It will help one to proceed confidently, knowing he or she is going in the right direction. The map provides warnings of sudden bends, hills, or obstacles; it will identify the hills on the right, the river on the left, and the village just passed through and the town ahead. Journeying into the human mind can be a difficult and dangerous project, especially without a map. Many have gotten lost; many have misinterpreted what they have seen. Many have seen but have neither recognized nor named what was right there in front of them; some returned more confused than ever before.

My aim in this text is to provide a detailed map of the human mind as oriented to truth and value. It begins with asking a question, leading to a sequence of activities on the way to a correct answer. Many things can be noted to the left and the right in that sequence. To use a GPS effectively usually takes some instruction and practice. I propose a special method to explore the human mind, which does require both a little explanation and lots of practice.

I acknowledge the help given to me on my own intellectual journey. This text is the product of a lifetime of thinking, teaching, writing, and reflecting. Dedicated professors introduced me to neo-Scholasticism in the 1960s, but by sheer luck our library was restocked and copies of Lonergan's *Insight* were included. He was my map for the rest of the journey. I have spent most of my life teaching philosophy in Africa, learning from my students. and developing the philosophy and pedagogy presented in this text. I owe a great debt of gratitude to the professors of Boston College where I defended my PhD and enjoyed five postdoctoral fellowships. I should acknowledge the late Father Joseph Flanagan SJ, who was chairman of the department of philosophy and sponsor of the fellowship program who became a mentor to me and many others. I continue teaching in Duquesne University and thank our dean, Jim Swindal, for time off to finish this project and our head of department, Ronald Polansky, for a manageable teaching load and encouragement to allow this work to come to completion. Finally, my thanks to Brock Bahler who copyedited the text in great detail and helped with many suggestions.

Introduction

Turn to the Subject

P hilosophy has always shown an interest not only in the objective world in which we live but also in the subject who is doing the inspecting. The Ancient Greeks referred to the Delphic Oracle, which advised each wise person "to know thyself." In the *Apology*, Plato, through the mouth of Socrates, espouses this aphorism as well as the famous admonition, "The unexamined life is not worth living." Thus, Socrates looked into himself and saw his own ignorance, but he also saw the struggle between vice and virtue, between sense and intelligence, and between the one and the many.

Augustine was wonderfully articulate in describing his own searching mind in his *Confessions*: his struggle with Manichean materialism and the existence of God; his struggle with sin, guilt, and his conversion to Christianity; and his struggle with the imagination and understanding. He was able to describe how his memory was a storehouse of images and ideas. His inner explorations helped him to understand how through illumination, one arrives at truth, and by analogy with the processes of the human mind, one can arrive at some understanding of the procession of the Word and the Trinity itself.

Jumping to the modern period, Descartes has been credited with a decisive "turn to the subject" in establishing the starting point of philosophy in the cryptic, "I think, therefore I am." Surely, here we find an indubitable foundation for a philosophy independent of religion, church, authority, or tradition. He turned philosophy in the direction of the human mind and its power and limits in knowing reality, and that has been the focus of much of philosophy ever since. The classical empiricists described in detail the activity of thinking, the conscious mind at work, the role of images and ideas, simple and complex ideas, laws of association, habits of the mind, and the limits of knowledge. Kant had a more complex theory of the human mind imposing a priori ideas on reality in the spheres of sensibility, understanding, and reason. He faced head-on the critical problem of whether we can know objective reality. Can we escape from subjectivity to objectivity? What are the a priori conditions for the possibility of human knowing? Existentialists were more interested in the subjects' feelings, in choice, in the drama and tragedy of human life, in angst, in boredom, in absurdity, and in meaninglessness. Phenomenology was motivated by a desire to return "to the things themselves" as Husserl famously put it, to start without presuppositions, to describe precisely and objectively the phenomena, to imagine variations, and to intuit essences. In contemporary times, postmodern philosophers espouse an "incredulity" regarding any grand projects or "metanarratives" as Lyotard famously called them. Content with the diversity of specific particular entities, they are suspicious of any truth claims whatever, and sensitive to hidden motivations (especially the lust for power).

How can we describe the spirit of our age? We are at home with subjectivity but with a wide variety of views about the ability of the subject to know. We have a multitude of theories about human knowing. We are familiar with the notions of consciousness, interiority, intentionality, interpretation, perception, and hidden motivations. The hermeneutics of suspicion usually trumps the hermeneutic of recovery. We revel in diversity. Fascinated by the particular, we are not interested in the abstract. We prioritize a spirit of universal tolerance. We also value self-fulfillment, self-transcendence, self-affirmation, and self-discovery. We are divided into contrary positions and incommensurable theories about human knowing. After two and a half millennia of the attention to the subject, we are still conflicted about how and what that subject can know about objective reality. Our turn to the subject is incomplete, truncated, conflicted, and fraught with misunderstanding. The aim in this text is to complete this turn to the subject and to move from authentic subjectivity to genuine objectivity.

Completing the Turn to the Subject

Subjectivity and objectivity are often seen as polar opposites. On the one hand, subjectivity is to be eliminated because it represents bias, personal opinions, twisted feelings, and ideology. On the other hand, objectivity is sought after because it represents truth, balance, solidity, and something we can all agree upon. I seek to use these terms in quite a different way in which they are viewed as reciprocal or complementary notions. There are good and bad elements in both subjectivity and objectivity. For example, subjectivity depicts the subject as conscious, as feeling, as desiring, as thinking, as knowing, as believing, as criticizing, as valuing, as aspiring to higher things, as deciding, as loving, and perhaps more. At the same time, subjectivity implies bias, prejudice, ignorance, lust for power, lies, fraud, crooked arguments, unconscious motivations, hidden agendas, laziness, and much more. There is a similar duality in the term "objectivity."

My approach, then, is to include the totality of the elements of subjectivity and to discriminate between the beneficial and the harmful elements. I will describe the activities that promote full human understanding and the elements that tend to help or hinder that noble endeavor. A phenomenology of human understanding means, first of all, a full, detailed, precise, verifiable, and intelligent description of the process of human understanding, beginning with concrete examples and then moving on to an analysis and an identification of the common structure of all acts of human understanding.

By all means, we can learn about human understanding from epistemologists of the past and present: from cognitive psychologists, or from biographies and autobiographies of great scientists and philosophers that reveal how they made their discoveries. But in the end, the only way we know about human knowing is by introspection: by evaluating our own experience, by becoming aware of the processes of understanding as they unfold in our own minds. Studying frogs requires hands-on experience with frogs. Similarly, a study of human understanding begins with assembling individual examples of understanding. Unfortunately, I do not have access to the workings of the minds of other people, but I do have access to my own mind where the details, characteristics, and forces producing understanding can be identified. Contrary to common opinion, such introspection is not private and unverifiable, but rather, can and should be communicable and verifiable. Thus, I am proposing a journey of self-discovery, exploring and identifying the capacities of the human mind.

In the end, I suggest that this is the way to genuine objectivity. It does not lock us into subjectivity but reveals precisely the way to judgments of truth, and hence, the path to an objective, real world. The end result is a platform from which to expand into metaphysics, ethics, and a philosophy of God, and to develop understanding in common sense, in the sciences and practical applications on a firm foundation.

Advantages and Contributions of this Approach

The term "understanding" can be used in many senses with a variety of nuances. Studies of these specialized meanings in particular contexts and in specific detail can be very valuable. However, this text focuses on the core philosophical meaning of understanding, from the broadest and deepest point of view, to reveal its structure and role in knowing. Here I will outline some of the advantages of such a general approach.

1. *Understanding "Understanding."* In order to teach a course, it is not enough for the educator to personally understand the material; the educator must also comprehend how to communicate the material to others. To do that it helps to understand "understanding." We all have little eureka moments when we move from being puzzled to seeing the solution. We know vaguely what understanding is, but we need to identify the details, conditions, characteristics, and implications of this most basic act of human intelligence. My approach will identify individual acts of human understanding and analyze the structure that is common to all acts of human understanding. Then, I will differentiate types of acts of understanding as I identify direct insights, inverse insights, higher viewpoints, reflective, and deliberative insights. My goal is to move from a vague notion of understanding to a precise and explicit identification of its characteristics and types.

2. *Method.* As a result of grasping the process of understanding, I will be able to suggest an appropriate method and criterion for coming to correct conclusions in all areas of the search for truth. Understanding is central to common sense, science, philosophy, and technology. Is there any discipline in kindergarten, grade school, high school, or the university that does not involve understanding? If I can show precisely what understanding is, surely I can make a contribution to progress in all of these disciplines and all other areas of specialization. Understanding and the method of understanding underpins everything.

3. *Personal Foundations.* I propose this as a journey of self-discovery, an invitation to take possession of one's own mind, and to recognize the power and limits of the mind. Through this journey, I believe we can learn to understand ourselves. The evidence for all that is asserted in this text is our own minds and our experiences of understanding or misunderstanding. My position is based on this personal self-appropriation of how we actually understand and know. I do not propose this as an exercise in abstract analysis and synthesis, or in logic, scholarship, or the history of philosophy. Nor does this account of human understanding rely on political correctness, the latest ideas from French intellectuals, the authority of a tradition, or from admittedly great minds like Kant or Lonergan. Because we can understand for ourselves the source and basis for all human knowing, we have a standpoint from which we can criticize and evaluate every other position put before us. Hence, the aim of this book is to help readers to be in a position to confront many skeptical trends in contemporary culture and sort out the

authentic from the inauthentic. Most of these contemporary trends arise from a misunderstanding of the process of human knowing. If we acquire a personal grasp of understanding and its proper unfolding, we will also be in a position to identify the source of such misunderstanding.

4. *Diversity and Unity*. Nowadays, it is common to stress the diversity of mentalities, cultures, and philosophies. That is fine. In many cases diversity is an enrichment. But underlying such diversity lies the other side of the coin: what we have in common in the basic human act of understanding. Human understanding has a common structure and process. From Socrates to Sartre, from America to Japan, from young to old, and from male to female understanding involves a question, attending to data, the emergence of an idea, and expressing that idea. It involves a critique of the proposition or hypothesis and a conclusion that is affirmed based on evidence and arguments. In many cases of understanding, there is often a further question of value that arises and is answered after deliberation in a judgment of value. This is the common substructure of what it is to be an intelligent human person. Diversity does not mean irreducible chaos. There is diversity, but underlying all the diversity of human cultures lies a common factor of human understanding, from which all of these various positions have emerged.

5. *Common Source*. Understanding is such a primordial human activity that it is relevant to all things human. It is the source of language, culture, social institutions, common sense, science, philosophy, history, progress, economics, and so on. In addition to understanding operating in the spheres of truth and value, forms of intelligence are in operation in sports, art, music, poetry, conversation, dialogue, comedy, communication, literature, prayer and worship, and in so many other daily activities. It is imperative to understand what this basis is.

6. *Higher Viewpoint*. Every individual act of understanding unifies and organizes that which is understood. For example, if a person is reading a detective story, upon discovering the true perpetrator near the end of the book, every clue and red herring in the story falls into place. The whole story becomes clear—the distractions, the false alibis, and the reason for everything. If the reader does not understand the plot, the story will be a very confused tale of murder and mayhem; with understanding, however, it all falls into place. Or once an individual understands that chemical elements are distinguished from one another by their atomic weight, the person can now comprehend the unfolding of the periodic table and where every element in the universe fits into that table and why. Or if one is watching a game of football and does not understand the rules, then it will all seem to be a pointless exercise. But once the spectator understands the rules, it can become meaningful, dramatic, and even exciting and sophisticated.

Likewise, if we understand "understanding," then we have something that unifies and organizes the whole process of all human knowing. We can then unify and organize all that is to be known. We can attain a kind of universal viewpoint that sees from one perspective how all of the parts are related in the one whole of human life in an evolving world.

7. *Philosophy.* This text is intended to be a contribution to philosophy, not psychology. Empirical science is a much envied discipline because it seems to have found a method that produces cumulative and progressive results. There is more or less unanimity among scientists worldwide about their methods, their terminology, what they have achieved, and what remains to be discovered. It keeps advancing not just in theory but in the technology made possible by scientific discoveries. Scientists from all countries of the world can collaborate on projects like the International Space Station or the Large Hadron Collider. Philosophy, by contrast, does not seem to have a commonly accepted method. It does not have a commonly accepted terminology. It is characterized by verbal disputes, mutual incomprehension, conflicts, and spirited disagreements. It is very hard for philosophers to collaborate on any project. By chapter 9, I will have presented a common base for all philosophies and whether they represent a deeper understanding or a misguided misunderstanding.

8. *Verifiability.* This text promises to deliver a method for philosophy that should yield cumulative and progressive results. Scientists discovered a method of formulating theories that could be verified by reference to empirical data. Philosophers must use the same method, but instead of applying it to the data of the senses, they must apply it to the data of consciousness. Epistemologists must turn to the introspective data on the experience of asking questions, thinking, conceiving, understanding, formulating, criticizing, judging, and evaluating. They must verify their theories with reference to what actually happens when we understand and know. If epistemology can be verifiable, a metaphysics that flows from it will also be verifiable. Philosophy is subject to a criterion of verification just as the empirical sciences. What this text is promising is a verifiable epistemology followed by a critical philosophy that yields cumulative and progressive results!

Sources

The reader is entitled to ask from what background or tradition this text emerges. Where do these extraordinary claims come from? The context is really two-fold: Bernard Lonergan and the phenomenological tradition. Bernard Lonergan, SJ (1904–1984) was trained in the Scholastic tradition with roots in Aristotle and Thomas Aquinas. He wrote a series of articles on the epistemology of Aquinas, which were published in *Theological Studies* and then in book form as *Verbum, Word and Idea in Aquinas*. Having discovered a complete, detailed, and accurate metaphysical account of knowing in Aquinas, he thought that it would be a good idea to make this available for contemporary culture. As a result, from 1949 to 1953 he wrote a little book entitled *Insight: A Study of Human Understanding*. This was a transposition of the metaphysical categories of Aristotle and Aquinas into the psychological categories of the present day. He identified the meaning of the metaphysical terms in reference to the subject's experience of the activity of knowing. He is not normally associated with phenomenology and has his own critique of Husserl in that text.

However, in part one of *Insight*, Lonergan provides a phenomenological description of the process of knowing. The first part is called "Insight as Activity" and answers the question: what are we doing when we are knowing? In those 400 pages he is doing nothing more than accurately describing, in detail and with many examples, the activities involved in human understanding, including the conditions, characteristics, and implications of these activities. The authority for all of his statements is the subject's own experience of asking questions, struggling to arrive at the solution, finally grasping the point, and expressing this in a definition or a judgment.

I will make few explicit references to Lonergan in this text. However, my work is profoundly influenced by the ideas, method, and terminology of *Insight*. I am not claiming credit for these insights for myself. Most of this text is entirely derivative; it is an exercise in communication rather than original thinking. Lonergan himself said that the point of reaching up to the mind of Aquinas in his own life profoundly changed him. Likewise, my own efforts to reach up to the mind of Lonergan since 1961 has profoundly changed me.

The second influence is phenomenology, which specializes in descriptions of subjective states. This tradition has produced a phenomenology of perception,[1] a phenomenology of spirit,[2] a phenomenology of the person,[3] a phenomenology of jealousy,[4] a phenomenology of literature,[5] a phenomenology of visiting the zoo,[6] and so on. It is time for a *Phenomenology of*

1. Merleau-Ponty, *Phenomenology of Perception*.
2. Hegel, *The Phenomenology of Spirit*.
3. Sokolowski, *A Phenomenology of the Human Person*.
4. Giorgi, *The Descriptive Phenomenological Method in Psychology*.
5. Natanson, *The Erotic Bird*.
6. Garrett, *Why Do We Go to the Zoo?*

Human Understanding! Understanding is such an integral part of our cognitive experience that it deserves more attention. Phenomenology allows one to perform qualitative and interpretive studies; the study of human understanding is both of these. Phenomenologists are at home with subjectivity and objectivity, intentionality, consciousness, introspection, and limiting one's conclusions to what is warranted by the data. Lonergan, similarly, is at home with these terms, and seems to have been doing what phenomenologists could have been doing from the beginning.

By phenomenology, I simply mean an accurate description of the phenomenon of understanding from the subject's point of view. I do not want to get involved in disputes over phenomenological method or transcendental reductions. I do not presume any of the other positions of the phenomenological tradition. It is a tradition in which everyone seems to add his or her own individual twist. I hope I will be extended the same latitude. I do want to offer accurate, rich, verifiable, and detailed descriptions of every aspect or stage in the unfolding of human understanding. Is there a structure and pattern common to all acts of understanding? That is what I am looking for. I will use any available and useful sources for the study of human understanding: biographies and autobiographies describing how new discoveries actually occur; psychological research and reports on intelligence, insight and genius; and philosophical theories about the scope and limits of human understanding. Above all, I will depend on my own experience of the act of human understanding. From description, I will move to analysis and synthesis.

What Kind of a Book Is This?

This text is not a demonstration of deep scholarship or a show of erudition. There is a place for demonstrating one's expertise and detailed familiarity with a writer or a period, but that is not my aim. It is not about the history of philosophy. After all the history has been done, there is a time for the philosopher to be a philosopher and to take a stand on the basic questions of philosophy, namely, the reality of the world, the limits and possibility of our knowing, distinguishing true and false, or distinguishing good and bad. That is real philosophy for which the history is merely a preparation.

Consider this text as a map of the mind. A map guides one along the right path, identifies what is to the right and left, and explains which way to turn when one reaches a crossroads. Without a map, everything appears to be chaos, and one can easily get lost. The mind is also a seeming chaos, but with a map one can name and identify what is on the right or left and determine what road to take and what to expect. The human mind is the terrain and the point of reference. This book is about discovering the power of the human mind to inquire, to understand, to judge, and to reach objective reality. It may seem simple from that point of view, but it is difficult to describe the processes of the human mind. It is easy to focus on frogs or trees or stones but it is more difficult to focus on ideas emerging from images in one's own understanding. As the argument unfolds in each chapter, I will lay out a sequence of steps, the appeal to the evidence, and the clarification of terms. I keep it as clear and focused as possible. For more detail or depth, I defer to Lonergan's *Insight*. I have been teaching this approach for 35 years and know how it can transform lives. I can only hope that the reader is ready for the journey into self-discovery as a knower, in order to produce an examined life that is the springboard to cumulative and progressive results in philosophy.

Book Summary

Chapter 1 searches for a method by which we might systematically study the power and limits of the human mind to know truth and value. I argue that whatever way we look, in the end, the only method for studying human understanding has to be an introspective methodology. I consider the history of this much maligned method of introspection and the difficulties and dangers involved. I suggest that anyone who has written about the human mind has either implicitly or explicitly been using this method. I call it "self-appropriation" in order to confer the idea of self-discovery, taking possession and control of one's knowing capacity.

In chapter 2, I embark on the journey of self-discovery. The first distinction is relatively easy to grasp: that between the experience of being conscious (as opposed to being unconscious) and the experience of cognitional activities such as classifying, defining, questioning, understanding, expressing, criticizing, evaluating, judging, and verifying. The term "consciousness" is used in so many vague and confusing senses in various disciplines. I use it as the abstract noun derived from the simple experience of being conscious. To be conscious means to be aware, awake, alert, attentive; usually we are attentive to what we are doing, what we are seeing, who we are talking to. But our attention can be turned to our own feelings and thinking and knowing, and even focus on our experience of self. I introduce a simple, necessary distinction between consciousness and the conscious activities of questioning and understanding so that we can concentrate on these latter activities.

Chapter 3 and 4 make up the heart of my inquiry: a description and analysis of the basic human act of understanding. I start with the role of questioning, a somewhat neglected starting point of the act of understanding. Then, I try to identify the passive and active elements of understanding, the conditions of study and concentration, and the nature of insight, which comes suddenly and unexpectedly. Understanding differs from sensing in that it is not immediate, not simple, not direct, and not automatic. The key moment of understanding is when an idea emerges from an image. In colloquial terms, we refer to this by saying we get it, the light goes on, it all makes sense at last, or we find the solution. This is the oft-mentioned eureka moment. We do not forget these illuminations and they gradually transform our minds.

Human understanding develops in many ways that I explore in chapter 5. It becomes broader, becomes deeper, is formulated into language, moves from common sense to theory, and discovers ever higher viewpoints. Simply compare and contrast the mind of the infant, the adolescent, the university student, the PhD graduate, the specialist, the professor, and the wise and mature old person. The dynamic is the questioning; solutions to one problem only lead to further questions about related matters. The process is ongoing and the expansion is exponential and never ending.

Insights only give us bright ideas; insights are a dime a dozen. Insight is not yet knowledge. In chapter 6, I identify the act of critical understanding, which produces judgments of truth. Hypotheses or bright ideas are always followed by the question: is it true, is it correct, will it work? The brainstorming mode leads to the critical mode. The mind analyzes what justifies this affirmation that a proposition is true. I conclude that we know something is true if we have sufficient evidence and the evidence entails the conclusion.

Usually a discovery, an invention, or a verified theory will be open to many uses and abuses, applications, adaptations, and implications. What is it worth? What is it for? What can we do with this? I explore the question of value in chapter 7. The question of value naturally and spontaneously arises. How do we deal with it? Can we answer it truthfully? I conclude that the mind performs such evaluations most of the time and usually performs them quite well. Judgments of value neither come from arbitrary preferences nor from choices, nor from emotions, but from an act of deliberative understanding. People in Western societies constantly talk about values yet are often quite inarticulate in answering the question: what is a value? This chapter clearly explains where they come from and how to distinguish responsible from irresponsible judgments of value.

At this point in chapter 8, I place all the discoveries about the process of human understanding together into a diagram. This makes clear how the sequence of activities that constitute human knowing and valuing unfolds.

I identify four levels of operation, each with its own characteristic products that parallel the other levels. I define each activity in relation to the other activities in the diagram and offer an explanation of the process of knowing. Many dynamic parts constitute one whole.

If I am correct in this account of understanding, I should be able to shed some light on misunderstanding. In chapter 9, I speculate as to why there are so many fundamental disagreements and conflicts between philosophers, especially about human knowing. Surely such intelligent people should be able to talk over their differences, correct what is wrong, and come to an agreement as to what is right. But it is not so in the real world; thus, I consider the deep source of misunderstanding in the unstated imaginative assumptions and feelings of philosophers.

All of the above comprises what is a phenomenology of human understanding, that is, an accurate description of the act of understanding from the point of view of the subject. But some might dismiss this as folk psychology and of no relevance to real philosophy. However, if I have discovered the power and limits of human knowing, then we can embark on a journey of using that power to know. Hence, I shift the point of view in order to posit three strategic judgments that are the foundation of a critical realist epistemology and philosophy (chapter 10).

The default position of many philosophers is that we cannot know objective reality. I disagree with this view on the basis of these three judgments: I am a knower, this is a tree, and I am not this tree. On this basis, one can affirm the objectivity of what is known. I claim that authentic subjectivity leads to genuine objectivity (chapter 11). I define the meaning of subject and object in contrast to one another, which leads to a realist philosophy based on judgments of truth rather than unstated imaginative assumptions.

Finally, in chapter 12, I sum up what has been accomplished under the title of "the mind recovered." I conclude that I have fully presented a foundational position of human understanding, which can be developed in any specific direction of human science, scholarship or discipline. I have set forth a universal method for common sense, for science, for human science, and for philosophy. It could be the beginning of a philosophical tradition that really yields cumulative and progressive results.

1

From Introspection to Self-Appropriation

STREAKING IN SYRACUSE

The famous story of Archimedes is first related by Vitrovius in the following manner: King Hiero of Syracuse had received a crown of gold, which was beautifully decorated, as a tribute from a visiting dignitary. The king wanted to know whether the crown was made of pure gold or whether it was mixed with baser metal, such as silver or copper. He asked Archimedes to find out without melting down the crown. We are told that he worked on the problem to the point of exhaustion and finally decided to relax in the public baths. Floating in the water, perhaps wondering why he was floating, he suddenly realized that if he weighed the crown in water he could discover whether the crown was adulterated or not. He ran naked through the streets of Syracuse, shouting, "Eureka! Eureka! I have found it! I have found it!"

This image of the naked Archimedes streaking through the streets of Syracuse shouting, "Eureka!" has become an enduring symbol for having an insight, a eureka moment, an act of human understanding. He understood the idea of density, the relation between volume and weight, and hence the laws of what would float and what would sink. Furthermore he discovered a technique to apply these principles and solve the problem of the crown.[1]

1. However, how did he apply these insights to determine whether the crown was adulterated or not? It is unlikely that it consisted of Archimedes realizing that he could immerse the crown in water, measure the displacement, and thence know the volume of the crown. He would know what an equal volume of pure gold should weigh and could determine immediately if there was a discrepancy. This procedure was rather elementary and was presumably familiar to Archimedes already. Galileo points out that such a method of measuring the volume of the crown would not have yielded the precision needed for the subsequent calculations. More likely, the idea was to suspend the crown by a thread on one side of a balance and suspend a similar weight of pure gold on

Technicalities aside, it is clear that Archimedes got an idea. He understood: it came to him, not while working, but while relaxing. The moment was preceded by concentrated thinking, experimenting, and measuring. It was followed by further experimenting, formulating the concepts explicitly, checking the procedure, confirming the results, and realizing that the concepts of density and flotation applied universally to all material bodies.[2]

The Need for a Method

F ast forward two millennia to a philosophy lecture in a seminary in Dublin in 1961. The subject was psychology and the topic at hand was human knowing. The textbook consisted of a neo-Scholastic form of Thomism, written in Latin, which presented dogmatic theses on all aspects of human knowing, proving them summarily and firmly rebutting contrary opinions.[3] The subject was being taught in Latin, which made it additionally difficult for the professor and the students. The theses were systematically presented and defined human knowing through a series of concepts, namely, active and passive intellect, phantasms and forms, impressed species and expressed species, material and immaterial reception, potentially intelligible and actually intelligible, three different kinds of abstraction, three levels of abstraction, identity and difference, and much more. The theses and arguments were justified by reference to Aristotle, Aquinas, and the Scholastic tradition. We—my peers and I—laboriously worked our way through the definitions, the connections, and the sequence, all of us trying to answer Aristotle's simple question: what is thinking? Aristotle answered this question using the concepts of metaphysics. He understood what he was referring to when he used these concepts. It was epistemology being done by using the concepts of metaphysics. Sadly, these concepts are not part of our Western culture at large, and we have largely lost touch with the original meaning.

---

the opposite side, and then submerge both weights in vessels of water. If the crown was pure gold the two sides would continue in balance, as equal amounts of water would be displaced. If the balance tilted on the side of the pure gold it meant that the crown was mixed with silver or copper, which are lighter than gold and would displace more water. Implicit in the procedure are the notions of density, namely, the relation of weight to volume, and the notion of the laws of flotation.

2. This overview of Archimedes has been adapted from Hirshfeld, *Eureka Man,* 73–78.

3. Gredt, *Elementa Philosophiae.*

What is amazing is that although it was an analysis of human knowing, no one thought to refer, in any way, at any point, to actual experiences of human knowing. Studying the interrelations of concepts, one might have been studying the workings of a sausage machine, a jet engine, or a hydraulic pump. It was all purely theoretical and abstract. Imagine what might have been possible if an example like that of Archimedes was introduced and the above concepts lined up with his actual experience! But no one thought to do so—neither the textbook, nor the professor, nor the students. The reference was always back to historical texts, justifying or rebutting the definitions and arguments. We were studying human knowing without any reference whatsoever to particular, real, examples of human knowing— surely not a great pedagogical strategy! Imagine an astronomer studying the heavenly bodies without ever actually looking through a telescope, or a biologist studying frogs without ever examining an actual, live frog. But that was what we were doing!

What continues to amaze me is that philosophers continue to formulate theories about human knowing without the slightest reference to describing the actual experience of human knowing. Textbooks on epistemology regularly present five to ten different theories of knowledge on the assumption that the only way to discriminate between them is arbitrary choice. But theories are usually based on data and facts. One chooses between theories on the basis of how they account for the data and the facts. To ask the question, "Which epistemology is true?" presumably means to ask whether this theory adequately explains, orders, and accounts for the various experiences involved in the process of knowing from beginning to end. It is actually an empirical question, namely, a question about what actually occurs. Is there a real difference between images and ideas, as Hume denied? Well, is there a real difference between chalk and cheese? For the latter question one can refer to examples, experiences, and characteristics of chalk and cheese. For the former question one will refer to the experience of knowing, the activity of imagination as contrasted with the activity of understanding. One might mentally line up examples of images and line up examples of ideas. Are they the same or are they different? Plato seems to have held that understanding is really just an act of remembering. We can examine such a claim: line up real examples of remembering and note their characteristics. Then, line up real examples of understanding (such as Archimedes) and note the different characteristics. Compare the two. Are they the same?

Not only is there still a reluctance to attend to the experience of knowing, some philosophers rule out of court any reference to mental activities since they are deemed to be private and unverifiable. Introspection is deemed to be a very dubious, private, unverifiable, unreliable, and idiosyncratic method. However, the consequences of refusing to attend to mental activities are rather drastic: First, any epistemology is unhinged from any data that might verify or disprove the theory. Theories could spawn at will with no control, no criterion, and no way of distinguishing true from false. Second, the procedure of teaching neo-Scholastic epistemology in terms of a string of concepts with no reference to verifying experiences would be quite normal and unobjectionable. Repeat the words and forget about the meaning. Third, if cognitional activities are determined to be private and unverifiable, then one remains confined to studying the manifestations of such activities in words, gestures, and activities. It might become rather difficult to distinguish between a robot and a human being, a computer and a human mind. We would be condemned to studying the surface of things and not the source or cause of the origin of theories, language, art, and science. Fourth, without any understanding of human knowing, then it is hard to establish the methods, limits and conditions of knowing. It would be difficult to make any pronouncement on the method of the sciences or the possibility of a method for philosophy. The consequences of not studying the activities of human knowing are too absurd to merit further attention.

Between 1943 and 1949, Lonergan studied in great detail the epistemology of St. Thomas Aquinas, convinced that the tradition had lost touch with his thinking and had gone badly astray into a form of conceptualism. He was thoroughly familiar with Aquinas, quoting him roughly five hundred times in the *Verbum* articles. He became convinced of two things: that Aquinas was absolutely correct in his metaphysical treatment of the acts of sensing, understanding, and judging; and that Aquinas could do this only because he paid attention to his own acts of human understanding. Aquinas could use Aristotle as a reference, but there were times when he had to disagree with him. On such occasions, his reference was always to the experience of knowing. His argument for the unity of the human intellect was simply, *hic homo intelligit*: this man understands.

That was a fine historical study. But then Lonergan took another step forward. He wrote *Insight* on the principle that the metaphysical categories of Aristotle and Aquinas should be translated into the psychological categories of contemporary discourse. It is not enough to depend on the authority of Aquinas in order to provide an adequate account of human knowing. One must pay attention to the actual experiences of human knowing by oneself and by others. *Insight* is based on the principle that every statement made about the activity of the human mind must be backed up with evidence: the experience of others and oneself, real-life examples, and empirical evidence. No astronomer can make affirmations about pulsars unless they can be supported by sightings, photographs, data, calculations, and evidence. Why should epistemologists be freed from this constraint?

My aim in this chapter is to justify a method of introspection, to recognize our awareness of cognitional experience, to show how it can profitably be the locus for the foundation of philosophy, and to explain how it can be verifiable and a topic for conversation and communication. In short, the theme of this chapter is to try to nail down a methodical introspection, which will provide verifiable assertions about human knowing.

Difficulties in Studying Human Understanding

If one wants to know about frogs what must be done? It is not very difficult to realize that one has to get frogs from some source, study their activities, their eating habits, their mating, and their growth. One must observe them in all stages of life: birth, life as tadpoles, the emergence of legs and moving onto land, reproduction, and death. One has to study the parts: limbs, organs, sensitivities, diseases, croaking, aggressiveness, sociality, and so forth. Then, one collects various species of frogs, their subspecies and varieties. One must learn about the evolution and history of the species. After all of this and more, one might be an expert on frogs.

Similarly, if one wants to know about human knowing, what must be done? One begins by collecting examples of human understanding. One must study the thought process of others and compare and relate them to one's own experiences of discovery. One must study the ways in which all acts of human understanding conform to the same structure and yet have different content, different applications, and are specific to different times and places. One will have to assemble a variety of examples of understanding and knowing in common sense, in science, and even in philosophy. Because human understanding is a different kind of reality from that of frogs, the approach will have to be appropriate to the subject matter. Human knowing can be understood in the same way that we understand frogs; however, we do have to make an allowance for the difference in subject matter. It is imperative to identify the special difficulties that would seem to arise in studying human understanding

First, the main differences are derived from the fact that understanding goes on inside our minds and not outside in the external world. Our natural orientation seems to be outwards toward the data of sense. All of our five primary senses are oriented to objects that are seen, heard, tasted, touched, or smelled. The objects are usually outside. Scientists are quite happy dealing with their various specializations on the world of the outside. We are at home studying frogs, but not so comfortable studying understanding. Mental activities are different from frogs. They take place in the head. They cannot be seen, touched, heard, smelled, or tasted. Yet they are conscious: we know what we are thinking about, dreaming about, or searching for. The instruments used in the physical sciences are not of much use in reporting on what goes on in the mind. How then does one use his or her mind in order to double back and observe the mind itself in action?

Second, frogs can be trapped, controlled, experimented on, and are still there to be observed the next day. One can easily identify what is the object of study in the case of frogs. But acts of understanding are not so easily marked off from their surroundings. Understanding seems to be involved in just about everything we do as human beings. There is no department of the university that does not embrace understanding as at least one of its aims; there are few departments where obscurantism is preferred to understanding. It is involved in most human interactions. We rejoice in the growing understanding of the child and celebrate its entry into the world of language. We experience our own progress in understanding from grade school to high school to college. From the time we get up in the morning to when we lay our tired heads down to rest, we are understanding what we hear, reacting to what we see, and evaluating just about everything. Is it possible to define an activity that is so pervasive, so constant, and so ubiquitous?

Third, understanding is an activity: it takes time, proceeds through stages; is fleeting, and comes and goes. How can we pin it down, stop its motion, and freeze it so that we can focus on it? But if you freeze it, it is no longer an activity of understanding, no longer dynamic. We are so accustomed to the scientific method and so at home in it; but is it possible to apply the scientific method to something that keeps hopping about? It is not so easy to devise experiments with the act of understanding.

Fourth, there seem to be different kinds of acts of human understanding. There is an understanding of language: we rejoice at the child's first words. We learn to understand what objects will sink and which will float. We understand the probability of rain tomorrow. We understand the necessity of positing something as true if the evidence and circumstances warrant it. We understand the difference between justice and mercy. Many more examples could be provided.

Fifth, it seems that the act of understanding is not one single activity but a series of related activities. It takes half an hour to complete a crossword puzzle, perhaps twenty minutes to do a fiendish Sudoku. It takes a week to write a good article but at least a year to put together a book. It seems that knowing is not a single, simple, direct act of the mind, but rather, is a temporal sequence of activities that finally issue in knowledge.

Sixth, some hold that introspection is impossible on the basis that one cannot be studying frogs and at the same time observing oneself studying frogs. How can someone simultaneously observe oneself while being engaged in the process of scientific knowledge? How can someone do two things at the same time? How can someone's attention be directed outwards and inwards at the same time? Understanding "understanding" would seem to be impossible on that basis.

These difficulties exist, but they are not insurmountable. Moreover, the topic is of such importance and centrality that we are obliged to use whatever method is possible to make whatever contribution we can to understand understanding. Although there are difficulties, the enterprise of studying human understanding promises much. If we can pin down the meaning of understanding, surely we will be able to know "knowing" and then the known. Understanding is such a key element in language, culture, science, common sense, theology, and technology that if we get a handle on understanding it will illuminate everything else.

Despite the difficulties, if we want to study human understanding, it would seem inevitable that we use some form of introspective methodology. Biology can use microscopes, test tubes, petri dishes, and solutions of this and that because their object of study is there on the desk. If we want to study the activities of the human mind, we must in some sense look inwards, focus our attention on the mind and its workings, identify activities, find relations of cause and effect, and draw our conclusions. In light of this, I will try to work out a procedure of introspective analysis that will be surrounded by checks and balances and can be subject to review by others.

Introspection: Uses and Abuses

My contention is that introspection is the only way to study human understanding and it has been used either implicitly or explicitly in the past to do so. It has been used by philosophers, more explicitly by psychologists, and surreptitiously by cognitive neuroscientists. If we are going to use this method we are well advised to learn from the past. Introspection has a checkered history of use and abuse. Needless to say, we need to recognize the abuses so that we do not fall into the same trap. In the following pages, I discuss the role introspection has played in philosophy, in psychology, and in neuroscience, albeit briefly.

Introspection in Philosophy

Some might suggest that if we want to learn about human knowing that we consult the classical philosophers and the theories of knowledge that they have proposed. One could study Plato for instance, his theory of remembrance, his divided line, his myth of the cave, his knowledge of forms, and the value placed on the four kinds of knowledge. But where did Plato get these ideas? Where did he get this theory of knowledge as recollection, of this idea of the senses being illusory and of true knowledge in knowing the forms? One could answer that he got some of these ideas from Pythagoras and others from Parmenides. But where did they get their ideas? And where did their predecessors get their ideas? At some point long ago, a human being made the first attempt at describing his or her own experience of knowing and formulated some primitive account of what knowing is. At least implicitly, that individual utilized introspection.

Plato may have learned from his predecessors, but why did he pick some ideas and reject others? Why did he modify the rather extreme position of Parmenides? He must have attended to his own experience of knowing and found that it did not fit with the monism of Parmenides. His reference to his own experience could only have been cursory, because if it had been more systematic and critical, he would not have held that remembering is the same as understanding. He might have given a more differentiated account of the development of knowledge than the myth of the cave.

Aristotle disagreed fundamentally with Plato and set off on a different path. He affirmed that all knowing begins in sensing, that images are necessary for understanding, that the intellect takes the initiative in order to make what is potentially intelligible to become actually intelligible, and that there is an aspect of knowing that is active and an aspect that is passive or receptive. He recognized a process of abstraction of forms from images. He recognized an intellectual memory; when we understand an idea we do not easily forget it.[4] Where did he get this theory of knowledge? It is quite original in most of the elements, so it does not appear that he inherited it from anybody. It is quite sophisticated and seems to have stood the test of time. The most likely explanation is that he paid serious attention to his own experience of understanding and learning, the experience of his students, and his teaching and discussions. These were the cognitional data on which he built his theory. He used introspection and the results demonstrate that. However, he was not in a position to objectify the method as introspection. One can use a method implicitly without being able to define that method.

---

4. All these ideas are to be found dispersed in Aristotle's *De Anima*, book 3.

It has taken another two millennia to formulate the notion of introspective methodology.

John Locke and David Hume both used an explicitly introspective method and provided some details on the various processes of knowing. Locke wrote roughly 560 pages in his *An Essay Concerning Human Understanding*, while Hume wrote a more modest 120 pages in an *Inquiry Concerning Human Understanding*. They dealt with such notions as understanding and imagination, ideas and images, simple and complex ideas, the association of ideas, consciousness, representations, the origin of ideas, modes of thinking, ideas of cause, substance, relations, truth and certainty, judgment, freedom, and so on. Unfortunately, the method and conclusions were subject to empiricist preconceptions. Nothing was to be allowed that would go beyond the sensible. The underlying idea was to explain human knowing in natural terms: everything was to be derived from the senses and the sensible without any reference to spiritual realities, souls, universals, ideas, or occult entities.

The group of modern philosophers who come nearest to an introspective methodology would seem to be the phenomenologists. There one finds a focus on such themes as consciousness, intentionality, subjectivity, synthesis, perception, description, a return "to the things themselves," presuppositionless thinking, intuition, judgment, transcendentals, method, the ego, understanding, and truth. I studied phenomenology hoping to find a common, rich harvest of data and understanding about the sequence of mental activities that result in knowing truth and value. However, what I found was a splintering into different terminologies, different methods, different interpretations, and different specializations. No common core position or conclusions seem to have emerged from these individuals as to what happens when we understand correctly.

Some phenomenologists seem to be more interested in difference than in what is common to all acts of understanding and knowing. Particularities, of course, are interesting and concrete and detailed and need to be studied. However, the question of what is common to all correct understanding is even more necessary, legitimate, important, and valuable. The text most similar to my own project would be that of Hannah Arendt's *The Life of the Mind*.

Philosophers have always implicitly and later explicitly appealed to a method of introspection. They have sometimes done it well and sometimes badly, or incompletely. My hope is to appropriate and build on the successes of these predecessors and to avoid the dead ends and the ambiguities. I will work out my own method, implement it, and judge it by its results.

Introspection in Psychology

The discipline of empirical psychology started in the late nineteenth century with a primarily introspective method. Wilhelm Wundt founded a psychological laboratory and laid down the fundamental principles and methods of psychology for its first fifty years. This was introspective psychology. Psychology at the time relied almost entirely on introspective data. The method required (1) inducing experiences in oneself; (2) describing the resultant mental states; and (3) trying to find sequences, causes, and effects of the mental states. It was the psychologists who conducted the experiments on themselves, although they sometimes used other subjects. Untrained subjects were judged to be incapable of the precision and reflective skills of the psychologists. They tried to reduce all mental states to a few basic types, which when combined, produced the wealth of experiences in the human mind.[5]

This approach was abandoned around the 1920s largely because the varying schools could not agree on anything. It foundered particularly in the controversy over imageless thought. Oswald Külpe (1862–1915) of the University of Würtsburg suggested that imageless thought was possible and his subjects reported having thoughts without corresponding images. This was a revolutionary suggestion as it was accepted wisdom that thinking was a stream of associated images of various kinds. E. B. Titchener in Cornell University defended the orthodox view that thinking was done through images and that there is no such thing as imageless thought. He claimed that the subjects of Külpe had not been able to discern images that are subtle, elusive and faint; but the images were there all the time. Subsequently, introspection was abandoned in favor of behaviorism, psychoanalysis, and phenomenology. Apparently about 50 percent of contemporary psychologists accept introspection as one legitimate method in psychology.[6]

One stream of psychologists has focused on the topic of insight, sometimes called studies of creativity. By insight they refer to eureka experiences, or aha moments when the solution of a problem hits us, or the "light" goes on in our brains. These are typical examples of acts of human understanding; Archimedes is an archetypical example. It is a common psychological experience and is particularly prominent in the lives of famous inventors or geniuses. The method in these studies involved asking subjects to describe their own acts of understanding. In other words, they were asking subjects

5. See Schwitzgerbel, *Perplexities of Consciousness,* chapters 5 and 7.

6. See Kukla and Walmsley, *Mind.* This is a simple, historical introduction and overview of schools of psychology.
See also Giorgi, *The Descriptive Phenomenological Method in Psychology,* chap. 2.

to perform introspection, and then they collected and correlated the reports. This stream of investigation seems to have been started by Graham Wallas in the *Art of Thinking* (1926). He identified four phases in the process of discovery, namely, preparation, incubation, illumination, and verification. This became a standard way of identifying the process of arriving at new ideas, discovering solutions to problems, inventing, and understanding.

Eliot Hutchinson in *How to Think Creatively* (1949) set about elaborating this schema in a professional, scholarly manner. He distributed detailed questionnaires to 250 of the most famous thinkers and artists of the time, including Bertrand Russell, Somerset Maugham, Aldous Huxley, and Arnold Bennett. His subjects included artists, scientists, poets, and philosophers. The questionnaire was to provide information as a statistical and experimental study of the process of artistic and scientific creation. The questions concerned when and how and under what conditions creative ideas popped into the mind; how much effort is put into it; and how they would describe the experience of discovery, their study methods, the process of revision and their feelings during the process. He renamed the four phases set forth by Graham Wallas as (1) preparation, (2) frustration, (3) achievement, and (4) verification. I will briefly summarize this schema of phases.

1. *Preparation.* The artist or scientist starts with a vague notion of what he is aiming at. The question has not been formally defined. What is needed is to formulate the question clearly. One starts with a kind of hunch. Chaos and confusion reign. Idleness and indecision predominate before starting a big work. Different kinds of errors are made at the beginning and the person might set off in the wrong direction. Finally, some suggestive starting point for a creative idea emerges and one proceeds.

2. *Frustration.* Frustration is also called "renunciation" or "recession." There is a period of frustration when the solution to the problem seems elusive. These are strongly emotional, and if not handled correctly, can lead to giving up the project. It can also lead to repression, the attempt to forget. It can lead to neurosis, to a breakdown of the personality, a nervous breakdown. It can also lead to regression, apathy, the feeling of inferiority, indifference, and depression. The person may seek a substitute goal that is more easily attainable. Inherent in the very process of creation are the seeds of defeat and self-destruction. There is a way of normal, effective adjustment to these emotions, which usually involve a turning to unrelated interests, a purposive laying aside of the problem. "The attainment of this masterful idleness is in fact the hardest part of the creative discipline."[7] Hutchinson continues: "When the creative desire is active, intense, aroused, but for

---

7. Hutchinson, *How to Think Creatively,* 81.

the time being restricted in freedom of expression, the chief psychological symptom is tension."[8] Typical of the creative process of understanding is this phase of frustration, tension building up, and an effort to relax the tension and allow the insight to appear.

3. *Achievement.* First, there is the fleeting intimation that insight is about to appear. Such insights must be allowed to come: "Such intimation constitutes, in fact, one of the most unanalyzable experiences of creative life."[9] Often the occasion of the insight can be quite accidental and from totally unrelated pursuits: "In the case of insight the process must wait upon purely chance factors, since there is no prediction as to just what element or just what kind of experience will release the repressed ideas, the character of the creative system being largely unknown."[10] However, Hutchinson insists, intellectual discovery is in no sense an accident in its fundamental mechanism. Periods of rest, mild distractions, quiet meditation, listening to the radio, driving a car, or walking up and down can all help the release of the insight. Even sleep and dreams can be the occasion for insight to occur.

Finally, there is the moment of creation: "That moment often brings with it ideas in such profusion that one is not only astonished at their number, not only startled by the vividness and ease of their appearance, but also largely at a loss to capture them."[11] Thought seems effortless. The subject experiences great exhilaration and release of tension, jumping about in excitement, and the like. This experience occurs in both the arts and the sciences even though one is imaginative and emotional and the other is logical and technical. At the highest point, art and science have much in common. Typical emotions at the moment of creation are joy and enthusiasm, excitement, and the relaxing of tension.

4. *Verification.* No matter how clear the insight, the future of the project is still extremely uncertain. Insight gives way to systematic work that is exacting, continuous, and largely uninspired. The critical attitude takes over and patient, exacting verification must be carried out. This may involve revision of the creative idea or even abandonment of the idea as useless. The critical stage is as important as the creative.

Such is the account of a professional psychologist working with questionnaires from 250 of the most famous contemporary thinkers in England and America in the 1940s. Every case involved the emergence of an insight with an accompanying release of tension and joy. The eureka experience

8. Ibid., 84.

9. Ibid., 88.

10. Ibid., 113–14.

11. Ibid., 134.

is not purely emotional; actually, the emotion is a byproduct of an act of human understanding. It shows clearly that the act of human understanding takes place in the context of other activities and can only occur after preparation and some frustration and must be followed by a critical phase. This is how we get new ideas.

In a somewhat related field, which might be called heuristics, authors gave directions as to what one should do in order to understand or solve a problem. This was not in terms of following strict rules but in terms of general directions, structures of thinking, and proceeding, which should normally lead to a solution. George Polya, the great mathematician also distinguishes four phases in solving mathematical problems in a slightly different way. For him the stages are the following: (1) understanding the problem, (2) devising a plan, (3) carrying out the plan, and (4) looking back. He presents a kind of heuristics, namely, a general framework to be used to solve any mathematical problem: how one should proceed in order to have the best chance of understanding.

At about the same time, Jacques Hadamard in his *The Mathematician's Mind* (1945), worked out his own four phases: (1) preparation, (2) incubation, (3) illumination, (4) and verification. He was inspired by Henri Poincaré who experienced such moments of insight, and Hadamard also experienced the same phenomenon himself. He tried to analyze the role of the unconscious in the emergence of discovery. He asked other mathematicians, including Albert Einstein, to share their experiences with him.

Karl Popper in the *Logic of Scientific Discovery* (2002) continues this line in terms of general recommendations on how to proceed in the various stages of the work. Similarly, William Ian Beveridge in *The Art of Scientific Investigation* (1950) gives general advice on how to organize work in a laboratory for the solution of a problem. I am sure there are many more texts along these lines, but these would seem to be typical. Working from these scholarly works, there are more popular, simple, contemporary books on the theme of how to obtain creative ideas.[12]

This line of study is still alive and well as is shown by Robert Sternberg and Janet Davidson's *The Nature of Insight* (1995).[13] It is a 600 page study by thirty psychologists on detailed aspects of the insight experience. It focuses on four different approaches, namely, (1) the challenge of solving puzzles, (2) the experience of creative invention, (3) the study of the minds of great thinkers, and (4) the search for metaphors for understanding insight. These

---

12. See, for example, Foster, *How to Get Ideas*; Young, *A Technique for Producing Ideas*.

13. See also Rothenberg and Hausman, *The Creativity Question*; Rothenberg, *Creativity and Madness*.

are empirical studies carried out by professional psychologists on detailed aspects of the process of understanding. The articles discuss the role of chance in getting ideas, the use of the imagination, how to organize thinking, the suddenness of insight, the role of the unconscious, the influence of affects, fixation and liberation, and theories of insight. Such a study provides body and background to many of the ideas in this book, which I can only treat in a perfunctory manner. I will try to briefly sum up what can be learned from this wealth of psychological research.

First, these are very detailed studies of various aspects of understanding. But there is no overall grasp of the role of understanding in knowing and its importance. There are many descriptions but little analysis of the parts or a synthesis of the whole.

Second, these are empirical psychologists and not philosophers. My interest is in the implications of the activity of insight for a theory of knowing. Where does it fit in? Some authors consider insight as a special case and do not relate it to other, more routine acts of understanding. None of these psychologists fit it into a complete philosophical theory of knowing.

Third, the role of imagination is recognized. We are advised to think outside the box, manipulate the diagram, explore possibilities, and think creatively. They clearly establish the importance of imagination in getting a new idea.

Fourth, the four stages seem to be accepted by all and do make a positive contribution to understanding understanding. It means that understanding takes time, that different activities are involved, and that there are aspects that are active and others that are passive. There is an unconscious element present in conditioning which images, or data, or memories, or clues pop into the mind, when one is searching for solutions.

Fifth, there is a recognition of the affective dimension of the process, namely, desire, frustration, determination, joy, and the release of tension.

Sixth, introspection on the part of the interviewees was taken for granted as a valuable tool. 250 questionnaires were distributed, which asked about experiences of discovery and how, when, and where it happened. Detailed questions about study habits and productive procedures were posed and answered in great detail. The subjects readily complied. They answered them, sometimes in great detail. No one claimed that introspection was impossible, that they could not answer the questions, or that such accounts are private and unverifiable.

Cognitive Neuroscience

Neuroscience has become the most popular, current way of studying the mind. They harbor great hopes of finally explaining thinking and consciousness. Most cognitive neuroscience presumes a background of materialism and assumes that the mind is the brain. It has been spurred on by computer science, by MRI imaging, and by other measuring devices that can image the electrical impulses in the brain. This is a short assessment of what might be expected from this source in illuminating the activity of understanding. How and to what extent can the study of the nerves and the brain help us to understand the activities of the mind? In what way does my approach of describing mental activities differ from the method of neuroscientists?

First, there is a clear interrelation and dependence of the operation of the mind on the correct functioning of the brain: a healthy mind in a healthy body. A high fever inhibits thinking. It is hard to do philosophy if one is starving, or has malaria, or is too tired, and so forth. In old age, neurons start to die off and the result can be seen in loss of memory and dementia. Certain diseases have a distinct imprint on the brain, such as epilepsy, Parkinson's, and Alzheimer's. The presence of these diseases can be identified in scans and MRIs; drugs can help to alleviate the symptoms, but as far as I know, not to cure them. Other drugs such as ecstasy, cocaine, heroin, and marijuana can induce altered states of consciousness in the brain, whether it be hallucinations, ecstatic feelings, or freedom from inhibitions. If one has a headache, aspirin can alleviate it. A general anesthetic injected into the body can render the mind unconscious in seconds.

Second, however, the thinking behind neuroscience has often been on the lines of a materialist, reductionist philosophy of mind. The claim is often that the brain is equivalent to the mind. The hope is that once they have mapped all the neurons, synapses, connections, and structures of the brain, they will have explained all consciousness, thinking, feeling, and knowing. They hope to show how the electrical, chemical, biological, and neurological reactions in the brain determine thinking, feeling, and consciousness. Hence, the ambition is to control and predict thoughts and feelings in terms of brain reactions. The claim is that all of the activities of the mind can be explained in terms of activity in various parts of the brain. The hope is that with further research and mapping tools that the brain will be shown to be a complicated computer. The computer for them is a ready and suitable model for the working of the mind and much effort has gone into Artificial Intelligence in the hope that the hardware and software of the computer will provide a ready model for the working of the brain. There is no room in this view for autonomous truth claims, responsible value judgments, and subsisting persons or selves or subjects. These somewhat extreme positions represent classical neuroscience which is being challenged and modified by more contemporary thinkers such as Iain McGilcrist.

I am not yet in a position to argue the philosophical issue of reductionism, and materialism; I might be able to make some comments after I have established a critical realist position in the concluding chapters. For the moment, I am prescinding from philosophical stances. Whatever the contribution neuroscience might turn out to be, it does not and cannot do without introspection and the kind of description of mental activities that I am proposing in this text. It does not invalidate, or replace the need for descriptions of mental activities. Let me explain why that is so.

Third, neuroscience aims to identify physical parts of the brain and find a direct correlation with activities such as language use, concepts, memory, and the other functions of the mind. They aim to find a causal link between activities of neurons and synapses and the activities of thinking and information processing. They use subjects who have suffered physical damage to parts of the brain and study which mental functions have consequently been impaired. My understanding is that such correlations between mental skills and parts of the brain has had limited success. The brain has been found to be plastic, that is, mental functions can be performed by different parts of the brain and specific parts of the brain can perform a variety of functions. Many parts of the brain are involved in the simplest of mental activities.[14]

Fourth, neuroscience seems to offer a way of studying mental activities that would be fully scientific, measurable, verifiable, and repeatable. It seems to escape the need for introspection. But in fact it does not and cannot. The neuroscientist focuses on the neurons and synapses in the brain, the organs of the brain, and the localization of functions in the brain. They use very sophisticated scanning techniques that measure the activity of neurons in various parts of the brain and map these activities and print them out for all to see. The typical experiment would be to set up a subject to watch a video clip. As the subject is watching the video clip the various instruments map and measure brain activity. The hope is that the various visual and audio stimulants in the video clip will correlate with the map of the simultaneous brain activity and then we will be able to read the brain. This presupposes that the subject provides an accurate and correct description of his or her reactions, feelings, and perceptions. It presupposes that the subject is doing what he or she is supposed to be doing, namely, attending carefully to the

14. McGilchrist discusses this relationship in chaps. 1 and 2 of *The Master and his Emisary*

video clip. That presumes that the subject is not tired and daydreaming, not in a joking mood and thinking of something entirely different, or not trying to sabotage the experiment for the fun of it. It is only the subject who knows because the subject is the only one with privileged access to the activity of his or her own mind. Even if the subject claims to be attending to the video and following instructions, people have been known to utter untruths. The subject is the only one who can give an account of his or her thought processes in order to correlate them with the brain scanning that is going on at the same time. All psychological experiments with subjects, such as role playing or simulations, find that they are dependent on the subject to honestly, precisely, and accurately report on his or her feelings, images, and thoughts during the experiment. The experiment depends on the fidelity of the subject in following instructions and the ability of the subject to accurately report on reactions, feelings, and decisions required by the experiment. In other words it depends on the introspection of the subject.

Fifth, the approach I am presenting is different from that of the neuroscientist. I intend simply to describe in detail the conscious activities of the mind, such as questioning, imagining, understanding, and knowing. If these activities occur, then they are possible. It is not my task to explain how and where neurons, synapses, and electrical impulses make thinking possible. It is not my task to show how and where images and ideas are stored in the brain. We can remember images, ideas, and concepts, but my concern here is not to discover how this is possible. The point simply is that they are preserved. Undoubtedly, these activities depend in some way on the brain, but that connection or correlation is not my concern at the moment. Neuroscience has a valuable contribution to make to illuminate those sorts of very difficult questions about thinking. Putting it simply, neuroscience works from below upwards: from neurons and synapses to thinking and feeling. My approach is from above downwards: start by describing the act of understanding and leave it to somebody else to explain the biological and neurological infrastructure that makes these activities possible.

A good example of mutual enrichment between neuroscience and philosophy is presented by Iain McGilchrist in *The Master and His Emissary*. There he spends the first chapters on the neuroscience of the divided brain and identifies the functions of the right brain and the left brain. Then he explores the history of philosophy and culture to indicate how one style of thinking characteristic of left brain sometimes dominated; whereas, at other times another style of thinking characteristic of right brain took over.

From Introspection to Self-Appropriation

Mindful of the checkered history of the use of introspection, but mindful also that it is the only avenue open to us, I will now lay down certain guidelines as to how it is to be used. How can introspection be turned from being private and unverifiable into a reliable, fruitful, communal, and verifiable method for the study of the activities of human understanding? Philosophy, psychology and even neuroscience, directly or indirectly, explicitly or implicitly, all depend on a method of introspection. This should really not be surprising. Human understanding is a series of mental activities, which are hidden from the outside observer but are accessible to the subject in which these activities occur.

However, introspection does not mean going off into a corner, closing one's eyes, and working everything out in splendid isolation. It does not mean being cut off from discussion, teaching, and writing, or from studying the history of philosophy and engaging with the great philosophers of the past. Extroversion suggests looking outside; introspection suggests looking into the self. But looking is not a very suitable metaphor for knowledge of self. Looking is not knowing; it is surely part of knowing but not the whole of knowing. Although I have shown that introspection is valid and possible, I want to move it into a wider context. Think of introspection not as an occasional exercise, but rather, as a reflective, philosophical way of life.

I suggest the word "self-appropriation" rather than the term "introspection." Introspection suggests "looking" into one's mind, which is not quite the goal.[15] Appropriation adds the notion of taking possession of one's own mind, understanding, and judgment of truth and value.[16] Appropriation is broader and deeper than introspection. Introspection might be thought of as somehow detached. It is like looking at the mind through a microscope as if it were some foreign object, a shift of awareness from outside to inside. Appropriation is the Socratic "Know thyself" brought to its ultimate conclusion. We know ourselves by taking possession of our own minds and by taking responsibility for what we do with it. To appropriate one's intellectual activities is to become aware of them, to be able to identify, name and distinguish them, to grasp how they are related, and thus, to ob-

---

15. Searle thinks of introspection as *seeing* what is going on in the mind. But obviously we cannot *see* perceiving. Therefore, he concludes, we cannot know what is going on in the mind and such attempts at introspection has led to truly appalling mistakes: "One thing you cannot see when you see anything is your seeing of that thing" (Searle, *Seeing Things as They Are*, 107). He continues: "Many truly appalling mistakes . . . would have been avoided if everybody understood you cannot see or otherwise perceive anything in the subjective perceptual field" (ibid.).

16. Morelli uses the term "self-possession" (Morelli, *Self-Possession*).

jectivize or make this process explicit. Therefore, I will sometimes use the term "intellectual self-awareness" as well as self-appropriation.

It is common enough in spirituality and counselling to become aware of one's feelings, motives, character, and personality. A large area of psychotherapy seems to be concerned with bringing unconscious, repressed feelings and traumas back to consciousness so that they can be dealt with. Becoming aware of one's feelings puts one in a position of being able to identify and heal those thoughts that are damaging and to reinforce and enhance those that are positive and loving. There are various movements based on techniques to achieve self-awareness in these different fields. It seems to be very acceptable and even fashionable.

Intellectual self-appropriation is a more difficult challenge. In itself, it is not entirely new, but to make it the explicit method of one's whole philosophy is new. It does seem to promise a great deal; if the appropriation of one's feelings and motives can be so healing and rewarding for psychological growth, then it seems warranted to expect that the awareness of our activities in understanding will be able to purify, strengthen, and guide those activities as well.

My theme is to consider how to complete the turn to the subject in a fruitful manner. Modern philosophy is at home with the notions of consciousness, subjectivity, the psyche, the self, affectivity, *ressentiment*, hidden agendas, lust for power, sublimation, repression, unconscious motivations, and the like. Literature abounds in acute descriptions of feelings, inner conflicts, and the inner richness underlying banal events. I am more interested in this inner life than the sequence of events that make up the story. One could narrate the events of one day in the life of Mr. Leopold Bloom in one page, but in *Ulysses,* James Joyce covers 600 pages in describing his daydreams, feelings, ambitions, hopes, extravagances, passing thoughts, opinions, reactions, and likes and dislikes. We can describe our feelings, our ambitions, our hopes and dreams, our fantasies, and our aches and pains with great detail and precision. Surely we can equally well describe the unfolding of our acts of understanding. Inwardness seems to be an idea whose time has come.

Self-Appropriation that is Communal and Verifiable

What kinds of activities are necessary in order to do self-appropriation? How does it become communal and verifiable, as opposed to private and unverifiable? In this section I reposition introspection by placing it in a wider context, making it a collaborative affair, and ensuring that its affirmations are based on sufficient evidence.

Communal and Verifiable

Insights occur everywhere that humans interact. They occur in a family context where weary parents answer the incessant questions of a growing child. They occur in the pub where arguments swish here and there, dogmas are propounded, facts are evinced, insults are thrown, and great liberty is taken from the rules of logic. Wherever conversation takes place, provided it is a dialogue and not a monologue, understanding is always present. The laboratory for understanding understanding, is not some psychological-experimental laboratory but wherever human beings communicate and talk together. All reading, watching movies, playing games, doing work, or using the computer include the activity of human understanding in some way or another.

The classroom situation is particularly a laboratory for human understanding, particularly when understanding is the topic. It is possible to teach epistemology by way of self-appropriation. It does require a special pedagogical approach using examples, projects, and illustrations that invite the student to identify their own questions, their own imagination and intelligence, their own reasoning processes, and their process for reaching their own conclusions. Understanding is not taught according to the theories of Aristotle or Kant or Husserl, but rather, according to the spontaneous exigencies that arise in the intelligent mind when confronted with a problem. Students take very well to a methodical self-appropriation. It gives them foundations. They do not have to rely on the authority of Aristotle or Derrida or the professor. The evidence is in their own experience. They become confident, autonomous thinkers, sure of their foundations. Nothing that our distorted culture throws at them can undermine these foundations.

It is not only possible but very rewarding. When I teach epistemology, one of the exercises I do is ask the students to name fifty different mental activities. It takes a while to get going but once they start there is no stopping them. A typical class might produce something like the following, given in no particular order: criticizing, dividing, comparing, contrasting, analyzing, synthesizing, thinking, knowing, feeling, questioning, seeing, hearing, classifying, understanding, revising, remembering, imagining, clarifying, stating, affirming, judging, sensing, denying, evaluating, loving, deciding, reporting, describing, explaining, solving, contemplating, meditating, praying, daydreaming, studying, researching, learning, reading, listening, observing, paying attention, suggesting, proposing, positing, concluding, hoping, believing, adding, and subtracting. Who says we cannot talk about mental activities?

The students recognize each of these activities as specific, distinctive, mental activities. No one in the class has any difficulty recognizing each activity as distinctive and as activities that they perform every day. It is not rocket science to perform these activities or to be able to recognize how they are distinct from one another. However, they do not yet recognize how they fall into a sequence and a pattern. Is there a way of grouping these activities together? Is there a sequence in which these activities occur? Where does the process of knowing start? Maybe Aristotle's "all philosophy begins in wonder" is a clue. And so my students might agree that the process begins in a question. A question about what? Where does the content come from? What experience provoked the question? What did not make sense in that observation? At this, they might agree that questions usually arise in the context of sensing and experiencing phenomena that we have not yet understood. Activities of questioning and activities of sensing seem to form categories that initiate the process of knowing.

What do we do next? We try to understand, and most of the activities described above are done in the effort to understand examples, thinking, contrasting, analyzing, clarifying, and the like. These activities seem to be necessary on the way to understanding. Through the use of any manner of resources, eventually an idea comes. But we are not usually satisfied with any old idea: it has to work, it has to be true, and it has to solve the problem at hand. And so we move to the critical problem: is it true? Here we perform activities such as criticizing, affirming, verifying, checking, reviewing, weighing the evidence, and examining the reasoning in order to arrive at a conclusion, an affirmation, a statement, a truth.

It is not hard to see that there is a structure and a pattern to this sequence of activities. They can be categorized into four groups: (1) asking questions; (2) sensing, imagining, and remembering; (3) understanding, which encompasses most of the activities mentioned above; and (4) criticizing, evaluating, or judging. We do not usually affirm unless we have understood the ground for the affirmation. The ground for an affirmation is usually some sensible evidence and inferring the conclusion from the evidence. Students can do it. It is possible. It is very fruitful.

How then are descriptions of private mental acts verifiable? If I describe in detail how I solved a particular puzzle and present this to students, they are able to recognize the words, to identify the activity, and to know what I am talking about. If I ask students to describe their own acts of understanding, I can recognize what they are writing about. If one gives an example of remembering instead of understanding, then we discuss the difference between understanding and remembering. We identify the characteristics of each activity. We note that animals can remember but do not usually discuss ideas. Remembering implies knowing and having forgotten; remembering usually refers to particular times and places, whereas understanding usually produces ideas. They are distinct activities; it does not take long to distinguish them. The distinctions are verifiable. Only confusion will ensue, if they are not distinguished.

The same process can be applied to notions such as innate ideas, intuitions, perceptions, a priori categories, abstraction, and the like. Each of these notions can be discussed and evaluated in a classroom situation, in a group discussion, or in written articles or books. The procedure would involve, describing concrete examples of where these occur in one's own thinking, describing and defining the notion itself, discerning what function does this notion play in understanding, comparing with counterexamples, clarifying the meaning of terms, and finally, affirming or denying the role that these notions play in the actual unfolding of the process of understanding. Communication about cognitional activities can take place. It can lead to agreement, mistakes can be recognized and corrected, and thus, descriptions of mental acts are verifiable. Explanations of the relationship of cognitional activities to one another can be shown to be correct, accurate, and true by reference to each person's awareness of their own experience—in other words, by way of self-appropriation.

Developing a Technique

Naming mental activities at random does not result in a theory of knowledge. But given the basic facility in describing subjective experiences, can we not erect this into an explicit technique in order to systematically study the activities of understanding and knowing? Some think it is impossible because one cannot do two things at the same time, namely, understand something and simultaneously attend to the activities of understanding. It is quite true that it is difficult to attend to a task and examine the performance of that task at the same time. It is difficult to work on an intellectual problem while observing these activities of trying to find a solution. Introspection can only really work if it is retrospection.[17] First, we confront a problem, struggle by all means to solve it, find the solution, and relax. Second, we can shift our attention back to the experience as it unfolded, including the hints and guesses that point to the solution, the false clues and hunches that lead to a dead end, the flash of insight, the putting together of the pieces of the solution, and the realization that we had solved the problem.

Footballers make instant judgments and decisions in the throes of the game as to whether to pass, to run, or to turn. Days later, while watching the

17. Ryle admits the authenticity of retrospection even though he has little time for introspection (Ryle, *Concept of Mind*, 166–67).

video, the coach and the team will analyze the decisions: Why did I do that? What was I thinking? Was I being selfish? Should I have passed the ball? All the movements, decisions, and judgments of the players are subject to this retrospective analysis.

Chess players have a tradition of a post mortem. Chess requires intense concentration, quick analysis over the board, and the ability to see five to ten moves ahead, balancing strategy and tactics. But in the end, one player shakes hands with the other and resigns. The two can now go over the game together. In conversation with one another, they may talk about their questions and concerns: Why did you make such and such move? Did you not see the danger to your King side? It would have been better to take the pawn on move thirty. I was afraid you would play h6. Professional analysts can also give their opinions, lines of play, and analysis of various positions and what was the critical move that led to the loss. We can identify our insights and oversights. We can explain our thought processes. We can give the idea behind a certain move.

Self-appropriation then is to be conceived in two phases. In the first phase we actually tackle a problem, working at it until we find the solution. In the second phase, we remember the stages of the struggle; describe them in detail; identify the relevant images, data, examples, diagrams, and what was helpful or harmful; and pin down the emergence of an act of understanding. At first there is a puzzle, a quandary, bits and pieces that do not fit together; after the emergence of insight there is unity, meaning, coherence, and satisfaction. We can identify these phases for ourselves.

It is best to take real problems encountered in daily life as a basis for analysis. Remember writing an article and how the process unfolded from the first vague notion, to the research, to the ordering of the material, to the review process, to further research, to copy editing, and finally, to revising and polishing. There are many moments of acts of understanding coming together and adding to one another and correcting one another. Or we could take simpler examples such as fixing the refrigerator, identifying the noise in the attic, or learning a new function on the computer. These examples have the advantage that they are not contrived; they are part of the flow of real life.

Alternatively one can do mathematical or crossword puzzles, or play a game like Sudoku, bridge, chess, or draughts. These have the advantage that they are very precise, and it is clear when one has arrived at the correct solution. In these examples, one can easily contrast the difference between the experience of seeing without understanding and the flash of insight where everything—image, idea, question, and solution—comes together. The more precise and simple the puzzles are, the better.

We have all experienced the joy of getting the point, whether by solving a puzzle, fixing something, finding the cause, understanding a detective story, or understanding calculus. But describing how one arrived at the solution is the harder next step. To do so, we need to be able to answer questions such as: what or who was helpful along the way? What was a hindrance? What feelings arose during the process? What tricks proved successful? What discernible method was utilized?

Students can describe their own acts of understanding. The descriptions can be rough, vague, confused, careless, inattentive, distracted, biased, fabricated, or imaginative. I often give students an exercise to describe the movements of the heavenly bodies. The first descriptions are usually somewhat chaotic, contradictory, and even totally at odds with reality. Some students would say the heavenly bodies are not moving, or that they are moving in circles, or that they are dancing in circles, or that they are appearing and disappearing at random. After a review and reflection, I ask them to try again but to do it systematically this time: get a fixed point of reference, check the time, check observations every hour, establish directions (north, south, east, and west), and be intelligent! Good descriptions demand attention; the act of describing calls for intelligence and for discipline. Descriptions can be perceptive, accurate, detailed, precise, prolonged, and verifiable—or the exact opposite of these characteristics.

That is the kind of description needed in the self-appropriation of thinking, knowing, and valuing in philosophy. Describing will pave the way for distinctions and divisions. When the heavenly bodies are systematically observed, one can begin to distinguish between fixed stars, planets, meteorites, satellites, and airplanes. When the activities of the mind are closely described, one can distinguish between sensing, understanding, feeling, evaluating, and judging. We are aiming at accurate, detailed, systematic, and precise descriptions of cognitive activities.

Conclusion: An Empirical Method for Philosophy

In conclusion, I propose that we elevate self-appropriation as described above into an explicit empirical method for recovering human knowing. It can be applied systematically and can resolve any and every question we can ask about human understanding and knowing. It has to be made explicit, and applied consistently and critically. It is not easy; it does not come spontaneously. It does demand discipline and effort. It is easier to describe the movements of the heavenly bodies than it is to describe the invisible landscape of our minds at work. I have made a few preliminary distinctions above to show that the method works. In the next chapter, I will make a further fundamental distinction between consciousness and activities. I started this chapter describing a pedagogy where understanding was treated as an occult, abstract mystery, defined in metaphysical terms. Appropriation reminds us that the process of understanding is quite accessible and that everything we say about understanding and knowing must be verified in our own experience.

2

Consciousness as an Experience

MEDITATION ON SILENCE

"Silence is the great revelation," said Lao-tse. . . . To take in the revelation that silence offers, you must first attain silence. And this is not easy. Let us attempt to do this in our very first exercise.

I want each of you to take a comfortable posture. Close your eyes. I am now going to invite you to keep silence for a period of ten minutes. First you will try to attain silence, as total a silence as possible, of heart and mind. Having attained it, you will expose yourself to whatever revelation it brings. At the end of ten minutes I shall invite you to open your eyes and share with us, if you wish, what you did and what you experienced in these ten minutes.

. . . Most people discover, to their surprise, that silence is something they are simply not accustomed to. That no matter what they do they cannot still the constant wandering of their mind . . . These wandering thoughts of yours are a great revelation, aren't they? . . . The fact that you were aware of your mental wanderings or of your inner turmoil or of your inability to be still shows that you have some small degree of silence within you, at least a sufficient amount of silence to be aware of all of this . . . As silence grows it will reveal to you more and more about yourself. Or more accurately, silence will reveal yourself to you. That is its first revelation: your *self*.[1]

---

1. de Mello, *Sadhana*, 13–14.

What is Consciousness?

Thus far, I have outlined a method of describing mental activities, which I have called a critical introspective method or self-appropriation. Such a method is possible because we are conscious, we are in control of our consciousness, and we can shift the focus of our awareness from outside to inside. The first application of this method concerns identifying this notion of consciousness and distinguishing consciousness from the study of mental activities, which I will proceed to do in detail in subsequent chapters. The very basis of this method is that human beings are conscious and that awareness, though usually oriented outward to physical objects, can be turned inward to describe and identify mental activities. Many hold that this is impossible, in which case I would have us do the impossible.

The word "consciousness" is used in many senses, but I use it with clear reference to concrete experiences, in order to demystify what is really a simple matter. "Consciousness" is often used in a very general sense to refer to everything that goes on in the head. I am hopeful that a more precise definition of consciousness than that is possible. Often it is considered that consciousness is knowledge, and that it includes perception, understanding, deciding, and knowing. Consciousness is often used in the sense of sensitivity to racial, religious, justice issues, sexual discrimination, that is, consciousness of bias, consciousness of racial inequality, consciousness of economic inequality, and so on. My limited interest in consciousness is simply to personally identify the ability to shift the focus of consciousness from objects, to mental activities, and to the self.

The path to understanding is usually by way of precise definitions of terms. My aim is to distinguish the experience of being conscious from conscious activities such as thinking, knowing, and deciding. My procedure is to differentiate the experience of being conscious, from the many conscious cognitional activities that we perform. Later, I will move from differentiation to integration.

Consciousness as Experience

To be conscious is commonly understood to mean to be awake, to be aware, to be alert, to pay attention, to notice what is going on, and to react to phenomena. To be "unconscious" is to be unaware, to be asleep, to be under anesthetic, or to be knocked out through a blow on the head. The word "conscious" is grammatically an adjective; it must go along with a noun. Thus, we talk about a conscious act, a conscious person, a conscious decision, or a conscious animal. Or one can say: he is conscious, I am conscious, I was not conscious, and so on. "Consciousness" is the abstract noun made from the adjective. It simply refers to the state of being conscious or aware. It can become an abstract, obscure, philosophical term, but it simply refers to the common experience of being aware, as opposed to the state of being unaware. "Conscience" is a noun referring specifically to our awareness of moral guilt or righteousness; it has the same etymology but is narrower in its application than simply being conscious.

Etymology

The Latin origin of the word "conscious" is from *conscire*, or, knowledge that goes along with. Aquinas uses the word *conscientia* to refer to conscience, but for him it is an activity of the intellect telling the subject what is the right thing to do. I do not think Aquinas had an equivalent notion of conscious or consciousness simply as an awareness. It appears that these terms were first used by Hobbes and Locke. In the nineteenth and twentieth centuries, they were commonly used in philosophical vocabularies. Even though it is a very simple notion, philosophers contrive it to make it difficult and to misconstrue its import. The big mistake seems to be to think of consciousness as the same as knowing, as any kind of activity that goes on in the head, as some kind of faculty, as a concept to be defined, or as something abstruse and mysterious. On the contrary, consciousness is an everyday experience; it is simply the experience of being aware, awake. It is to be conscious as opposed to being unaware, asleep, or unconscious. My method of self-appropriation encourages the subject to attend to this experience in the self before proceeding to analyze and define it.

Experience

Consciousness is first of all an experience. We do not produce it; we find ourselves in it. It is simply the experience of being conscious as opposed to being unconscious. This chapter began with a little meditation from Anthony de Mello; his focus is on conscious awareness. I am devoting a whole chapter to identifying precisely the experience of being conscious. To begin, it helps to have an experience that is concrete and fresh and to refer everything that is said here to that personal experience. I am not talking about some obscure, philosophical concept but about what it means to be a conscious, human person. For the moment this is a phenomenology of the experience of being conscious, simply as such. Thus, I will spend some time identifying the experience of being conscious and then later consider the activities of sensing, feeling, questioning, understanding, knowing, valuing, deciding, and loving, which are usually conscious.

In teaching I used to approach the topic of consciousness with some trepidation, laden with bibliographies, references, definitions, and distinctions. The students would be equally in awe, brows furrowed, furiously taking notes, grappling with this most difficult of concepts. In my more mature years, I now begin with an exercise in awareness, a simple meditation, usually the one suggested at the beginning of this chapter. Students reported that it is quite difficult to attain complete stillness of the mind; it is easy enough to suspend thinking, but not so easy to stop images, memories, fantasies, and feelings that are flitting about, attracting us like little sprites. The point of the exercise is that whatever success you can have in arresting activities, there always remains some activity, with a conscious self, trying to be silent. Assuming that the students do not fall asleep, there is always a self that is aware—a subject that is conscious. The self is still around, whether that self is silent or distracted by plans for a night out. Consciousness is first and foremost a simple experience of awareness, of being conscious. That simple experience must be identified before moving on to the definitions! Consciousness is such a basic, simple, primordial, pervasive experience that it is difficult to put into words and articulate correctly. It is like what St. Augustine said about time: "We all know what it is but nobody can define it."

In conscious cognitional acts, such as thinking or deliberating, we are clearly aware of what we are thinking or deliberating about. But at the same time, in the same activity, we are immanently aware of the self, who is the subject of the activities. Consciousness is a quality of activities. Some activities such as thinking and deliberating are conscious; some activities such as digesting and growing are usually not conscious. To be conscious is simply to be aware of the subject at the same time as being aware of the object of the activity. Consciousness is not another activity added on to the activity of thinking; it is immanent in thinking.

There is one awareness, which is normally focused on the object, with the subject implicit in the background. Consciousness is one awareness but it has two poles, namely, a primary awareness of the object and a concomitant accompanying awareness of the self as the subject of the awareness. If I am aware of typing on this computer, my main concentration is on the thoughts, sentences, keyboard, screen, and so on. But there is a concomitant awareness that it is I who is the self who is typing, I who is the self who is thinking, I who is the self who is looking. The key characteristic of consciousness is this experience of the subject concomitant with the experience of the object. It is nothing more complicated than the experience of watching a football match, but at the same time being aware that it is *I* who is watching the match. The double awareness is immanent in the activity, that is to say, the awareness is not separate from but part of the activity. There is one activity but two poles of awareness, an objective and subjective one.

To be conscious is not in itself an activity; it is something that goes along with an activity. This is the import of the word "immanent," which implies concomitant, going along with, part of, accompanying. It is not a quick look at an object and then a quick look at the self. Looking is a particularly inappropriate metaphor for consciousness; looking is an activity, consciousness is an experience. The uniqueness of consciousness comes from this characteristic of awareness of an object, concomitant with an awareness of the subject, in the same activity.

Some might argue that machines can see or hear—that copying machines can see, print, and reproduce a text or that computers can hear the human voice and respond to commands. They might conclude that machines and computers are therefore conscious. But few people would call these activities conscious. What is missing is the concomitant awareness of the self which is conspicuously absent in a machine.

Not Knowledge

To be conscious is an experience and not yet knowledge. It is given rather than achieved. One does not have to study philosophy to be conscious. A child who is awake is conscious; an uneducated person is usually aware of what they are doing and the self who is doing it. Aristotle was conscious of what he was doing while writing the *Nichomachean Ethics*, but he was not able to articulate a definition of consciousness. Descartes wrote about the subject as a substance but did not identify the experience of consciousness; however, he was conscious nonetheless. Consciousness occurs long before one is able to define consciousness. Theories about consciousness come after the experience. Before any further step is taken, this experience must be clearly identified. It is a very simple experience, but perhaps that is the difficulty; we take it for granted.

Animals are conscious or unconscious just as human beings. Dogs are sometimes asleep and therefore unconscious. There is a difference between a dog that is awake and one that is asleep. To say that a dog is conscious is not to say that it is thinking or knowing or remembering. These would be separate assertions. That animals are conscious and what is the range of their cognitive abilities are two distinct issues.

Obviously, animals are conscious, provided they are awake, alert, attentive, and aware of their surroundings, as opposed to being asleep, under anesthetic, or severely concussed. To the second issue, I would answer: animals show every sign of sensing, feeling, remembering, and imagining, but no sign of asking questions, understanding concepts, or intellectual knowing. This position will be explained later; for the moment I just emphasize that "to be conscious" is quite different from "to be thinking."

Some philosophers seem to think that it is impossible to be conscious of two things at the same time in the same act.[2] But this is because they think of consciousness as a knowing, an activity in itself, knowing something outside and knowing something inside at the same time. That is indeed impossible but these are misinterpretations of the simple experience of being conscious of an object and at the same time being conscious of the self who is looking at the object. My appeal is not to any theory or concept but to the simple experience. It is possible, because it is happening all the time.

Primary and Secondary Focus

Usually the focus of our attention is primarily on the object; it is only secondarily an awareness of the self. Explicitly we focus on the object; implicitly there is an awareness of self. When we play football, solve a problem, dig a trench, or study philosophy, awareness of self is only an implicit part of our awareness. But it is there in the background, an experience, immanent in the activities, implicit, indirect, and concomitant. "I am seeing the tree" is a rather simple, conscious operation. The main focus is on the tree as the object of seeing and awareness. The activity is basically seeing but will usually involve some activities of understanding and identifying. Immanent in the seeing is an awareness of the self as the one who is doing the seeing. It is not a question of imagining what consciousness looks like but of identifying a very simple experience.

When using the sense of sight, humans usually focus on a central object but have peripheral vision up to about 170 degrees. In other words, we can notice a movement at nearly right angles to us even though we are looking directly ahead. Similarly, we can be centrally conscious of studying, but peripherally conscious of pangs of hunger. We may be focusing directly on driving a car, but we are also listening to music, smoking a cigarette, and even answering a telephone call—and being immanently aware of the self who is the subject of these activities.

2. Ryle, *The Concept of Mind*, 158.

Degrees of Consciousness

There are degrees of consciousness in that we can be well aware that we are studying but not so well aware that the chair is very uncomfortable. One can distinguish what is unconscious, preconscious, and subconscious. Psychologists will offer variations in the meaning of these terms. The unconscious is what cannot be brought to consciousness or only with difficulty; it is repressed or denied. The preconscious is what can be recalled to consciousness easily and freely, what is stored in the memory and imagination. The subconscious seems to be what is just below the threshold of consciousness. But there is a gradation of awareness in each case. Motives can be explicit, implicit, or more or less unconscious. Semi-consciousness would refer to someone who is half conscious, such as someone who is very sick or is just waking up. There are also abnormal states of consciousness that occur in psychoses, neuroses, paranoia, split personality, and so on. There are also altered states of consciousness induced by drugs of various types. There are hypnotic states of dissociation. We are focused on normal process of human conscious activities and not attempting a comprehensive treatment of abnormal or exceptional states of consciousness

Levels of Consciousness

I have already noted how any group of normal students are able to name fifty or more mental activities and to divide them into natural groupings such as experiencing, understanding, judging, and evaluating. The activities they name are conscious, cognitional activities. But there is a different mode, a variation in the affective dimension, when moving from sensing, to questioning, to knowing, and to matters of conscience involved in deliberating. Hence, we can say that the consciousness characteristic of activities of sensing is an empirical consciousness. It is a level of consciousness characteristic of acts of feeling, imagining, seeing, hearing, and fantasizing that are detached from any intellectual questions or tensions. These are conscious and intentional activities but are similar to those of the higher animals; they are purely biological, sensitive, and empirical.

Questioning introduces a new dimension as we seek understanding and meaning; I call this the level of intellectual consciousness. Acts of thinking, comparing, analyzing, and the like are conscious but embody a consciousness characteristic of rational animals. They introduce a new feeling of intellectual tension: an eros of the mind, a desire to know.

A further dimension is introduced when we judge—what could be called the level of rational consciousness. Judging means taking a stand, reaching a conclusion, affirming or denying. We accept responsibility for our judgments; we defend them because they are very personal. They constitute what we are as knowing human subjects. It is embarrassing when we discover that we are mistaken in our judgments.

Finally, there arise questions of value judgment: what is the best course of action? Is this action right and just? Can we serve both God and Mammon? Matters of conscience arise and we feel obliged to do the right thing. This could be called the level of responsibility for our judgments, decisions, and actions. We wrestle with our feelings, we are conflicted in our choices, or we are pulled in different directions, but in the end we choose and make ourselves become moral or immoral human persons. I will define these levels of consciousness in greater detail after dealing with the cognitional structure and can demonstrate the importance of distinguishing these levels or dimensions.

Stream of Consciousness

One can talk about a stream of consciousness. It is an experience of being swept along through imagining, remembering, fantasizing, and feeling with one thing leading to another in a pleasant daydream. We are aware at different levels, in different degrees, and our focus keeps moving. When we are studying we find ourselves distracted by thoughts of football, home, and friends. We are moved along by a stream of images, ambitions, hopes, fears, and feelings; with a start, we bring ourselves back to the library. Most modern fiction is written in this style, recounting events from the point of view of each subject. We follow the characters from the inside, see the world as they see it, and follow their every stray fantasy, association, or thought.

An Experience of Unity

We perform many different activities including eating, feeling, seeing, thinking, deciding, and loving. But we are conscious that it is the same self who is performing all of these activities. Some activities depend on others, as thinking often depends on seeing. But what connects thinking to seeing? It is the one self who is doing both the seeing and the thinking. This is the unity of consciousness as given. It is the same self who gets up, has breakfast, drives to work, gives a lecture, feels tired, assigns grades, sees, understands, evaluates, judges, and might even pray to his or her God. It is an experience of unity throughout many different kinds of activities.

It is also an experience of continuity over time. When I wake up in the morning I usually do not have to ask, "Who am I?" I am conscious of a continuity stretching back fifty years of the same self, of doing and failing, of feeling and thinking, of being healthy and sick, and of being joyful and sad. I can remember many of the feelings, events, successes, and failures of the distant past. Many things have changed but this sense of self does not seem to have changed. There is an experienced continuity, a sameness—the same self, but growing, changing, moving, taking on various tasks, and moving through life's stages: infancy, childhood, adolescence, early adulthood, mature adulthood, and late adulthood. The same identical subject uniting a great variety of activities, stretched out over time.

Sometimes in life we experience disharmony between elements of the personality. We are involved in too many activities and we cannot get it all together. Or there is conflict between professed priorities and actual performance, or between financial and moral aspirations. Then, we have to work at integration, restore harmony, and achieve unity. But it is the same self who experiences tension and disharmony, the same self who gets it together in terms of integration and maturity.

I am describing the experience of the self as one of the poles of consciousness. This experience unites the past with the present, thinking and deciding with feeling and doing. We are prescinding for the moment from questions of the ontological status of the self. For the moment, allow me to describe the experience of unity conferred by the sense of self at the center of all awareness and activities. My descriptions are a mere sketch of the landscape; one could go on and on forever describing the experience of the self that unites a lifetime of variegated experiences and activities. Disagreements about consciousness often arise because of the difficulty of describing it accurately and the fluid meaning of the terminology.

Givenness

Consciousness is an experience that is given. We do not teach children to be conscious. We do teach them to be conscious of the danger of fire, or of their manners in front of guests; but if they are unconscious, this is rather fruitless. If it is not there, we cannot make it come to be. We ask them to pay attention, but that presupposes that they are attending to something else. We do not produce consciousness by philosophical concepts or human effort. We can expand or contract our consciousness, dissipate or alter our consciousness, and focus or heighten our consciousness; however, if it is not there to start with, we cannot produce it.

Analysis and Definition

Lonergan defines consciousness simply as "an awareness immanent in cognitional acts."[3] This can be utilized in order to summarize the essential points of what I have been describing as the experience of being conscious.

First, awareness simply means being conscious, awake, alert, or attending to. Human consciousness has a two-fold polarity, a subject pole and an object pole. There is an awareness of the subject and an awareness of the object at the same time, which is immanent in the activity.

The subject pole can be referred to as a self, a person, or an ego. Nothing more is involved here than the sense of self, which every normal human person seems to experience when he or she is conscious. For the moment, all that is being suggested by the self is the experienced self, which seems to be continuous over time and place, and seems to be the focus of unity of all the various activities performed by the person.

The object pole is very general and all-encompassing. All the cognitional activities that I will be describing are intentional. They intend an object: seeing intends the visible, understanding intends the intelligible, sensing intends the sensible, and evaluating intends values. The activity would make no sense if there were not this intention of the activity. I am not taking a stand on the question of subjectivity or objectivity here. I am simply noting that intentional, cognitional activities are transitive, that activity passes over into an object. In English grammar we distinguish between transitive and intransitive verbs. The verbs we are talking about are transitive. They are also in the active voice rather than in a passive voice, which is the difference between knowing an object and being known by another person.

Second, the awareness of subject and object is immanent in an activity. It may be a cognitional activity, it may be a volitional activity such as deciding, or it may be an affective activity such as loving or hating. In any cognitional activity such as thinking, there has to be a subject who is doing the thinking, and there has to be something that we are thinking about. There has to be a mediating activity to have consciousness. All cognitional activities are normally conscious, such as, knowing, questioning, experiencing, sensing, remembering, imagining, seeing, understanding, judging, and evaluating. Other activities such as deciding, relating to a person, praying, or loving are also conscious and intentional even though they are not in

3. Lonergan, *Insight,* 344.

themselves cognitional. Feelings can be conscious or unconscious, intentional or nonintentional.

Third, consciousness of self is immanent in the activity of knowing an object. By immanent, I mean that it is essential to, concomitant with, not separable from, and an integral part of the activity. I have been differentiating between the various aspects of consciousness, and now I put the parts together again. Consciousness is one experience of a self being aware of an object in a cognitional act. If one of the elements is missing there is no consciousness.

Fourth and finally, is there such a thing as pure consciousness? In other words, can one be conscious and not be performing some mental activity? Can one have awareness in a totally empty mind? Can the self be aware of the self without an object or activity? This is an empirical question and not a theoretical one. Does it happen or does it not? In my view, there does not seem to be a direct experience of the self as subject without a mediating activity. In the minimal consciousness of dreams, there is an awareness of the self as a participant or observer; however, these are mediated by activities such as being chased, falling off a cliff, flying an airplane, and so forth. Upon waking up in the morning, the person gradually remembers where he or she is, what time of day it is, and what things have to be done that day. The person becomes conscious of the self through these acts of remembering and anticipating. In meditation, such as the one suggested at the beginning of the chapter, directors recommend a focus on breathing so as to quiet the mind and prevent distractions. But the sense of the self remains, as it is immanent in the conscious activity of breathing. All consciousness of self seems to be mediated through sensitive, cognitional and volitional activities. In higher states of meditation, mysticism and ecstasy there may be an unmediated awareness of God as a cloud of unknowing but it is beyond our purpose to discuss that here.

I have belabored this notion of consciousness, because the method of self-appropriation depends entirely on recognizing this ability to shift one's awareness from objects to activities, and from activities to the self. Allow me to summarize this shifting of awareness from objects, to activities, to the self.

Normally, the focus of our awareness is on objects or on activities that we are performing in the world. I am conscious of the keyboard, some rough notes, a computer screen, a mouse. I am not doing any explicit self-reflection. The self is very much in the background. All I am trying to do is get words on paper. Most of our daily activities are in this ordinary mode of extroversion: getting to work, washing the dishes, serving clients, teaching class, repairing automobiles, or playing golf. These are mostly conscious activities, but the focus is on the work, the object, or the outside, while the awareness of self is in the background.

In a more reflective mood, we can shift the awareness from objects to the activities going on in the mind. We can identify these activities, name them, identify them, and define them. We can reflect on our thinking: a penny for your thoughts. We can reflect on our seeing: did I really see what I thought I saw? We can prescind from the objects and attend to the activities. The objects can be a quasi infinity. We can think about anything, but the thinking is much the same in all of these cases. We can see anything in the range of visible light, but the activity of seeing is the same in all cases. The activities are simple, basic, and common; they are recurrent, forming familiar patterns. Most of this book will focus on identifying these cognitional activities and getting them in a sequence.

Can one shift the focus of awareness from the activities to the self? If this is achieved one has an awareness of the subject as object. It can be done. We can be self-conscious. The self can be the focus of awareness. We can identify, name, and define the experience of the self. But it is the self as object and not the self as subject. We can move from consciousness of the self to knowledge of the self. I use the term "self-consciousness" to indicate this explicit self-awareness of the self as object and not in the sense of embarrassment at being the focus of attention.

Clarification by Contrast

I have offered a phenomenological description of the experience of being conscious. I have added some analysis with the aim of searching for the essential characteristics of consciousness. These seem to include the following: the necessity of a subject, or self, or person; the necessity of an activity of experience, or sensing, or understanding, or knowing, or some other intentional act; and the necessity of an object, including the awareness, understanding, or knowledge of that object. That is all that is presently necessary in order to be able to distinguish consciousness from conscious cognitional activities. One cannot go very far in understanding if everything that goes on in the mind is just one big undifferentiated blob. The first distinction, then, is between consciousness and cognitional activities. I will follow this with many other crucial distinctions between the activities themselves. Everyone should be able to identify all of these distinctions in their own awareness of their own minds.

I have not yet attempted to develop a theory of consciousness, nor have I attempted to explain how consciousness is possible in terms of the

brain, such as the chemical, biological, and neurological conditions necessary for the emergence of consciousness. I have not traced the evolution
of consciousness and its function in the survival of the fittest from earliest
times. All of these questions are legitimate, but my only aim is to first get a
handle on the extent and limits of human consciousness and human knowing. Then, one might be in a position to tackle those difficult questions.
Others have not been so reticent, and I present a few contemporary views
for the purposes of clarification by contrast.

First, Susan Blackmore's work *Consciousness* seems to be representative of the empiricist, linguistic, analytic tradition. She starts by posing the
problem of the bridge, the *pons asinorum*,[4] between the subjective and the
objective, the inner and the outer, or mind and reality, which everyone is
trying to cross. She presents Descartes's dualism: the mind that is nonphysi-
cal and nonextended, while the body and the rest of the physical world are
made of physical, or extended, substances.[5] She appeals to Nagel's famous
question—what is it like to be a bat?—as a question that is equivalent to
asking whether a bat is conscious. Slowly it becomes clear that she is trying
to explain all of the activities of the mind in terms of changes in the brain.
Later, she considers the sense of the self, beginning with Hume's position
that the self is just a bundle of sensations.[6] We imagine that the self is a continuous, permanent entity, but for Blackmore it is really only a succession
of sensations. She discusses William James, Antonio Damasio, and Daniel
Dennett who are considered experts on consciousness. She concludes that
we can reject any persisting entity that corresponds to our feeling of being a
self.[7] On that basis, it is not hard to dismiss conscious will, or willing, as an
illusion. She follows with some thoughts on altered states of consciousness
and the evolution of consciousness. The conclusion is boldly stated:

> Consciousness, then, is a grand delusion. It arises through ask-
> ing such questions as "Am I conscious now?" or "What am I
> conscious of now?" In that moment of questioning, an answer
> is concocted: a now, a stream of experiences, and a self who ob-
> serves it all, appear together, and a moment later they are gone
> . . . If you go on to believe that you always were conscious, and
> construct metaphors about streams and theatres, then you only
> dig yourself deeper and deeper into confusion.[8]

4. Blackmore, *Consiousness*, 2.
5. Ibid., 4.
6. Ibid., 67.
7. Ibid., 81.
8. Ibid., 131.

Allow me to make a few short comments.

The topic of consciousness is posed in terms of the inner mind knowing outer reality. That poses the whole problem of objective knowing and not the specific question, what is the meaning of being conscious?

If knowing is the same as feeling, then the conclusion that the self is an illusion would be valid. But do we know through feeling? Is knowing the same as feeling, as seeing, as touching? Is knowing the same as being conscious? These are the questions I explicitly address in this text.

The reasoning is interesting. She cannot find any satisfactory explanation of consciousness neither by herself nor in the authors she consults. She seems to conclude that if it cannot be explained, it cannot be possible; therefore, it is an illusion. My approach would be quite different based on the principle that if it happens then it is possible. I am conscious and some of my best friends are conscious; usually my students are conscious. It is a relatively common experience in my community. Not only are we conscious, but we also ask questions, think, reason, and distinguish true from false. We are doing these things all of the time. We perform these activities, and therefore, it is possible. I offer an explicit exposition of the reality of the subject and of the object of knowing in chapters 10 and 11.

Second, in contemporary science and philosophy, the most common misconception of consciousness is to bypass the element of experience and immediately engage in a discussion of the concept of consciousness. If we talk about concepts with no reference to experience, then we can formulate, compare, define, and divide concepts in whatever way we wish *ad infinitum;* however, we have no criterion of truth because we have bypassed the experience to which consciousness is referring. For example, Eugene Webb's *Philosophers of Consciousness* compares the concept of consciousness as found in Polanyi, Lonergan, Voegelin, Ricoeur, Girard, and Kierkegaard. Such comparing, contrasting, and distinguishing can be done forever; however, it ends up with nothing unless it refers back to the experience of being conscious. The discussion becomes a verbal tangle without a basis in experience, a formulation of a concept without reference to examples.

Third, Daniel Dennett is a materialist and tries to explain consciousness in terms of neuroscience, cognitive psychology, and artificial intelligence. He is typical of a large group of contemporary materialist philosophers and scientists who have the difficult task of explaining consciousness and thinking within the bounds of their materialist presuppositions. Dennett's thesis is:

> Human consciousness is itself a huge complex of memes (or more exactly, meme effects in brains) that can best be understood as the operation of a *"von Neumannesque"* virtual machine implemented

in the parallel architecture of a brain that was not designed for any such activities. The powers of the virtual machine vastly enhance the underlying powers of the organic hardware on which it runs, but at the same time many of its most curious features, and especially its limitation, can be explained as the by-products of the kludges that make possible this curious but effective reuse of an existing organ for novel purposes.[9]

I am not sure that this or any other computer-generated program will enlighten us on the nature of human consciousness. Neuroscience has a valuable contribution to make to understanding the biological and neurological conditions for the possibility of consciousness. But to imagine that reductionist neuroscience by itself will understand consciousness is like a person taking pictures of New York City from a helicopter and claiming, "Now we understand how the city works." Computers may have enormous and expanding memories; they may have great powers of computing and calculating. They may process streams of incoming data in seconds; however, they are not conscious and never will be conscious. There will never be a machine that is capable of simultaneous awareness of self and of an object, immanent in cognitional or volitional activities. If these reductionist neuroscientists did de Mello's exercise at the start of this chapter, they might realize how far they are from replicating that simple human experience of being conscious.

Fourth, John Searle is a biological naturalist. He claims: "Consciousness is a natural, biological phenomenon. It is as much part of our biological life as digestion, growth, or photosynthesis."[10] He challenges the terms in which this discussion has often been conducted—such as mental, physical, dualism, monism, or materialism—as these terms fix one into a mindset of unreal problems. He claims that we will understand consciousness when we understand in biological detail how the brain does it. He is trying to turn the mystery of consciousness into a problem that can be solved. There are also many dualists such as the physicist Roger Penrose and the philosopher David Chalmers, who see no way out of Descartes's dualism and learn to live with it.

Is consciousness a mystery, as Searle suggests? If in principle a tradition rules out a study of mental activities as intrinsically private and unverifiable, then the mind will remain in the mysterious shadows of the unknown and unknowable. If one lumps everything that goes on in the head in one undifferentiated blob, then it is hard to look forward to a clear, differentiated understanding of the workings of the mind. If, while ruling out a study of

---

9. Dennett, *Consciousness Explained*, 210.
10. Searle, *The Mystery of Consciousness*, xiii.

mind, one continues to use it in life, science, and philosophy, one cannot but foresee confusion and contradiction. The way out of that is by way of an explicit focus on the activities of the mind, clear distinctions between consciousness as experience and the conscious activities of questioning, experiencing, understanding, judging, and evaluating. That is the way to clarity; that is the way of self-appropriation.

Neuroscientists usually try to explain consciousness, to provide the cause of consciousness, to explain its role in evolution, to identify what part of the brain is responsible for mental activities, and to sort out how the physical effects the mental. This is a very difficult set of questions, and I think most would admit that they have not yet been answered in a satisfactory way. Fortunately, these are not yet the questions of concern here. My question is to describe the experience of being conscious, to identify the characteristics of that experience, to distinguish that experience from other activities of the human mind, and then to describe in detail cognitional activities. Having put together a comprehensive view of the activities involved in human knowing, we can then face the critical question of subjectivity and objectivity. After that, I believe we are in the clear to distinguish the physical from the mental, dualism from monism, the sensible from the intelligible, and what is real from what is of value It seems to me that one needs a sound epistemology before entering into and solving metaphysical problems. Most of the above thinkers presume that knowing is sensing, or seeing, or feeling; most are working in a framework of materialism or dualism. There is very little recognition of understanding and passing judgments as distinct and different cognitional acts. But that is the crux of the issue.

Defining Basic Terms

One of the difficulties in speaking about mental activities is that there is no accepted, well-defined terminology in which to do it. Words slip and slide and one becomes unsure of his or her location or of what the author is trying to say. Words like consciousness, subjectivity, understanding, imagination, knowing, facts, interiority, real and ideal, image and idea, representation, impression, perception, conception, abstraction all have a variety of shifting meanings. The only way I can deal with that is to define my own use of terms when they are first encountered. The empirical referent of such definitions is often personal experience. Now that I have presented a method of self-appropriation, I can utilize it to make some basic distinctions. In the following, I clarify the distinction between (1) data and facts, (2) data of sense and data of consciousness, and (3) activity of knowing and content that is known.

Distinguish Data from Facts

The word "data" is most commonly used in the sense of data of the census, economic data, population data, or a database. In these contexts, it means information, a collection of facts, or figures. However, in philosophy it has a special, narrow meaning. In philosophy the term "datum, data" means simply what is given in experience. That is the etymology of the word from the Latin verb, *do, dare, dedi, datum*, which means "to give." The given is what is simply experienced, before naming, before interpretation, before understanding, and before conceptualizing. It is an experience simply as an experience, before any intervention or addition of intelligent activity. We see a shape, but for a moment we do not know whether it is a rock or a person. A professor writes an equation on the board. We can see it but we do not understand what it means. A child sees a dog, but does not know that it is a dog. We can see Chinese characters, but unless we know Chinese, it is nonsense to us. Data in this sense is what is given, meaning that nothing has been added by intelligence, by preconceived ideas, or by naming. Sometimes, we use the expression "raw data" to emphasize that nothing has been added by naming or interpretation.

There seems to be a sequence in which we first sense an object, and only then can we recognize, name, and understand it. We can catch this sequence in our own experience, but it is difficult to be aware of that brief moment when we sense but do not understand. In adults the activity of intelligence has permeated everywhere in the mind and influenced our interpretations and classifications. All of our reactions to what we see are influenced by previous learning and understanding. But a small child is seeing everything for the first time, hearing as well as we do, but understanding almost nothing. The given is an important notion in philosophy and especially epistemology because it seems to be the beginning of knowing—it is that about which we ask questions. Sensing is largely passive; sense datum is received. We open our eyes and we see what is there to be seen. Later, we will question, name, interpret, and understand, but at that first moment we receive something for which we are not responsible; we do not make it come into existence or present itself.

However, if we ask questions about what is given and try to understand and know what is happening, we are moving beyond sense data and heading toward facts. Facts are not given. Facts are a result of questioning, understanding, and affirming. Dogs do not question, name, understand, and affirm. Only humans sense, understand, and affirm. Facts are complete increments in knowledge, units of knowledge, or pieces of true or false information. True and false are categories that do not apply to experiencing sense data. If one sees something and wonders whether it is a rock or a person, then intelligence has come alive and the person is moving to an affirmation, which might be true or false. A fact is a complete increment in human intellectual knowing and requires questioning what we have sensed, in order to recognize, name, interpret, and judge it to be true or false.

Linguistic analysts have difficulty with this distinction between what is given in sensation and what is added by naming and understanding.[11] They do not pay much attention to the process of knowing, and thus, do not realize that knowing is a series of distinct cognitional operations starting with data and concluding in a true fact. They consider knowing to be a single simple operation which they usually name a perception or an intuition. I would simply appeal to self-appropriation. Moments of experiencing happen in my life before I understand; any students I have taught agree that they too have experiences of sensing without understanding. Perhaps more attention to what actually happens in the mind would help resolve the issue.

There is then an enormous difference between sensing the data of sense and affirming a true fact. This text will be an extended analysis of how we move from what is given in sensation to what is affirmed in judgment.

Distinguish Data of Sense from Data of Consciousness

Data of sense refers to the data given in the experience of the senses, imagining, and remembering. The senses are oriented outward; it is extroversion. By definition the senses sense the sensible: what is seen, heard, touched, tasted, and smelled. Our natural, spontaneous orientation is by way of extroversion to what is sensed. The physical sciences take the data of sense as their special field of operation.

Data of consciousness is what is given when we shift our attention from objects of sense to the activities and feelings involved in sensing, understanding, and knowing. We can focus our awareness on mental activities rather than on objects out there. When we are asked by a counselor to describe our feelings, we seem to be able to do so: we turn our attention inward, focus on our feelings, name them, and describe them. When we are asked to describe our dreams we can with some effort concur. We can describe our hopes and dreams, our aches and pains, and our joys and sorrows. We can focus on feelings or on cognitional activities. When we focus our attention on the activities of our mind, we are focusing on data of consciousness. Just as the biologist can be conscious of frogs and dogs, so we can be conscious of the activities of seeing, hearing, questioning, understanding, criticizing, and affirming. We can

11. McDowell, *Mind and World*, 13–23. Cf. Arianna Betti, *Against Facts.*

also focus on our sense of self, our felt identity or single center of consciousness, while it performs various activities and perdures over time.

Data of consciousness is simply given in experience, before selection, interpretation, or understanding. The experiences of feelings, activities, and the self are first of all simply conscious, and then we can try to understand and define them. The first time we attend to mental activities, we find a jumble of confusing and overlapping activities, which do not seem to have any order or sequence. But once we start naming, describing, isolating, and identifying the activities, they begin to fall into recognizable patterns of interrelated activities. The process of self-appropriation starts with this given data of consciousness with a view to understanding the invariant pattern of relations existing between the activities.

I can shift the focus of my attention to my own thoughts, desires, and feeling and have a direct immediate awareness of them. I cannot become aware of another's thoughts and feelings, except mediately through his or her expressions and my external senses. I have privileged, direct, immediate access to the data of my own consciousness. Nobody else has such access to my inner life. Nobody can see directly what is going on in there. I can tell lies and get away with it. Self-appropriation can only be done by the self who takes initiative and responsibility. Nobody can do it for another person or force it on him or her.

Scientific theories about climate change for instance stand or fall by the evidence that is presented and the connection between the evidence and the conclusions. The evidence in that case is from the data of sense, actual temperatures, actual percentages of greenhouse gasses, figures for extreme climate events, and so on. Theories about human knowing stand or fall on the evidence presented, and the connection between the evidence and the conclusion. This evidence is based on the data of consciousness. Is understanding the same as remembering? Do we have a priori ideas of space and time? Are intuitions the same as acts of understanding? Do we have intuitions? These and all questions about human knowing are answered correctly only by reference to the data of consciousness.

Distinguish Content from Activities

Usually, the orientation of our conscious activities is outward toward external objects, to the content of our knowing. The infant is almost entirely oriented by way of the senses toward objects to be grasped, touched, thrown, or put in the mouth. We are most at home in the world of objects attained through the senses. Our senses massively orient us outward toward what can be seen, heard, and touched in the external world. When asked to give examples of acts of understanding, most students give practical examples, such as how to mend a leaking pipe, how to deal with mosquitoes, how to discover short cuts to make work easier, or how to fix a computer glitch.

Can we focus on the mental activities themselves, rather than on the contents? Can we become aware of the mental activities by which we perform operations? If we can talk intelligently about our dreaming, can we similarly talk intelligently about our thinking, understanding, and knowing? It is my contention that we can; this is the key to recovering an awareness of the process of knowing. What actually happens when we understand something? What kinds of activities are involved? What comes before and what comes after and what is the usual sequence of events? These questions can only be answered by shifting our awareness from the contents to the activities of our minds.

Even though it is difficult to shift attention from content to activities, there is a preliminary indication that this could be a very fruitful way to go; it might also give us the kind of integrating unity that we are seeking. The possible content of the act of seeing is for all practical purposes an infinity; there is no limit to the number, shape, color, or size of the objects that might be seen. But the seeing is the same activity in all cases and for all contents. We can remember a multitude of events, persons, feelings, experiences, words, and names; however, the activity of remembering is the same in all cases for all contents. We can imagine an infinity of shapes, sizes, colors, and sounds; we can combine data from the five senses in any way we like; we can spin tales of science fiction, great literature, and dramas; but the activity of the imagination is the same in all cases, for all contents. We can question everything—the known and the unknown, even every book in the library—but the basic form of questioning remains the same for this infinity of content. We can understand so many things—all the sciences, all the books in the library, all the languages of the earth, and all the databases in our computer—but in every case, it is the same act of understanding. We use the word understanding in all cases. There is one act of understanding and an infinity of contents to that same, single activity. We judge the truth or falsity of many propositions every day. The contents may vary enormously between what we read in the newspaper, what we hear from our friends, what our teacher tells us, and what we read in our textbooks; however, the act of judging is the same in all of these cases. Finally, we evaluate professors, meals, books, climate, and computers. We evaluate from the point of view of health, from the point of view of efficiency, or from a moral or religious point of view; yet the act of evaluating is much the same in all cases.

The content of our knowing overwhelms us. Knowledge expands exponentially in all directions. We are swamped by new information, recent discoveries, broadening horizons, and increasing specializations. Our knowledge of objects overflows libraries and encyclopedias, but there is one set of activities by which they are all known. If we can get a grasp on how these different activities of seeing, understanding, conceiving, and judging combine into authentic human knowing, then we will in some way be able to grasp a unity behind all the differences in contents. The sequence of activities by which we know and evaluate is forever the same, deals with all fields in the same way, and has a basic structure and simplicity that does not change whatever the content. If we can get a handle on this simple sequence of activities, then we can confer an extraordinary unity on all that is known and that is to be known in all fields of human inquiry. That is the aim of this book—to isolate and identify that sequence of activities, questioning what we have imagined, remembered or sensed, in order to understand, judge, and evaluate correctly.

Understanding as an Activity

We are familiar with physical human activities such as playing football, eating a meal, teaching a class, driving from New York to Washington, cutting down a tree, building a house, mowing the lawn, and so on. They are unproblematic, but allow me to identify some of their characteristics so that we can be clear about the nature of an activity.

1. The activity has a beginning, middle, and end. In football, the game begins and ends with a whistle. In between, the game is composed of furious actions of defending and attacking, passing and tackling, throwing and kicking, and victory and defeat.

2. The activity has a purpose, an end, goal, or reason. Some activities are for pleasure or entertainment, some are for survival, some are for medical reasons, and some are necessitated by the need for cleanliness, hygiene, and the like.

3. Activities take time and are extended over time and place. It takes a few hours to mow the lawn, a year to build a house, and about half an hour to eat a meal.

4. Usually activities are deliberately chosen and freely embarked upon. They are conscious activities. They do not happen to the subject, but the subject chooses to make them happen.

5. Usually there is a correct and incorrect way of performing the activity. There is a good way to play football and a bad way, an intelligent way and a stupid way, a successful way and a way that usually ends in failure. There is a time and a place for cutting down trees. There is also a right way, so that it does not fall on anyone. There is also a wrong way in which people can get hurt.

6. Activities are often complex rather than simple. There are many activities of a football team, with specialists in various positions working for the advantage of the whole. Even a simple activity like jogging involves different activities from the legs, arms, lungs, and muscles.

7. These activities can be observed, described, understood, and known. The press will be able to describe the key moments in a football game. The crowd can understand what is going on. They can know that the coach made a mistake in certain decisions or that players failed to perform their specific duties.

8. Activities can be analyzed. The coach will review the video and obtain the statistics on tackles, kicks, passes, assists, and scores. Who did what they were supposed to do? Who failed and why?

Clearly, we recognize that such physical activities are conscious, purposive, willed, and performed well or badly as the case may be. Similarly, cognitional activities share most of these characteristics even though this fundamental activity is not visible.

1. An assignment to write a paper or an article has a beginning, middle, and end. If a student is assigned an essay topic by a professor, what does the student have to do? Well, it helps to understand what the professor wants and expects. Usually it will involve research, reading, and taking notes. Often the student will go through a period of confusion and frustration when the essay does not come together. With more thinking, discussing, and revising the outline becomes clear. The student's points fall into place, he or she writes a rough draft and polishes it up, references are inserted, and behold a work of genius. Any intellectual task, solving a problem, doing a homework project, or writing an article has a beginning, a middle, and an end.

2. Intellectual activity is purposive. There is a deadline to finish an assignment. The student's long-term goal is to graduate. More concretely, my phone will not work and I do not know how to fix it. I set about concentrating on the problem, exploring possible solutions, rejecting those that do not work, finding a helpful hint, applying the advice,

and bingo, it is fixed! To accomplish the purpose requires that I push myself at that point when I might be tempted to give up.

3. Cognitional activities take time. A bachelor's degree usually takes four years, a master's degree takes two more years, and a doctorate will take three or four more years. To write an article will take a month. To write a book will probably take a year or two or three. The quality of chess games is dependent on the amount of time allowed for each move.

4. The self is free and responsible for his or her own mental development. One enrolls in a university, has a deliberate plan to get a degree, and desires to enter a specific profession. These are conscious decisions.

5. There is a correct way of thinking and an incorrect way, a good way of writing an assignment and a bad way. Normally a professor would recommend that the student read the relevant articles; go over lecture notes on the topic; think of what the student wants to say; be critical and clear; stay within the number of pages allowed; and include an introduction, argument, and conclusion. Professors are often disappointed when students do not do the assigned readings, do not have their thoughts in order, and clearly have not understood what they are talking about.

6. Knowing is not one single activity, but a sequence of activities. Studying biology involves listening to lectures, thinking about definitions, memorizing material, doing experiments, observing results, and looking through microscopes. Through this process, one learns, understands, questions, criticizes, and much more. Knowing biology involves various kinds of mental activities. The same is true with problem solving, doing philosophy, or playing chess. Delivering a lecture, writing a book, reading a book, and discussing in a group all involve a stream of different mental activities. Mental activities do not take place on their own but usually in conjunction with other activities. Reading involves physical seeing as well as understanding and evaluating. Lecturing involves standing and speaking as well as good communication. Writing an article involves typing as well as critical thinking.

7. Mental activities can be named and identified. A typical junior-level college class will be able to name thirty such activities in fifteen minutes. These are each specific mental activities that we are usually involved in thinking, writing, or teaching. Understanding is just one of these activities, but it is central and many other mental activities can be classified as specific kinds of acts of understanding.

8. Cognitional activities can be analyzed, broken down into parts, and put into a sequence; they occur in a pattern of relations. That is what

I am attempting in this manuscript. We need to identify each of these activities, locate them within a sequence of other activities, then see the whole process as human knowing. Typically, this involves starting with a question, moving through research, observation and collecting data, understanding the results and clearly articulating it into words, verifying and checking the results, and evaluating and deciding what to do next.

Human knowing then is not some simple, single, activity of perceiving or intuiting, but a series of activities. Human knowing seems to start with a question and end with an answer; it is purposive; it is discursive; it takes time; it is a sequence of activities that can be broken down into parts; the activities can be done well or badly. Just as we can analyze playing football into its constituent parts so we can analyze the process of knowing into a sequence of parts. That is what I am setting out to do. Later, when we have understood, I will synthesize the parts into a whole

Conclusion

One of the problems in discussing mental activities—consciousness, intentionality, subjectivity, perception, and the like—is that the terminology does not have a precise, defined, universally accepted meaning. My first tasks then have been to provide a precise definition of the notion of what it means to be conscious and consciousness and its various characteristics and to distinguish this strictly and clearly from activities that might be conscious or unconscious.

All of this is included in the project of self-appropriation. Everyone is invited to recognize in their own experience the points that have been made in this chapter. The goal is to take possession of our own minds. This involves distinguishing the experience of being conscious and the many cognitional activities that we can perform. Consciousness is not a big mystery; it is the simple state of being awake, aware, and alert. I am now moving on to discussing and defining many cognitional activities, most of which are conscious activities that one can identify in one's own awareness. But activities are different from the state of being conscious. Remember that "conscious" is an adjective; it must go along with a noun as in a conscious act—a conscious person, a conscious decision, a conscious motivation. One could say much more about consciousness, but my only purpose has been to show that the method of self-appropriation is possible because of our ability to shift the focus of consciousness, from objects to subjects, from content to activities, from data of sense to data of consciousness, from sensing to understanding.

3

The Basic Act of Understanding (Part 1)

AND THAT WILL SETTLE THE MANICHEES!

There is one casual anecdote about St. Thomas Aquinas which illumi-
nates him like a lightening-flash, not only without but within. For it
not only shows him as a character, and even as a comedy character, and
shows the colours of his period and social background; but also, as if
for an instant, makes a transparency of his mind. It is a trivial incident
which occurred one day, when he was reluctantly dragged from his
work, and we might almost say, from his play. For both were for him
found in the unusual hobby of thinking, which is for some men a thing
much more intoxicating than mere drinking. [He was invited by the
King Louis IX of France to a banquet and he felt obliged to attend.]

. . . Somehow they steered that reluctant bulk of reflection to a
seat in the royal banquet hall; and all that we know of Thomas tells us
that he was perfectly courteous to those who spoke to him, but spoke
little, and was soon forgotten in the most brilliant and noisy clatter in
the world: the noise of French talking. [The banquet proceeded with
the usual pomp and ceremony.]

. . . And then suddenly the goblets leapt and rattled on the board
and the great table shook, for the friar had brought down his huge fist
like a club of stone, with a crash that startled everyone like an explo-
sion; and had cried out in a strong voice, but like a man in the grip
of a dream, "And that will settle the Manichees!" [Some consternation
ensued but King Louis kept his cool.]

And he [King Louis] turned to his secretaries, asking them in a
low voice to take their tablets round to the seat of the absent-minded
controversialist, and take note of the argument that had just occurred
to him; because it must be a very good one and he might forget it.[1]

---

1. Chesterton, *Saint Thomas Aquinas*, 49–51.

Introduction

Finally, it is now possible to describe the basic act of human understanding in this and the following chapter. There would seem to be a basic act of understanding, which is the prototype of all acts of understanding. It is possible to divide acts of understanding into genus and species. In these two chapters I describe the genus; in subsequent chapters I will describe the species, namely, particular forms, or kinds or variations of this basic act. There, I will identify such species as reflective insights, inverse insights, deliberative insights, introspective insights, and higher viewpoints. For the moment, I shall concentrate on the basic act and its characteristics.

I will be taking the position that there are five essential characteristics of the act of understanding: (1) it arises from the desire to know, (2) it has an active component, (3) it has a passive component, (4) it leads to an idea that emerges from an image, and (5) the idea passes into the habitual texture of the mind.[2] The first three of these characteristics will be treated in this chapter, and the remaining two will be addressed in the following. My treatment will follow these characteristics sequentially for the sake of good pedagogy. The reader is encouraged to keep in mind his or her own experience of understanding and, perhaps, focus on one specific occasion when he or she had a great idea and it worked.

First, some clarifications about terminology. The word "insight" is used in this text as a synonym for the act of human understanding; it conveys exactly the same meaning. It is not intended in any other way than a simple act of understanding. It is not intended in any mystical, religious, emotional, or mystagogic sense. It is not a conversion experience, a change of life experience, or a purely emotional experience. In the opening citation, Aquinas had an insight; he grasped an argument that he could use against the Manichees. It was primarily an act of human understanding, even though it was accompanied by his own excitement, not to mention the consternation of the guests.

I will exercise great caution using the word "intuition." Intuition in ordinary usage can mean, a guess, a hunch, or a feeling for a solution without any philosophical implications. There is no problem with that general usage in those contexts. However, in a philosophical context the term "intuition" often refers to acts of knowing through the senses or acts of intellectual knowing, which are interpreted to be simple, direct, and immediate contact between the knower and the known. Descartes, Kant, Bergson, and Husserl seem to have used the word to imply that knowing is a simple, single act of

---

2. This is a slight variation on Lonergan's five characteristics of insight outlined in Lonergan, *Insight,* 28. The difference is merely pedagogical and not substantive.

contact between a subject and an object. This is almost the polar opposite to what is referred to as insight. Whether we have insights or intuitions is an empirical question that I hope to resolve through this description of the act of understanding.

I use the terms "intelligence" or "intellect" as cognates with the act of understanding. Aquinas used the term *intelligere*, meaning simply "to understand." To be intelligent means to be able to understand quickly, easily, and critically. For the most part, we have little difficulty distinguishing between those who are intelligent and catch on fast, and those who are unintelligent and struggle to catch on at all. Psychologists have much to say about intelligence, measuring intelligence, intelligence tests, intelligence quotient, multiple intelligences, emotional intelligence, and the like; their usage sometimes differs from what I present here. There is intelligence involved in art, in music, in religion, and in various other areas of life. There is intelligence involved in most of our activities in one way or another. Howard Gardner identifies seven kinds of intelligence: musical intelligence, bodily kinesthetic intelligence, logical-mathematical intelligence, linguistic intelligence, spatial intelligence, interpersonal intelligence, and intrapersonal intelligence.[3] My focus is on intelligence involved in the process of knowing truth and value whether in common sense, science, or philosophy. Examples taken from aesthetics or religion introduce extraneous matter and confuse rather than clarify.

Where to Look

I pointed out the difficulties in pinning down a single act of human intelligence from the many acts we routinely perform. Here I will offer some brief reminders as to the kinds of insights that are most identifiable and helpful in the process of self-appropriation.

First, we are looking for examples of acts of understanding that are protracted, take time, and where we can identify the stages of preparation, frustration, breakthrough, and verification. The privileged place to study the act of human understanding is in discoveries, in the aha experience, in the eureka moment. In these kinds of examples the experience is very fresh and lively; we distinctly remember such experiences. We can describe them because the struggle to get them was long and difficult, and the consequences that flowed from them were momentous. It is likely that all of us have had a similar experience as the example of Aquinas at the royal banquet if not quite so dramatic.

3. See Gardner, *Multiple Intelligences.*

Second, I am taking these dramatic insights as prototypes of routine acts of human understanding, which we perform continuously for most of our waking hours. The wildly dramatic and emotional content of eureka experiences are not very frequent. We do not run naked through the streets every time we have an insight or disrupt royal banquets by thumping on the table. But when we understand the idea of density, we are performing exactly the same mental act of understanding as Archimedes.

Third, the more precise the problem and solution, the more helpful it is in identifying the characteristics of insight. Thus, we tend to favor examples from mathematics and science from simple puzzles, games, crosswords, and the like. Examples taken from philosophy, the social sciences, history, and economics tend to be vague, with no clear cut definitions or solutions. It is imperative to point out clear, precise, concrete, real examples of being faced with a problem and struggling to find a solution. Students can find suitable examples in the courses they are taking, the homework or assignments they are given, the problems posed in the textbook, and the solutions offered by the professor.

Fourth, new personal discoveries are to be preferred. Reading a book or attending a lecture involves thousands of acts of understanding, but they are routine, part of a stream, and taken for granted. For most of our waking life, this stream of acts of understanding are overlapping, presupposed, taken for granted, and go largely unnoticed despite the fact that they are actually informing our behavior and decisions. In this context it is difficult to identify an individual specific act of understanding. But with some effort it is usually possible to pick out one experience which can be isolated, described and analyzed. Students can usually write an essay to describe an insight that they have had recently. They can pick out an experience of being puzzled and what they did to reach a solution.

Fifth, some psychologists divide understanding into methodical and intuitive kinds. The methodical mentality is logical, plodding, a slow but sure way to a solution, such as in calculation or following rules. The intuitive mentality involves thinking outside the box, getting new ideas fast, being creative, and inventing new rules. It is easier to identify insights in the latter than in the former.

Sixth and finally, it is imperative to remember that self-appropriation is a two-fold process: first understand, then reflect back on the experience. Introspection is really retrospection.

Questioning: The Desire to Know

I begin with the first characteristic of the activity of human understanding, the much neglected act of questioning. Plato has Socrates say: "For this is an experience which is characteristic of a philosopher, this wondering: this is where philosophy begins and nowhere else."[4] Aristotle opens his *Metaphysics* with the statement, "All men by nature desire understanding."[5] He recognizes from the beginning the importance of this desire and realizes that we will not attain understanding without this deep wonder about the universe and about ourselves. I suspect his own personal experience of striving to understand through a lifetime of scholarship and reflection led him to this observation. He also recognizes the dynamic of understanding: just as light makes what is potentially visible become actually visible, so the active intellect makes what is potentially intelligible become actually intelligible.[6] He speaks in the terminology of metaphysics, but I interpret him as saying that intellect takes the initiative in asking questions about sense experiences in order to understand. That first act of intellect must refer to questioning, which seems to be the first manifestation of intelligence. Aristotle has a complete, differentiated metaphysics of the act of understanding. To understand is to think the forms in the images.[7] There are no innate ideas.[8] We cannot think without images.[9] To know is to become.[10] The challenge is to translate the metaphysical concepts of Aristotle into the language of psychology and then check our own experience to see if he is right. For the moment I focus on the question.

In contemporary culture we talk about the search for meaning, the love of wisdom, the spirit of inquiry, the quest for knowledge, the curiosity of children, the questioning mind, the eros of the mind, the thirst for knowledge, and wonder. We seem to recognize the importance of the desire to know in the unfolding of knowledge.

The desire to know is but one of a cluster of desires of the human heart. We have all sorts of sensitive desires for pleasure, food, recognition, success, advancement, and fulfillment. We have a desire for love, for happiness, for unity, for peace, for forgiveness, and for God. I am trying to identify one

4. Plato, *Theaetetus* 155d.
5. Aristotle, *Metaphysics* 980a1.
6. Aristotle, *De Anima* 430a15.
7. Ibid., 431b2.
8. Ibid., 430a1.
9. Ibid., 431a17.
10. Ibid., 429b5.

specific aspect of this cluster of desires for it is central to the purpose at hand. This desire to know seems to represent the first thrust toward understanding, so we should examine it carefully. Few epistemologists pay much attention to this desire, but it would seem to be important and constitutive of the activity of understanding.

The Desire to Know Emerges Spontaneously

The desire to know emerges spontaneously, naturally, and universally. In the traditional language of philosophy it could be called innate: it is with us when we are born but various expressions of it only emerge with the proper development of sensation, nerves, the brain, memory, imagination, and social relations. It could also be called a priori in the sense that it comes from inside and cannot be put there from the outside. However, the terms "innate" and "a priori" have so many unfortunate historical associations and insinuations that I try to avoid them.

The desire to know is evident in children even before they can speak. They can point, look inquisitive, or seek an explanation or a name. They handle and pull things apart; they drop them on the floor or put them in their mouth. They understand commands, names, sounds, and symbols even before they can speak. They can express what they like and do not like, what they are willing to do and not to do, and what they want and do not want.

Language is a breakthrough, for now they can name and refer to things that are absent, not immediately within the range of seeing or of hearing. Their world continues to expand with this expansion of vocabulary. They can refer to the past, present, and future. They can refer to people, even though they are absent, at work, or on a journey. The desire to know expresses itself in a stream of unending questions: what is this, why is that, where is the other?

The more interest and curiosity a person shows, the more learning and understanding that is achieved. The more a person wants to understand, the more they will understand. If a person is interested in dinosaurs he or she will usually put in the time and the effort to learn about them, to see the fossils, and to study the various species. Success in understanding is usually proportionate to the strength of the interest and questioning.

This emergence of curiosity, language, and understanding is considered normal. If it does not happen then something is wrong. Psychologists like Piaget have worked out the sequence of cognitional achievements appropriate to each age group. Malnutrition, genetic disorders, disease, a deprived environment, and many other factors can hinder the development of understanding.

The question arises from inside the child; the adult provides the content of the answer. We cannot make children ask questions, but parents and educators can provide answers and stimulate curiosity. If they do not show interest in the first place, information is not much appreciated. If the questioning does not arise from inside, there must be an obstacle somewhere that has to be removed.

This emergence of the desire to know happens in all cultures, in all nationalities, and in all states, languages, and races. It was part of past human behavior, continues in the present, and presumably will be a part of human activity in the future. Even without a formal educational system, the desire for understanding manifests itself and expresses itself in questions. It is unavoidable. To be human is to want to understand and to know.

The Desire to Know Propels the Search for Understanding

The desire to know is the dynamic behind the search for understanding, from the beginning of the process to the end. The process of knowing is an interrelated sequence of activities: from preparation, to frustration, to achievement, to verification. The most difficult stage is that of frustration when the insight just will not come. The desire to know is the dynamic that drives the simple question into the research, study, work, and frustration in order to finally reach correct understanding. The desire to know in a person can be a silly, superficial curiosity with little strength, or it can be a deep, determined impulse that endures through frustration to find the solution. The desire to know is one part of our general desire for meaning, for understanding, and for truth and value. The desire to know is part of our desire to love and be loved and to be and to become a fully human person.

The Desire to Know Can Be Pure

The desire to know in itself is pure and disinterested. Our motivation can be as pure as snow in that we just want to understand and solve the problem for the benefit of all humanity, regardless of self-interest. There is such a thing as pure science, that is, discovery for the sake of discovery, truth for the sake of truth, progress in understanding as an end and satisfaction in itself. We spend trillions of dollars sending probes to Mars and Pluto, on building colliders, on research and development, and on new telescopes because we want to understand the basic working of our universe. The discovery of the Higgs boson confers no immediate financial benefit; it is simply the last piece remaining to support the standard model of particle physics.

More often motives are mixed. One's motives may be raw selfishness, private ambition, hatred of one's adversary, a desire to make a profit, a desire to become famous, or the desire to achieve a Nobel prize. All of the work can be done for personal gain. The motivation of an act might be to shock, insult, abuse, denigrate, make fun of, or even deliberately lead others astray. Are we publishing to get tenure or because we feel we have something to contribute? Or is it for the funds, the royalties, or the fame of being read and in the limelight? We might be writing to show how clever we are. We might be seeking novelty for its own sake, looking for farfetched connections that entertain rather than advance the cause of understanding. They might be deliberately obscure to give the impression of intellectual depth.

There is a dark side to the desire to know. It might be in terms of getting power over the ignorant or the weak. Knowledge is power according to Francis Bacon. Knowledge enables advertisers to manipulate people through the media, administrators to control their employees, and politicians to pull the wool over our eyes. Seeking knowledge might be intellectual hubris, an ambition to be like God. It might be arrogant, assertive, or twisted. The educated are sometimes rich and powerful. The ulterior motives of the desire to know is a common theme of postmodern philosophy.

The Desire to Know is Unrestricted in Scope

Questioning is in principle unrestricted. One of the characteristics of questioning is that it has no limits; in principle questioning goes on forever. One can ask questions about anything and everything. I offered a hundred dollars to any student who could come up with a topic or thing or area of being about which we cannot ask questions. The hundred dollars is still safe in my pocket. To claim that questioning is restricted is self-defeating, as it is an act of questioning the range of our questioning.

We can ask about the unknown, the unintelligible, chaos, infinite universes, God, demons, or sense and nonsense. We can ask about probability, the irrational, chance events, or random happenings. There is nothing that is in principle completely outside the scope of human questioning. Of course, asking questions is no guarantee of getting the desired answer. Sometimes, we aim for a partial understanding rather than a complete understanding. But it is important to recognize that we intend knowledge of everything. Aristotle defined intelligence as being capable of doing and making *all* things; he included everything within the scope of intelligence.[11]

---

11. Ibid., 430a15.

Questioning Involves Both the Known and Unknown

A question is always a combination of the known and the unknown. If one knows nothing, then he or she cannot ask a question. If one knows everything, there is no need for a question. A genuine question is always in-between. Sometimes I ask a group of students, "Do you have any questions?" and I am met with total silence. I tell them that either they understand everything and have no need for further questions, or they understand nothing and so cannot formulate a question. The question is part of a dynamic process from the unknown to the known, the unfolding of the dynamic of understanding and knowing.

We can distinguish between the pure desire to know and the formulated question. It is the pure desire to know that underlies all understanding and research. How we formulate the question is very important as it sets us off in a particular direction. The formulated question might be heading in the wrong direction. For centuries, scientists were asking about the cause of motion. This was not helpful and led to theories of pushes, impetus, and all kinds of imaginary solutions to the question. It was Galileo and Newton who realized that the fruitful question was rather: what is the cause of changes in rest or motion, namely, Newton's first law of inertia? There are also nonsense questions, which do not make sense and are not looking for understanding. For these, we do not expect an intelligent answer.

There are always more questions than answers, and that is the way it will always be. The more we discover about subatomic particles, the more questions we become capable of asking. Now that scientists have found the Higgs boson, they are already inquiring about how many kinds there are. The more we know about the universe, the more questions we can ask about the things we do not yet know.

Obscurantism is the refusal to ask questions about certain matters, which are too delicate or possibly upsetting. It is a stubborn refusal to question long-held assumptions, to consider new possibilities, or to face the implications of new discoveries such as climate change. It is a love of darkness rather than of light.

The Desire to Know Involves Intentionality

The question establishes the criteria that must be satisfied by a correct answer. A crossword puzzle requires a word that responds to the clue, and correctly spelled, fits into the assigned squares. In Sudoku, one must find the ordering of numbers from one to nine, which are not repeated in any box or horizontal or vertical line. One knows that the answer is correct if it satisfies these conditions. One does not usually have to look up the answers at the back.

Another way of putting this is that there is an intentionality to questioning. The question is intentional in that it intends a particular kind of answer. Many questions are questions for understanding, for intelligence, for information, or for ideas. What? Where? When? How? These questions represent seeking for information about particular topics. They intend further understanding or knowledge or intelligence about the matter. Any answer that does not contribute to better understanding is deemed irrelevant. A different type of questions asks whether it is true or correct. This question is looking for a yes or no answer, or perhaps, something in between; either way, it is looking for verification.

There is a heuristic structure guiding the question toward the answer. It is most evident in algebra, where it is an art form. Algebra entails a general three-step process. First, name the unknown (call it x). Second, combine the knowns and the unknowns in as many equations as possible. Third, manipulate the equations to find the value of the unknown in terms of the already known. The same kind of structure is involved in any question that is looking for an answer.

Usually when we are working on an intellectual problem, such as writing an article, we can sense when we are doing well and when we are doing poorly. We can sense that an outline is emerging, that it makes sense, that it is backed up by the material, and that we are making positive progress toward a worthwhile article. On the other hand, we can also sense that things are not working out as we anticipated. Too many counter examples are cropping up, the outline is getting more complicated and convoluted, or the conclusion is getting murkier and more doubtful. We begin to have second thoughts about whether the project is worthwhile. We sense these encouraging or discouraging feelings. We sense whether we are getting nearer to an answer to our questions or further away.

The criterion that we have reached our goal is that the stream of relevant questions dries up. Our questioning is satisfied. We have closed off any other possibility; closure is reached. We have enough evidence to back up our conclusion, the arguments are solid, and counter arguments and data have been taken into account.

The Desire to Know is Essential to Understanding

It would seem that the desire to know is a constitutive element in knowing. The desire is not peripheral, it is not extrinsic to the knowing process. It is an essential dynamic at the heart of the process. We have many desires: for satisfaction, for food, for comfort, for security, for friendship, and so on. However, the desire to know is unique, precisely in that it is a desire to *know*. It is distinct from all other desires. It seeks understanding and knowledge and is satisfied only when such goals are attained. If there is no desire, then there is no knowing. If we do not ask the question, we do not get the answer. To have a desire to know is to be already on the way to the goal.

We Are Conscious of the Desire to Know

The desire to know is a conscious feeling. We are conscious of our acts of remembering and can experience and describe acts of forgetting and remembering. We are conscious of our acts of understanding and can experience and describe what led up to it, or what hints and images helped us to understand. The desire to know is a state rather than an activity and has to be described as a feeling. It is a conscious feeling, because we can be aware of our feelings and describe them in great detail.

We have already spent several pages describing the desire to know. This description is not taken from books, authorities, or conventional wisdom, but from personal experience. We are conscious of our desire to know and can experience and describe our determination to understand. We are conscious of our perseverance, our moments of frustration, and our excitement when we feel the breakthrough coming and the complete joy of insight. In those cases when we feel that we have found the correct solution and know that we have dealt with all possible objections, we feel satisfied with the coherence of a piece of work; we have closure and a correct solution. On the other hand, we can be conscious of our lagging interest in a topic, our indifference, our laziness, our giving in to other desires, or our dissatisfaction with sloppy work and a dubious solution. There is no doubt that the desire to know is conscious.

Is it appropriate to call the desire to know a feeling? All other desires seem to be described as feelings, including love, hunger, lust, and ambition. Feelings provide momentum and drive to the eros of the mind. Without such feelings our determination would be paper thin. Those who pursue a life of scholarship, teaching, researching, and writing are not emotionless cyphers. It is only intense passion that enables original works of science, mathematics, or philosophy to be embarked upon and brought to completion. I would conclude that a desire to know must be described as a feeling.

However, is it the same kind of feeling as any other, or is there something special and unique about the desire to know? There are sensitive feelings and intellectual feelings, and the desire to know fits into the latter category.

Sensitive feelings are biologically based, neurologically based, and sensitive. They belong at the level of sensation; they are experienced by numerous nonhuman animals. These feelings are often transient or superficial, but they can also be very strong. Feelings such as hunger and thirst, likes and dislikes, pleasures and pains, and satisfactions and dissatisfactions, would seem to be sensitive feelings.

We have outlined above some of the characteristics of the desire to know as a feeling. The desire to know is innate and a priori; it arises in everyone. It is unrestricted in scope and constitutive of the process of knowing. It is the source of language, culture, science, and philosophy. It intends and normally leads to understanding, truth, and value. It is the criterion by which we judge between true and false. We do not say such things about sensitive feelings. Intellectual desire seems to be what makes us human and distinguishes us from nonhuman animals who do not ask questions or have insights.

The topic of human feelings is one with many complexities, ambiguities, and possibilities of misunderstanding. I have dealt with this topic in greater detail elsewhere.[12] I think I have said enough to identify the desire to know as unique to humans and different from every other desire. One cannot possibly understand the process of human understanding without an appreciation of the role of desire to know that is expressed in a continuous stream of critical questions.

The Desire to Know Can Wane

If the desire is so strong why are we not all consumed by the desire to know? Why does it seem to wane and even die? We have many other desires and a host of other feelings. The desire to understand can easily be snuffed out, bogged down, and overcome by other stronger feelings. The vocation of the intellectual, the scholar, the researcher, or the original thinker is a difficult calling with many uncertainties and challenges. I suppose for most of us we cannot go on searching; thus, we settle down to a routine of conventional wisdom, import the opinions of others, close off our worldview prematurely, and resist anything that challenges our established position. But there are some who continue to ask questions. All of the great philosophers and scientists have been consumed by a passion for understanding. To them

12. See Cronin, *Value Ethics*. Chaps. 5 and 6 deal with the self-appropriation of feelings.

we owe a great debt of gratitude. They were giants. They pushed back the frontiers and continue to do so. We climb hesitantly on to their backs.

The Desire to Know is Both Personal and Communal

The desire to know can be noticed at the social level as well as the individual. Looking back at the history of the human race, we can identify the role of the development of understanding, knowledge, science, and technology. Part of it was theoretical and pure science; part of it was practical in seeking new techniques, drugs, technologies, medicines, and sources of energy. Our curiosity remains unbounded in unraveling our history, from the origin of the universe to our own present state. Our inquiry extends from the micro-world of smallest particles, to the macro-world of billions of galaxies that surround us. Research is not only for practical gain but to answer our deepest questions about the universe and the meaning of human life. Even if one is dubious about the strength of his or her own desire to know, there is no doubt about humanity's search for the meaning of human life and the universe we live in.

To summarize, then, the desire to know is the spark that initiates the whole process. It points in a certain direction, formulates a question, and sets the criteria for a correct answer. It guides the research to a certain topic; it brings focus and purpose to the study as we seek an answer to a particular question.

The desire pushes us through the difficulties and frustrations of not being able to find the answer; there is nearly always a period of confusion, frustration, and anger. Often we give up at this stage. Maybe there is no answer! At least we cannot find it. Then things begin to take shape, fruitful methods are found, other possibilities are excluded, insights begin to flow, and further questions begin to close off the issue.

Finally, we recognize the solution, the data falls into place, the criteria set in the question are satisfied, and no further relevant questions arise. We have finally gotten it. We feel delighted. Tension is released and we experience the full joy of discovery.

Active Element: Strategies for Thinking

The question starts the process toward understanding, but we still have work to do in order to produce acts of understanding. The second characteristic of the act of understanding involves the kinds of activities of the mind that we perform in order produce understanding. This is not particularly difficult or controversial. Most people recognize that in order to become an expert in some field, one has to work to get there. We need to be specific in identifying these positive activities before we move on to the passive element.

What do children ask questions about? What is it that arouses their curiosity? Besides the question, is there anything else that is needed to get the process of knowing underway? It is hard to ask questions about nothing, so we usually ask about things that we have experienced. Children can only ask questions about what they see, hear (or have heard about), touch, and experience. It would seem that our first questions must be about something we have experienced. There has to be some content about which we ask questions. So it would seem that two things are required for the beginning of human knowing: the question of intelligence and the data of experience. We ask about what we experience in order to understand. Our knowledge starts with this experience of the sensible. The sensible may be what we are actually experiencing at the moment, or it may be what we have experienced in the past and we now remember and imagine. Then, we can ask questions about what we have remembered and imagined. After further intellectual development, we can ask questions about ideas, laws, meanings, causes, and so forth.

In this later stage of intellectual development, we need a general heuristic of what is to be done to answer intelligent questions. Consider questions such as the following: Is the climate changing, and if so, why? Why did the dinosaurs become extinct? Is there life on other planets? Why will my car not start? A ten-page paper on the psychology of Virginia Woolf has been assigned: how does one proceed? What is the Higgs boson? What steps does one take to answer such questions?

In general, the first activity in all of these instances is to gather materials—to go to the sources, visit the library, read books, get information, and read literature on the question. The process involves taking notes, reacting to the reading material, picking out significant points, and noting things that are not clear. One might consult databases or check the internet. Some cases may involve performing original research, conducting experiments, sending out questionnaires, doing a survey, or making observations. The more research we do, the more we can focus on fruitful ideas and move toward an answer. In some cases, it will involve making calculations, finding correlations, writing down all the possible equations, and experimenting with possible mathematical laws. It may be necessary to invent new methods to find new information. One might systematically exclude irrelevant or unimportant images and data, or gradually converge on a range of options. In short, the first active stage in the process of learning involves the gathering and organizing of materials.

There are many strategies of thinking that can also help. Descartes recommended the method of analysis and synthesis: break a complex problem down into smaller parts, understand the smaller parts, and then put them together into a synthetic understanding of the whole. We often have to distinguish in order to unite, to differentiate in order to integrate, to take apart in order to put together again. Sometimes we work forward from the question and describe the kind of solution that would satisfy the requirements set in the question. Sometimes we work backward to examine the question itself, clarify the terms, manipulate the knowns, and see if we can anticipate the unknown solution. Thinking involves comparing, defining, dividing, describing, organizing, putting in order, and contrasting. In thinking, we may use metaphors, allegories, examples, illustrations, or diagrams. We make connections, dissect, explain, justify, criticize, expand, summarize, elaborate, focus, formulate hypotheses, and use strategies and tactics. Remember the proverb that genius is an infinite capacity for taking pains.

Plato likened thinking to an imagined conversation with an interlocutor. Imagine explaining something to a group of experts or a group of students. What examples are more appropriate? What are the questions and objections one is likely to encounter? Discussion with a group involves collaboration, teamwork, and the exchange of ideas through journals and books. The cross-fertilization of ideas is a big element in much research and discovery. Ask questions of those who might help; there are no foolish questions.

The strategy of intelligent questioning goes hand in hand with the work of memory and imagination. Look for examples which might help, for suggestive images, possible diagrams of connections, for similar cases and helpful analogies. Imagine possibilities; try to think outside the box. The imagination can be a great help in proposing the vital image; but on the other hand it can be a block. It is hard to imagine outside the box. Our imagination forces us in a certain direction and we cannot escape. Husserl recommended a method of imaginative variation.

I asked my students what they should do if they really want to understand something. One student immediately responded, "Take a hot bath." He had a somewhat too literal interpretation of the story about Archimedes. I suggested that he might pass through the library on his way to take a bath. This section on thinking as the active aspect of understanding is a mere sketch of something most people take for granted. Thinking takes many forms depending on the subject matter and the particular question at issue.[13] The history of any great discovery will show the work that is put

13. I can only refer the reader to some classics on the topic of thinking: Dewey, *How We Think*; Dimnet, *The Art of Thinking*; Kahneman, *Thinking, Fast and Slow*; Arendt, *The Life of the Mind*.

into it, the hours of labor, the lonely search, and the temptation to give up. Because discoveries in each field are so different, we have to recognize the infinite flexibility of human intelligence to deal with any topic, any kind of problem, and any challenge. What is important is to persevere through thick and thin. There is always this active element of gathering information, putting it in order, thinking about it and working toward a resolution. I now turn to the passive aspect understanding, of taking a break, relaxing, and allowing ideas to come.

Passive Element: It Comes Suddenly and Unexpectedly

In many of the examples given in Hutchinson's *How to Think Creatively*, the insight comes not when the subject is doing research, busily reading, or organizing notes, but in moments of relaxation when attention has shifted to totally different matters. Archimedes had his great insight, not in his laboratory, but while he was relaxing in the public baths. In all of the cases, the subjects described the experience as, "It came to me," or "It dawned on me," or with similar expressions. They received the idea suddenly and unexpectedly. This is what I refer to as the passive element in understanding. This seems to be an essential element: we receive the solution as a kind of a gift. Most people readily use the expression, "It came to me," referring to an act of understanding. It is an experience of receiving, a reception, as if a gift from we know not where. It happens more easily and often in intelligent people and slowly and with difficulty in the not so intelligent.

It comes suddenly and unexpectedly, but not immediately. We may have been working on a project for days or weeks, and we wake up some morning and suddenly we have it. It comes in a flash; it is a eureka moment and we recognize it as the solution, but it is not the solution we expected. Many such insights do come while we are working on a project, but many come in moments of relaxation while our conscious mind is actually devoted to other matters entirely.

It comes unexpectedly in the sense that it is not the kind of idea that you anticipated; the idea comes from outside the box. It is something new, a discovery, an idea grasped for the first time. A minute ago it was not there and now it arrives. We cannot force it to come, as we did not know what it was. It can happen in the oddest of places. Archimedes was in the public baths. Helen Keller was taking a walk in the garden. Aquinas had his insight while reluctantly attending a royal banquet. Others recount that they were walking by the sea or even asleep or dreaming. There is an aspect of understanding in which we are not fully in control; we have to wait for it to come.

It does not come automatically. We cannot put a precise schedule on when to get a new idea. New discoveries cannot be programmed. Sometimes in research or calculation or laboratory procedures one may do the work and automatically get a result. Following the rules leads to a diagnosis or solution. However, in cases of new discoveries there is a passive element. It is creative, and the new idea cannot be forced to come. Since the 1960s doctors have been telling us that they will have a cure for cancer in ten years. But when they do not know the solution, how can they predict how long it will take to find it? New insights are not deductions; there is no procedure in logic that can produce new discoveries. There are no rules to be followed that will automatically find new hypotheses. There are no algorithms to produce good ideas. We cannot predict and control the flow of new ideas. We can have heuristics that might point us in the right direction, but if discoveries could be found by following rules then we would all be little Einsteins. There might be guidelines and strategies, but there are no rules for creative discovery. The title of Karl Popper's book, *The Logic of Scientific Discovery,* is a bit of a misnomer.[14] If there were rules, then anybody could apply them and become great innovators.

We are not in full control of our stream of acts of understanding. The mind is not a machine: machines work automatically, predictably, on schedule, on time. We cannot control the process of learning in the same regular fashion. We ardently desire to understand, we do all in our power to make it happen, but then we wait and hope that it will come. All we can do is create favorable conditions for the occurrence of insights. We do the work, focus, concentrate, observe, and think. New ideas have to be given the opportunity to emerge. Taking a break, relaxing, thinking about something else, or abandoning our control over our thinking may allow that opportunity for new ideas to surface.

Most people are familiar with the notion of brainstorming. It is a deliberate relaxing of the critical faculty to allow what might seem to be outlandish ideas to surface. But it does allow a free flow of ideas. The free association of ideas can lead to new ideas and help someone consider all possibilities. As Sherlock Holmes said, "When you have eliminated the impossible, whatever remains, no matter how improbable, must be the truth."[15]

Joseph Hadamard speaks of conscious and unconscious processes in the act of understanding.[16] There is an element in the act of understanding

14. Popper does recognize that scientific theories arise from creative imagination, but he emphasizes the logic of induction and falsifiability.

15. Conan Doyle, *The Complete Sherlock Holmes,* 111.

16. Hadamard, *The Mathematician's Mind,* esp. chaps. 2–3.

over which we do not have full conscious control. Why do certain memories surface to help us when we need them, or refuse to surface? Why do some people think of certain possibilities and others do not? It is clear that there is an element of luck in the search for understanding. We might be lucky with the teachers we had, the books we found in the library, the friends that stimulated our thinking, or the images that helped us to find the idea. We can be lucky in choosing the subject for a thesis, in choosing to follow a particular course, or in following a hunch that proves to be fruitful and leads in the right direction. However, we might also devote our lives to a hunch that leads nowhere. There is this element of chance in the life of the mind, and we just have to live with it. It is difficult to talk about unconscious processes precisely because if they are unconscious, what can we know about them or say about them?

Even though we cannot force insights to come, we can create the conditions in which they are more likely to occur. These are mostly inner conditions in the mind rather than in outer circumstances. Primarily, it means to be continually asking questions, to be manipulating the data in the direction we think the solution lies. It involves looking at the problem from different angles, dragging up new images, testing examples, remembering similar situations, exploring possibilities, trying analogies, and starting again when we reach a dead end.

Students hear the same lecture but receive it in many different ways. They are in the same classroom, have the same equipment, and the same general educational background. They hear the same words but grasp different meanings. There is an old saying: "Whatever is received is received according to the mode of the recipient." It is the inner conditions of interest, attention, questions, images, habits, expectations, and abilities that determine how a lecture is to be received.

The inquiring subject sets the context into which new ideas will be received. A person who is familiar with mathematics will easily solve mathematical problems, but that same person may not be so good at crosswords or trivia questions. Someone with a good memory will be good at general knowledge questions, but he or she may have difficulty with math or logic. So much depends on one's previous education, the state of the development of the culture, one's age, and many other influences. Many people frequented the baths at Syracuse and experienced the sensation of floating in the water, but only one of them had an insight into the laws of displacement and density.

Nowadays we have wonderful equipment that should make it easier to write articles and books. We have word-processing programs, libraries at our fingertips, citation managers, dictionaries, and the like. One might think it is now easier to write books and do good philosophy. We have made so many advances in information technology. Outer conditions are much more favorable to research and scholarship. The Greeks and Medievals were writing on parchment in ink and each book had to be individually written. But can we really claim that the quality of thinking and writing today is better than in those days? Intellectual development depends on inner conditions of interest, concentration, devotion to truth, a focus on what is relevant, and an infinite capacity for thinking things through to the end. That is what determines the quality of thinking, writing, and new discoveries.

Conclusion

I have started a description and analysis of insight by identifying three essential components. (1) The question emerges from the desire to know and is a constitutive element in the process of understanding and knowing. (2) The question directs the activities of collecting and organizing materials that might provide an answer. (3) No matter how hard we try, we cannot force insights to come; rather, we merely create the favorable conditions for the reception of ideas, then wait and hope. I will continue in the next chapter to identify what happens in the mind when the actual moment of understanding arrives. How is understanding different from sensing? How does it pass into the habitual texture of the mind?

We can already see that understanding is a complicated activity that takes time to accomplish. All the assertions made in this chapter and the next are simply descriptive, factual statements about how the process actually works. It is not a theory about intellect or epistemology but a simple factual description. All of us can attend to our own acts of understanding in order to verify or deny these assertions. I have tested out these assertions on hundreds of students and all seem to recognize what I am talking about and agree that this is how they experience the act of understanding.

4

The Basic Act of Understanding (Part 2)

As was normal for a Saturday morning, I got to work at Cambridge University's Cavendish laboratory earlier than Francis Crick on February 28th, 1953. I had good reason for being up early. I knew that we were close—though I had no idea just how close—to figuring out the structure of a then little-known molecule called deoxyribonucleic acid: DNA. This was not any old molecule: DNA, as Crick and I appreciated, holds the very key to the nature of living things. It stores the hereditary information that is passed on from one generation to the next, and it orchestrates the incredibly complex world of the cell. Figuring out its 3-D structure—the molecule's architecture—would, we hoped, provide a glimpse of what Crick referred to only half-jokingly as "the secret of life."

We already knew that DNA molecules consist of multiple copies of a single basic unit, the nucleotide, which comes in four forms: adenine (A), thymine (T), guanine (G), and cytosine (C). I had spent the previous afternoon making cardboard cutouts of these various components, and now, undisturbed on a quiet Saturday morning, I could shuffle around the pieces of the 3-D jigsaw puzzle. How did they all fit together? Soon I realized that a simple pairing scheme worked exquisitely well: A fitted neatly with T, and G with C. Was this it? Did the molecule consist of two chains linked together by A-T and G-C pairs? It was so simple, so elegant, that it almost had to be right. But I had made mistakes in the past, and before I could get too excited, my pairing scheme would have to survive the scrutiny of Crick's critical eye. It was an anxious wait. But I need not have worried: Crick realized straightaway that my pairing idea implied a double-helix structure with two molecular chains running in opposite directions. Everything known about DNA and its properties—the facts we had been wrestling with as we tried to solve the problem—made sense in light of those gentle complementary twists. Most important, the way the molecule was organized immediately suggested solutions to two of biology's oldest mysteries: how hereditary information is stored, and how it is replicated. Despite this, Crick's brag in the Eagle, the pub where we habitually ate lunch, that we had indeed discovered the "secret of life," struck me as somewhat immodest, especially in England, where understatement is a way of life.[1]

Ideas Emerge from Images

In the last chapter, I described the questioning, researching, and waiting that precede understanding, which are the conditions for the possibility of understanding. I identified the first three characteristics of the act of understanding, namely, (1) the tension of inquiry, (2) the active element of thinking, and (3) the passive element of coming suddenly and unexpectedly. I now consider at length the fourth characteristic, namely, that insight pivots between the concrete and the abstract, between images and ideas. Continuing the description of the activity of understanding, I now come to the core of the matter: what happens at the precise moment of insight? There are a series of crucial questions that must be answered at this point.

Where do ideas come from? Historically three different answers have been given to this question. First, there are those who appeal to innate ideas; we are born with ideas in the mind and so new ideas are simply innate ideas surfacing into consciousness. Plato seems to have held this position and claimed we had ideas in our minds from a previous life. Second, empiricists hold that there is no difference in principle between images and ideas; if we can account for images we have accounted for ideas. Hume defined ideas as "faint images."[2] He explained how images came from sense impressions; from simple ideas we can form complex ideas and so on. The third position is the Aristotelian position: the active intellect abstracts ideas from images, which are then received into the passive intellect. I understand this to mean that we ask questions about what we have experienced in order to understand. When we understand, we grasp an idea in the image and so possess the form in the mind. Which of these three accounts is true? Is

---

1. Watson, *DNA*, xviii–xix.
2. Hume, *A Treatise on Human Nature*, 45.

there a fourth or fifth account? They cannot all be true. How are we going to discriminate between these positions? Let us look at examples of acts of understanding and refer to our own experience of acts of insight or aha experiences. What exactly happens when we understand? Is it the same as sensing? Is it the same as perceiving? What difference does it make? I will answer these questions, not by appealing to authorities, nor by appealing to conventional wisdom, but by examining concrete examples of acts of understanding. We can check our analysis against our own experience of understanding. I offer some preliminary observations about the examples of Archimedes, and Crick and Watson, which have already been presented.

Archimedes had a concrete, particular problem, a real time issue with peace or war hanging on the result. He had a laboratory and played with the crown, with gold, silver, lead, boats, weights, and measures. He was touching, seeing, heating, and weighing. Nothing seemed to work. The tension of inquiry drove him on; he was actively intervening to amass the information that he needed. Then he decided to take a break. The insight cannot be forced. Floating in the hot baths, it came to him. Suspend the crown on one side of a balance; suspend an equal weight of pure gold on the other side; submerge both in water and see what happens. Implicit in the procedure is the idea of density and the laws of flotation. And the rest is history.

Where did the ideas come from? Were they innate ideas surfacing to consciousness for the first time? There does not seem to be any evidence for that hypothesis. It also raises all sorts of questions about the origin of innate ideas in the first place. Innate ideas are unconscious, so it is hard to verify their presence or absence. The whole hypothesis is unverifiable and bordering on the absurd. Are images the same as ideas? Archimedes enjoyed many sensations in seeking the solution; he had images of gold and silver, images of floating and sinking, images of heavy and light, and images of big and small. But images did not solve the problem. It was the ideas emerging from the images, in response to the tension of inquiry that solved the problem. The images were sensible, concrete, and particular. The ideas were intelligible, abstract, and universal. The key idea was the relation of volume to weight, defining the density of any solid or liquid. What seems to have happened at that moment in the baths was that an idea emerged from a matrix of images.

Did it make any difference? It solved the immediate problem of his answer to the king. But more importantly it was now possible to formulate universal laws regarding what would float and what would sink. Archimedes, an engineer, was in the business of designing war ships and defenses against enemy ships, so it was of some importance to determine what sinks and what swims. Having mastered that idea, he was free to move on to other engineering principles of displacement, center of gravity, levers, and the like. It took a great effort to discover the idea of density; yet he could explain it to his students in five minutes. It passed into the lore of basic engineering principles up to the present day. It changed history.

One Saturday in 1953, James Watson is playing with cardboard cutouts as he awaits his colleague Francis Crick to arrive. He is jumbling the four forms of adenine, thymine, guanine, and cytosine in a three dimensional frame, like a child playing with Legos; he himself compared it to a jigsaw puzzle. He is looking for the structure of the DNA molecule. He realizes that a simple pairing scheme worked exquisitely well—A with T, and G with C. He controls his excitement and waits patiently for Crick. Crick realized straightaway that the pairing—combined with a double-helix structure— satisfied all the requirements they had to fulfill. A few loose ends were tidied up and biology would never be the same again; they had discovered the structure of the DNA molecule, a mechanism for storing hereditary information and a model for the replication of a cell.

Where did the idea come from? It is absurd at this stage to suggest it was an innate idea. Was it just a "faint image"? Watson was playing with cardboard cutouts by fitting them into a three-dimensional framework. But he was looking for a fit, his actions were not random, and certain requirements had to be satisfied. He tried putting the molecules on the outside of the structure, but it did not work. Then he got the idea of pairing them on the inside and it worked. He was using images (cardboard cutouts) to experiment with various combinations. He knew all there was to be known about DNA, but nobody knew its structure. How does he go from not knowing to knowing? He thinks of possibilities and tests them out. When they added the idea of a double helix, everything fell together, all the requirements were satisfied. They found it by being intelligent and reasonable. They went as far as they could with the information, imagining, and experimenting; they arrived at the key ideas and discovered that they worked—exquisitely. They could not see a DNA molecule; they did not know what it looked like. They did not find its structure by looking, but by thinking. Seeing leads to visual images. Thinking provides ideas. The ideas of pairing and the double helix emerged from the images presented by cardboard cutouts on a steel framework. Ideas are intelligible, universal, and abstract; images are sensible, particular, and concrete. The ideas discovered here, for the first time, apply to every living cell that ever was, is, or shall be.

Does it make a difference? The day before they had all the information they needed—all the cutouts and models and all of their previous experiments—but they had not found it. They were still in a state of tension, confusion, and frustration. Another push with the cutouts and it came together;

they had their great eureka moment. It took years of searching, information gathering, and research. But now they had found it, and they could pass it on to any class of undergraduate biology students in five minutes. It changed biology, genetics, and medicine forever and opened the way for further discoveries. They had understood correctly.

The above examples are just typical of the 250 subjects who described their intellectual experience to Eliot Hutchinson.[3] They all described similar experiences of the tension of inquiry, assembling information, doing experiments, thinking of possibilities, and ideas coming suddenly and unexpectedly. They all mentioned ideas as the center of this experience. This fits with studies of genius,[4] with the history of discoveries,[5] with later studies on the nature of insight,[6] with my own experience, and with the experience of my students. It would seem to me that ideas are not innate, that ideas are significantly different from images, and that ideas come as a result of the tension of inquiry. First, one must do the spade work of amassing information, observations, hypotheses, and experiments. Then there is an element receptivity: it comes. It seems that ideas emerge from images. That seems to be a fully adequate and satisfactory definition of the nature of an act of human understanding.

I claim that at the heart of every act of understanding, an abstract idea emerges from a concrete image. It is so simple. My task then in this chapter is to be very clear about what I mean by "images," be very clear about what I mean by "ideas," and be very clear about what I mean by "emergence." As I have been describing activities, I will continue to describe the activity of imagining, which pairs with images, as well as the activity of understanding, which pairs with ideas.

In a sense, this is the most important chapter of this book. I am trying to establish the precise difference between sensing and understanding. If I can do this successfully, then I am in a position to identify the nature of human understanding and how it is different from the sensing of animals and the bytes of a computer. If I can identify the facts about how human understanding takes place, I am in a strong position to formulate a theory about the human mind and how it knows. I would also be in a strong position to rebut incorrect theories about human knowing, not on the basis of ideology, but on the basis of incontrovertible cognitional fact.

3. Hutchinson, *How to Think Creatively*.

4. See Gardner, *Extraordinary Minds;* Root-Bernstein and Root-Bernstein, *Sparks of Genius*.

5. See Watson, *Ideas*.

6. See Sternberg and Davidson, eds., *The Nature of Insight*.

Contrasting Images and Ideas

As I have noted, David Hume defined ideas as "faint images." This immediately put ideas on the same level as images, which was his intention. The stated aim of his account of human knowing was to show that it can all be traced back to sensation, and that acts of understanding were really the same kinds of things as acts of sensation. He admits that we think we have ideas, but he explains this in terms of habits of the mind and the laws of association of images; it is just convenient to think we have ideas because it seems to make thinking easier. So the question arises as to whether we can classify ideas as the same sort of things as images. My appeal will be to the facts of cognitional experience. Anyone can identify examples of images and examples of ideas from their own experience and compare them along the following lines. I am working on the hypothesis that the act of understanding can be characterized as ideas emerging from images. It is crucial, then, to be able to clearly differentiate ideas from images. I have given some indication of this in the previous section. Now I wish to make this distinction very clear and distinct.

The issue is not between vivid and faint. Both images and ideas can be either faint or vivid or anything in between. We do have vivid images and also faint images. Vivid images would usually be relatively recent, easily remembered, and refreshed perhaps on many occasions. On the one hand, a visual image of a place can be very vivid, detailed, and accurate; it supposes recent familiarity with the place. On the other hand, we can have only a vague image of a place we went to a long time ago and did not stay there for very long. We have only a vague image of how to get there and a general picture of the layout of the place.

Ideas can also be very vivid or very faint; ideas can be clear and distinct, or vague and confused. Descartes can be considered the prophet of clear and distinct ideas. If we have a clear, explicit definition of a circle, of an efficient cause, or of equality, then we have a clear and distinct idea. If we have a vague notion of justice, peace, causation, or the spiritual realm, then we have a confused and indistinct idea. So the issue is not between vivid and faint, but between the nature of images and the nature of ideas. I suggest that they are different sorts of things for the following reasons.

Images are Particular; Ideas are Universal

Archimedes handled one crown, bathed in one particular place, weighed the crown in water in his laboratory, and gave the results to the king of

Syracuse on a particular date around 260 BCE. But the idea of density, the relation of volume to weight, is an idea of universal application. It can be applied to any situation, to any material, at any time, and in any place in the universe; in that sense, it is a universal law. We have many images of how to apply it in particular circumstances, but the law itself cannot be imagined; it is not an image but an idea. On the one hand, an insight deals with data and images that are concrete and particular: Archimedes had one chalice, one king, and one particular problem to solve. On the other hand, what the insight grasps is an idea, a relation, a universal, or a law that is abstract. The laws that Archimedes eventually formulated were universal, referring not only to this chalice but also to any other material body immersed in any other liquid, at any time, or at any place. The insight is constituted precisely by "seeing" the idea in the image, the intelligible in the sensible, the universal in the particular, the abstract in the concrete. We pivot back and forth between images and ideas, as we search for the correct insight.

Images are always of particular things, places, persons, or events. They can often be traced back to an original, direct sensation. They can be either vivid or vague depending on how much attention we have devoted to them. They are sensible, involving either visual, tactile, auditory, olfactory, or tasting capacities. We taste particulars, not universals; we see the concrete, not the abstract. We hear a particular performance of Beethoven's Pastoral Symphony; the same symphony can be performed in any place at any time, but it will be a different performance, a different instance of the same symphony. As time goes by, images tend to fade and we move from vivid to vague images. Even a vague image is still a sensible image of a particular person or a specific event.

We have visual images of letters, words, sentences, and books; we have audio images of the spoken word. But the idea of language is that of a relation between a sign and a signified, a sound and a meaning, a writing and the meaning conveyed by the writing. For language to work there must be a sound, a seeing, or a sign language. But there must also be a meaning conveyed by the sound, or the seeing, or the sign language. Dogs can see and hear but they do not have language. The letters are images, the sounds are images, but the relation between the sounds or letters and meaning is an idea. It is a very clever idea. Basic education starts with teaching the letters of the alphabet, then the words composed of letters, and the meaning of the words and sentences. As intelligence develops, the linguistic expression of thoughts, theories, judgments, and definitions will become more subtle and sophisticated. Books in themselves are just marks on paper; they are sensible and concrete. Dogs can see them, but it is only human intelligence that can get the meaning intended in the marks.

If it is true that an apple fell on Newton's head and he immediately understood the law of gravity, then we can again distinguish between the particular apple, the place and time, and the sensation of getting a bang on the head, all of which are sensible and particular. In contrast, the idea of gravity is of universal application. We can imagine being in a place of zero gravity and floating around in a capsule or space craft. We can imagine hopping around on the surface of the moon, where gravity is one sixth of that of the earth. But if we ask why these situations are different, we have to appeal to the application of a universal law of gravity to particular materials, at a particular time and place.

Images are Concrete; Ideas are Abstract

Socrates went around Athens searching for a definition of justice. Most people thought they knew what justice is, but when he asked for a definition his audience found it very difficult to produce a satisfactory definition. If they suggested a definition, Socrates would test it against concrete examples and usually find it wanting. Any concrete human interaction can be assessed against a standard of justice, but the definition of justice that provides this standard is abstract. Philosophy is full of abstract terms, such as form and matter, potential and actual, causality, intentionality, intelligibility, person, nature, essence, existence, ontic, ontological, Ontological, beings, being, Being, being as being, and the like. But if philosophy is about the real world, then these terms have to be applicable in some way to the concrete.

Physics usually begins in reference to concrete experiments that are carried out in a particular laboratory, or with concrete data that is collected from a particular telescope at a concrete time and place. Physics starts by understanding concrete data and usually ends in a further application to the concrete, for example, in the production of computers, satellite navigation systems, or remote-controlled drones and other technologies, which are all very concrete. But in between, the physicist will be working on abstract notions such as mass, temperature, force, waves, quanta, laws, equations, graphs, symmetry, invariance, matrices, equivalents, and the like.

Abstraction is a term that has a history going back to Aristotle. It has been much misunderstood and abandoned in most philosophies. However, the term highlights an important aspect of the act of human understanding. Abstraction can be understood as focusing on the important and bracketing—that is, abstracting from—the unimportant, focusing on the significant and bracketing the insignificant, or focusing on the relevant and bracketing the irrelevant. That is what we do when we understand; we do this all the time. The act of human understanding can be seen as successive stages of abstraction. The first stage is to abstract the relevant data from the irrelevant. For Archimedes, the color, the shape, and the symbols on the crown were irrelevant to his search. What was significant was the weight and the volume. The second stage is to abstract the idea from the image, to have the insight. Archimedes experienced this in his eureka moment at the baths. The third stage is to formulate the idea clearly and distinctly in a concept or abstract definition. This Archimedes did when he reflected on his insight and wrote down the definition of density and the laws of flotation. The fourth stage is to pick out what is true and to disregard what is false. Archimedes checked again and again to make sure that he was right. He excluded any other theories and verified his own. Similarly for ourselves, what we are doing when we are understanding is a process of abstracting the relevant from the irrelevant, the idea from the image, the explanatory from the descriptive, or the true from the false.

Abstraction can be either enriching or impoverishing. It is enriching if it leads to an understanding that is correct and can be applied back to the concrete. Mendeleyev set about organizing all of the known basic chemical elements and formulated the periodic table for the first time. It was an extraordinary, enriching insight into the sequence of increasingly complex elements, falling into neat columns and lines. Highlighting similarities and differences, it suggested questions about elements that had not yet been discovered and suggested the very structure of the elements themselves. Abstraction is impoverishing if it loses touch with the concrete, or if it remains in an ivory tower, separate and apart from the concrete. It is impoverishing if it becomes static and empty, if it becomes a formal conceptualism of definitions and divisions from which no concrete conclusions can be derived.

Images are Sensible; Ideas are Intelligible

Images are sensible because they are produced by the five basic external senses and the internal senses of memory, imagination, and coordination. Higher nonhuman animals have sense knowledge and use their memory and imagination to hunt, to build nests, to reproduce, to protect themselves, and to exploit their environment in order to survive and thrive. Their senses can be much more efficient and sensitive than that of humans. They can use instruments; they can make sounds that are warnings, calls, or expressions of emotion or aggression. They can learn by imitation, by association, by trial and error, by noticing sensible similarities, and even by accident. They can be taught tricks by dog trainers, horse riders, zoo keepers, and the like.

Association of reward and punishment are the principles of this training. All animal behavior can be explained in terms of physics, chemistry, biology, and zoology. Sensing is a matter of nerves, sense organs, brain neurons, synapses, and so forth. Animal knowing is limited to the senses, images, and memories. What makes the higher animals different from the lower is this capacity of sensation. To understand these higher animals is to understand this greater capacity for sensing, imagining, remembering, and learning.

However, nonhuman higher animals do not ask questions, do not have insights, do not get ideas, and do not formulate concepts. Ideas do not fit within the remit of biology or zoology. The only living creatures that have ideas in the strict sense are human beings and the proper study of humans is done in anthropology. Anthropology deals with the specific difference between higher animals and humans. It is only humans who use language, understand ideas, formulate laws, and verify whether the laws are true or false. I have defined understanding as ideas emerging from images. The brain is within the provenance of the neuroscientist, but sensation and the brain is but the infrastructure for the possibility of thought. There is a dependence of thought on its infrastructure of neurons and synapses. But something new emerges in thought. It is the idea, the product of intelligence, and hence the intelligible. If we want to understand the intelligible, then, we have to realize that ideas are different from images and that understanding is different from sensing.

We could perhaps argue that computers store images such as photographs, videos, music, text, and numbers almost without limit and can call them up at will. But computers do not store ideas and never will be able to store ideas; only human beings can do that. Everything in a computer is physical, mechanical, and subject to the laws of physics; it is intelligible but not intelligent. All the operations of a computer are performed by streams of electrons divided into bytes signifying zero and one and manipulated through processors. Whatever intelligence a computer has is a pale reflection of the intelligent human who designed and produced the computer. Computers follow rules that have been put there by humans; they follow rules automatically, mechanically, and without any trace of thought or deliberation. They can be designed to learn from mistakes; but that is just following more sophisticated rules. The creative thinking with ideas of humans is worlds apart from the mechanical rule-following of a computer.

In conclusion, then, we are using the terminology of image and idea in a strictly defined sense. Ideas are not just less vivid shadows of impressions, but they have quite different properties as noticed above. The justification of this distinction is our own experience of the activity of understanding. What happens in our mind when we grasp the formula that generates an infinite sequence? What happened to Archimedes when he grasped the concept of density? What happened to Newton when he grasped that a line or motion was a continuum? It is more than imagination. It is intelligence at work. The imagination produces images. Intelligence produces ideas and concepts. Although image and idea are closely interrelated in the process of human knowing, they are also clearly distinct entities.

Relating Images and Ideas

Having distinguished clearly between images and ideas, let us not make the mistake of separating them. It is a matter of common experience that we cannot think without using images. Spontaneously, if we are trying to understand something we appeal to examples, we construct a diagram, and we refer to a particular incident. If we are teaching we similarly use examples, tell stories, apply metaphors, and draw illustrations. By "image," here I include the vast store of memories, imaginations, and sense data given to us in experiencing. Insights emerge when we question certain aspects of that data. Ideas emerge from the images. Yet they are quite distinct from one another. The development of our understanding continues to depend on appropriate images. It is not as if once we got the idea, we were set free from the senses and imagination. The process of pivoting between the concrete and the abstract, the image and the idea, continues from science into philosophy.

Images may become more and more rarified but never completely disappear. The mathematician needs appropriate symbols to facilitate his procedures. The Romans used an extremely awkward system of mathematical symbols; it would be extremely difficult to perform operations of multiplication, division, roots, and so on, using such symbolism. They had to be replaced by symbols that were more flexible, more suggestive, and more functional. In the empirical sciences, as we shall see, it is necessary to construct images of atoms, diagrams of forces and vectors, and tables and graphs of data. Even in theology it would seem very difficult to think of God without some vague image of light, size, or power. In the end, we are perhaps left with the image of the word as the peg on which to hang the idea. Grand master chess players can play chess blindfolded and can discuss complicated positions without a board in front of them, but they still must use some minimal algebraic imagery to describe their moves.

The more appropriate the image, the sooner the idea will come; we need the images to reach the ideas. We have to manipulate, adjust, and add to the images in order to get the insight. Solving problems in Euclidean geometry usually involves a construction, bisecting an angle, drawing a parallel line, and so on. This is manipulating the image; when we hit on the right construction, we can usually grasp the solution. There will be much drawing and pencil work in solving word puzzles or crosswords or geometry, but the act of insight that comes at the end produces not an image, but an idea. Intelligence grasps intelligible relations; we see the connection and reach the definition. Newton's laws of motion are a statement about a series of interrelated ideas. They are products of insight. The insights would not have been possible without the experience of motion and the images associated with that experience, but the insight goes far beyond that experience to grasp intelligible relations that explains universal qualities of motion. The laws are universal and abstract. They apply to all motion of all material bodies of any location, at any time, and of any size.

Experiencing and understanding are distinct activities but are closely interrelated and interdependent. Although these two activities are distinct, they are not separate; they do not normally operate independently of one another. Often if we claim two things are distinct, it is assumed that they can be physically separated from one another. Experiencing is a distinct activity from understanding, but understanding cannot occur without the senses. Allow me to illustrate some of the many ways by which they are related.

It is possible for a subject to operate at the level of experience alone at least for a time; there is a sense in which experiencing can be separate from understanding. Experiencing and sensation are already operative in the child before intelligence comes to full fruition. The child is mostly a bundle of sensations, desires, and needs. At first there is just a flicker of intelligence. But the child is seeing, hearing, tasting, and smelling. Activities of experiencing can occur apart from the operation of understanding.

Understanding depends on the activity of experiencing. We cannot ask questions unless there is some content; there must be something about which we ask questions. We ask about what we have heard and seen, imagined, and remembered. We do not just understand; we understand something. What is that something and where does it come from? In all of the aforementioned examples, questions are focused on sensible data; there is an interplay between sensation and understanding. First, there is data that are seen and remembered; initially, there is no meaning, sense, or explanation for the phenomena. Later, there follows the moment of understanding the connection, the meaning, or the solution.

However, in a normal adult the sensitive side of us has been so penetrated and influenced by intelligence that it is quite difficult to identify a pure sensation, that is, a sensation that is in no way influenced by understanding, naming, or defining. Compare a cow and a man looking over a fence. Both have their eyes open, are conscious, and see in the physical sense. Are they seeing the same things? The same images are being transferred to the brain along an optical nerve in much the same way. The cow sees in a physical sense within the context of its biological pattern of experience and, with its imagination and memory, can perceive and react to things related to its needs and instincts. The cow can recognize grass, smell an approaching fox, and hear and fear rumblings of thunder in the distance.

The man sees, but he adds identification and naming to his seeing. He sees five different species of trees, he sees the smoke of the village in the distance, he sees the lack of nitrogen in the pasture, or he sees one of his sheep limping and speculates on the cause. The experience of the adult is so patterned by organizing intelligence; so shot through with definitions, identities, relations; and so transformed by the influence of insights that have become habitual that it is difficult to separate out a sensation that is a purely biological sensation. It is this synthesis of animal experiencing and emerging intelligence that constitutes the uniqueness of human knowing.

Human knowing combines elements of animal knowing with intellec-tual knowing in a new synthesis, not just a mixture. It is animal knowing to the extent that it is tied to the sensible and particular by way of the external and internal senses. It is intellectual knowing in the sense that the human intellect can grasp the intelligible, the universal, the necessary, the abstract, and the forms in the images. But human knowing is not just a mixture of these two forms of knowing; it is a synthesis in which both are involved in a new unity, a new interrelationship or interdependence. It is unique and complicated. Any attempt to reduce human knowing to the level of the sen-sible alone will fail, because it cannot account for the grasp of the universal. Any attempt to maintain that human knowing is purely intellectual will fail when we notice the dependence on the sensible and images. Human know-ing involves both images and ideas, both the concrete and the abstract. It is, perhaps, because it is so peculiar and so complicated that so many theorists have been tempted to oversimplify it, and thus, have failed to give a correct, comprehensive account of human knowing.

Conception and Perception

The term "concept" can be used in a variety of ways, sometimes vague and broad, sometimes very clear and distinct. I use the term in the sense that concepts are ideas that have been formulated explicitly and expressed in words, symbols, or definitions. A concept is a product of conceiving. A di-rect, simple insight into a particular problem usually comes first. We think about its implications, qualifications, and connotation and denotation, and then we put it clearly into words and formulate it as a definition or law. Archimedes had the correct idea of how to proceed when he was in the baths, but only later defined the concept of density and the laws of displacement. Ideas come first but are usually followed by concepts. Concepts are formulated ideas. Most people have an idea of what constitutes a circle and would be able to distinguish between a circle, an ellipse, and an ovoid. But many would not be able to define a circle correctly. When we formulate a definition of a circle explicitly, then, we have the concept of the circle. Both idea and concept are products of intelligence, not of imagination. Both concepts and ideas are universal and abstract. It is intelligence that grasps intelligible relations, meanings, solutions, and laws and expresses them in a formula or definition. I will discuss this activity of formulating concepts and definitions in more detail in chapter 5.

A concept is only a concept, that is, a creation of the mind in its purposive search for understanding. We can have strings of concepts, which cluster together to form a theory or explanation. We could invent concepts at will, which happens in the dramas of science fiction. But normally concepts are a stage in the process toward knowledge of the real world when we need to be quite clear about what we are talking about. Concepts are usually a means toward an end, rather than an end in themselves. Concepts in themselves are simply suppositions, hypotheses, or possible explanations. But they can also be the means by which we correctly understand the working of the material world. Any technical discipline requires concepts, but they are not the object of the science in question; they are the means the science uses in order to know the concrete.

Are concepts "that which" we know, or that "by which" we know? Normally concepts are that by which we know. Watson and Crick used the concepts of pairing and double helix to find the structure of the DNA molecule. Archimedes used the concept of density to solve the problem of the crown. Philosophers use concepts such as hylomorphism, subsistence, existence, and sublation in order to understand the universe and human beings better. Normally concepts are a means to better understanding.

Yet concepts can also be the direct object of our knowledge: a concept can be that which we know. In identifying the activity of conceiving, which produces concepts, concepts are that which we know. We can reflect back and make the concept the object of our understanding. That, after all, is what we are actually doing!

The terms "perception" and "percept" seem to be used to refer not to pure sensations, but to sensations influenced in some way by the perceiver. Studies of perception focus on ambiguous or illusory diagrams to examine how they are perceived by the subject. I tend to use the word "perception" to indicate not a pure sensation, but a sensation that is patterned by understanding. Psychologists are fond of certain images that challenge our perceptions—a stairway that can be perceived as from above or from below, or a sketch that can be either an antelope or a bird. This is sometimes used to prove that our knowing is subjective, that the same sensible data can be "understood" in two different ways depending on the subjective dispositions of the knower. On my account, this is simply an example of understanding imposing upon or interpreting how we see the images. There is no correct way of seeing such images; there is not enough data to resolve the issue. I avoid the term "perception," because it can be used to refer to simple sense perception, or it can refer to a full act of understanding or something in-between. In current philosophy, much attention is devoted to the study of perception and very little to the study of human understanding.[7] This is an imbalance that needs to be redressed.

The Notion of Emergence

I have spoken of ideas emerging from images. The notion of emergence has roots in classical Scholastic philosophy where the phrase was used, "When the matter is properly disposed, the form emerges."[8] There was a burst of interest in emergentism in the first half of the twentieth century in Britain and it seems to be experiencing a revival at the moment.[9] The term "evolution" implies a universe that is always gradually moving in small steps by way of adaptations and the survival of the fittest. It evokes the name of Charles Darwin and neo-Darwinians; unfortunately, it is also associated with antireligious sentiments. "Emergence" on the other hand implies new things coming from old, an upwardly directed dynamism that is universal and central to our understanding of everything in the universe. Emergence does not evoke the same emotional reaction as evolution and is philosophically neutral. Precisely how is the notion of emergence appropriate in the context of ideas emerging from images?

The prime example of the process of emergence is the emergence of ideas from images in the act of understanding. The pure desire to know

7. See Merleau-Ponty, *Phenomenology of Perception*. This is a very famous work and receives much attention but is not intended as a complete treatment of human knowing. See also Searle, *Seeing Things as They Are*. He proposes a kind of direct realism. But can one get a realist philosophy from perception by itself, but rather from the full activity of human questioning, experiencing, understanding, and judging?

8. Quoted in Lonergan, *Insight*, 285.

9. See Clayton and Davies, eds., *The Re-Emergence of Emergence*; Holland, *Emergence*; Morowitz, *The Emergence of Everything*.

operates on the data of sense, and from the images emerge ideas. This is a discursive process; it takes time and effort. It is not automatic and immediate, but is sudden and unexpected. There is an element of activity as we must fulfill the conditions for the possibility of insight to occur. But there is also an element of passivity, of waiting for the insight to come, of receiving the idea, the solution, and the definition. The process involves manipulating the image, looking at data, appealing to examples, remembering relevant experiences, looking for help, and finally, the insight comes: an idea emerges from an image. I have already described this process, so the important point is that it involves an appeal to our own experience of understanding, and not to an authority, a proof, or a dogma. This is the primordial experience of emergence, and it provides the template for all other occurrences of emergence. From this basic experience, we can formulate some of the basic characteristics of the process of emergence, namely, (1) something new emerges, (2) it leaves the previous levels intact, (3) it even enhances the value of the previous levels, and (4) it continues to depend on previous levels.

1. *Something new emerges. An idea* is autonomous and can exist on its own. An idea and an image are as different as chalk from cheese. The differentiation of intelligence from imagination hinges on this distinction between idea and image, so it is of some importance.

Although they are of different orders, it remains that ideas emerge from images. There is no other way for a human person to understand except by appealing to examples, experiences, images, and memories. Yet the idea that emerges is of a different nature from the image. Our human minds do not have direct, immediate visions of the solutions to problems. We are obliged to proceed by way of discourse, discursively, indirectly, mediately, step by painful step. Our ideas are mediated by language, sensation, teachers, experiences, events, efforts, attention, and the desire to understand. Eventually the required idea comes; it emerges.

The new is unexpected, unpredictable, and genuinely novel. For some mathematical problems, it is possible to apply the rules and find the solution automatically as a calculator will do; in these cases the solution can be found deductively and simply by following clear rules of operation. But where did the rules come from? Who thought of the rules in the first place? How did we learn to understand and follow the rules? The senses cannot formulate ideas. There is no way of predicting the emergence of the correct answer to the question. There is a surprise element in emergence; something new is being produced. Again, we can appeal to our own appropriation of the act of understanding. It is a process of moving slowly toward a solution, eliminating possibilities, setting down clearly what is required for the solution, setting down limits and conditions, and following up on clues. We feel that we are making progress, that we are on the verge to a solution. The signs are good, things are fitting together, but still we have not arrived at the solution. Then it comes and everything changes; the solution unifies the disordered mess and fits everything into place. It is obvious, a relief: how did we not see it before? There is continuity in that the process involves a steady stream of invoking examples, testing possibilities, clarifying criteria, working forward and backward until the solution emerges, and checking to make sure that it is correct. But there is discontinuity in that an idea is new, different, and superior to an image. A truly new thing has emerged, has come into existence, and is a reality of its own.

2. *The idea leaves the previous levels intact.* The images and the imagination continue to function according to their own laws and capabilities. They are still needed. We cannot continue the process of thinking without images and imagination. We are constantly pivoting from the abstract to the concrete, from general laws to particular examples. Emergence produces new and higher realities, but it does not destroy, negate, do without, or escape from that from which it emerged. Ideas need to be expressed in images, developed by way of examples, and taught in a system of pedagogically effective ways. The proper functioning of sensing, remembering, and imagining is necessary for the further development of ideas and propositions, concepts and systems. We cannot think without images.

3. *The idea enhances the previous levels.* The results of the process of emergence, far from denigrating that from which it emerged, considerably enhance the value of its preconditions. Sensitivity reaches its highest point of development in humans, not in beasts. There is a feedback effect of intelligence back on sensitivity. The power of the human imagination is more flexible and creative than that of animals because of the influence of intelligence. It is intelligence that manipulates images, draws diagrams, imagines possibilities, and formulates hypotheses.

4. *Understanding continues to depend on previous levels.* Is there imageless thinking? Aristotle insisted that we cannot think without images. Aquinas agreed and explained at great length how ideas depend on images. Titchener, an associationist psychologist, agreed that there are no imageless ideas. Some of his colleagues disagreed and there was a long debate and a parting of the ways.[10] My own experience is that we need images to think. The images may be examples, events, sense data, particular cases, diagrams, constructed images, or even words. If we are looking for a definition of justice, we can consider particular examples of corruption, fraud, distribution

---

10. See Kukla and Walmsley, *Mind*. This is a short introduction to the history of psychology.

of wealth, and the like, and at the very least, we are hanging on to the image of the word "justice." Plato described thinking as a conversation with one-self, but what language do we use in this imagined conversation? We think by using a language; ideas are represented by words.

The emergence of ideas from images is the prime example of emergence. The notion of emergence is also very fruitful when it is applied to our universe. In our commonly accepted view of our universe, atoms emerged from subatomic particles, higher elements emerged from simpler elements, chemical compounds emerged from combinations of elements, living things emerged from complex chemical matrices, animals emerged after plants, and intelligent life emerged from non-intelligent life. Some kind of dynamism operates in the universe just as the desire to know drives the process of correct understanding. In the history of the universe, genuinely new things arise, which are different, more complex, more developed, more differentiated, and more integrated than previous things. The new things continue to depend on the proper functioning of previous sets of things and enhance the value of such functioning things. Emergence occurs not automatically, not according to predictions or deductions, but unexpect-edly, according to probabilities. Mistakes, blind alleys, stagnation, and regression can occur in the universe, just as it can in the development of understanding. There is a fruitful parallel between the emergence of correct understanding and emergence operating in the real world, but it is not my present task to explore such a theme.

Ideas Become Habitual

Finally, we come to the fifth essential characteristic of insight: that it passes into the habitual texture of the mind. Someone may be wondering about the complex account of the act of understanding that I have presented: "Is it really that complicated? I can come to understand, more simply, quickly, and easily. Do I really have to go through all of these steps just to solve one clue in a crossword puzzle!" To be clear, I have deliberately taken pro-tracted, complicated insights as a basis for analysis, because it is there that we can more easily recognize explicitly the various steps involved in the process. But understanding becomes easier after that initial breakthrough; it becomes routine, easy, automatic, taken for granted, and habitual. Drama, excitement, and emotion often occur while understanding something for the first time. But then it becomes routine, easy, and even boring. The ex-citement dissipates. Having insights does not mean that we are perpetu-ally running around naked shouting, "Eureka!" When psychologists study insight, the experience is often considered as exceptional and occasional. They do not regard the acts of understanding involved in reading a book or listening to a lecture as insights.

The act of human understanding can be very dramatic, emotional, and exciting; but it can also be routine, go unnoticed, and become merged into a stream of thinking. But it is the same act of understanding sharing the same five characteristics that we are examining, but are now compacted into a habitual, routine operation. There seems to be little in common between the dramatic experience of Archimedes and the humdrum experience of listening to and understanding a lecture. But in my analysis, it is the same act of human understanding. In the latter experience it has passed into the habitual texture of the mind. For Archimedes it was dramatic, emotional, important, and exciting. Listening to a lecture may not be any of these things, but it must involve a stream of acts of understanding of the words, the sentences, the references, the gestures, the writing on the board, the information being communicated, and the ideas being expressed. It is always the same act of understanding—sometimes protracted and exciting, and sometimes simple and taken for granted. We can illustrate this in terms of (1) intellectual memory, (2) intellectual habits, and (3) the accumulation of insights.

1. *Intellectual memory.* Once we have understood certain ideas, they stay with us, and we can recall them easily. We can build on them and take them for granted. This constitutes the basis for the possibility of learning. A professor writing out his syllabus usually has a sequence of topics, the later building on the earlier. In the second half of the semester the professor takes for granted that students remember what was taught in the first part of the semester. If one is in the fourth year of a four-year course in pharmacy, the student is expected to remember at least the basics of what he or she learned in the first year. Pharmacists are pharmacists even when asleep; when they wake up they do not have to start from the beginning. They remember the laws, definitions, principles, and ideas that they have learned.

We take it for granted that we can read English and forget the years of learning involved in acquiring that skill. We had to learn each letter individually, and then each word; then, we learned to put them together in sentences with verbs, nouns, adjectives, and adverbs in the right place. Then, we understood paragraphs, chapters, and books. After years of developing these skills, we take it all for granted as we read a book and focus on the content, meaning, and message of the text. The ability to read is presupposed, a basic skill that has passed into the habitual texture of the mind. It is effortless, but that is only because each of the individual insights have coalesced and become part of the very texture of our minds.

Much the same thing happens in any area of competence when the learning process builds up a context of principles, laws, and relations that are taken for granted as a background when approaching any concrete problem. A professionally trained mechanic sees and hears the same as the lay person, but because of his habitual store of principles and theory, he can attach significance to data which for the layman is insignificant. Similarly, a doctor, an astronomer, a physicist, an exegete, or a historian all possess a store of theories, concepts, and procedures that have become habitual and which serve as a background for the understanding of each new concrete case.

Listening to a lecture, conducting a conversation, reading a book, or playing chess all require a continuous stream of insights. If we have performed these activities often, the movements of questioning, thinking, receiving ideas, the emerging of ideas, and the habituation of understanding happen quickly, easily, smoothly, and go unnoticed. It has become such because we previously put effort into it and now it has become habitual.

Because habituated activities are so easy, we sometimes do not recognize them as acts of understanding. We often do not notice how ideas have become so much a part of the habitual texture of our minds and influence our further interpretations and understandings. We can watch a game of football and understand and appreciate skillful play, because we understand the purpose and rules of the game. We take this understanding for granted because we were taught the rules and have extensive experience and practice in playing and watching the game. A person who sits beside us and does not know the rules or the purpose of football is seeing the same game that we see, but understanding nothing. To that person, it is just random running, kicking, and tackling. Similarly, if we understand the laws of gravity and Newton's laws of motion, we will know what makes a kite fly; in contrast, for children, it is still a mystery or magic. Along these same lines, I can hear nothing when I listen through a stethoscope, but doctors seem to find them very informative.

2. *Intellectual habits.* Aristotle defined a habit as an inclination or disposition to act or to think in a certain kind of a way. At first, it is difficult to perform the act concerned; it is not pleasurable, and it takes effort and discipline to do it. But he noted that as we become accustomed to performing the action it becomes easier, smoother, and in the end, pleasurable. He was discussing moral virtues and vices. In addition to moral virtues that apply to behavior, Aristotle identified five virtues that belong to the intellect: art, scientific knowledge, prudence, wisdom, and intuition.[11] These apply to the habits of thinking and illustrate how the act of understanding,

---

11. Aristotle, *Nicomachean Ethics* 1139b16.

which is difficult at the beginning, becomes easy and routine as it becomes habitual; it even becomes pleasurable. Good habits of the mind include clear thinking, critical questioning, serious research, not jumping to conclusions, thinking things through to the end, and leaving no stone unturned. There is a good way and a bad way to set about understanding. There are virtues of the intellect that become habits of the mind. The purpose of seven years of medical training is not to remember the Latin name of every bone in the body, or to remember the characteristics of every drug in the catalogue; the aim is to think like a doctor, to develop the mentality of a doctor, to form the intellectual habits that are proper to best practices in the medical profession.

3. *Accumulation of insights.* The ideas that pass into our minds change our way of interpreting, understanding, and reacting. Some think that the emptier the mind of the observer, the more objective the person will be in his or her observations. If the observer already knows something about the case, or already has ideas about it in his or her head, it is presumed that the person will be biased. Some admire the notion of theory-free observation. Some think of this as the way to being objective. I would call it the fallacy of the empty head. If my car refuses to start and I call a mechanic, is it an empty head that I am looking for, or one that is filled with theory of mechanics, practical experience of motor repairs, and habits of practical wisdom? If I have a pain in my stomach and go to a doctor, am I looking for someone trained in the medical profession and experienced in diagnosis, or some well-meaning but empty headed do-gooder?

Our minds are formed and informed by a multitude of ideas. Each of them has to be learned, appropriated, and incorporated into our view of the world. Education is the process of putting together the pieces, step-by-step, of a world of meaning. We can identify how some of these ideas were learned and how they are products of acts of human understanding. We take many aspects of our adult minds for granted, as if it were always that way. Let us think about our own educational process and how our minds were formed by ideas. As a result, we can uncover some of the familiar, fundamental ideas that we somehow take for granted.

Relations are ideas. A prime example is language. It is the relation between sign and signified that is at the heart of language. Letters have to be learned and remembered in preschool; learning each letter is a triumph of understanding and remembering. The underlying idea is the relation between the sign written on the board, the appropriate sound, and the cor- responding meaning. Put the letters together and the required relation is between a word and what it is referring to in the real world. Put sentences together and we make affirmations, convey definitions, and affirm true and false. We give meaning to language, and through language we understand our world of meaning. There may be many other ways in which language functions for communication—for commands, for play, for expressing emotions, and so on. I am concerned with its function in cognition and the development of human understanding. All use of language presupposes that we have grasped this fundamental idea of language as expressing meaning.

Relations can be mathematical. Counting introduces the ideas of equal, more than, less than, double, triple, one-third, 50%, the square root of five, and the like. More sophisticated math introduces the ideas of nothing, minus quantities, surds, infinitesimals, irrational numbers, proportions, and probabilities. Each of these is an idea from which we work out rules and perform operations that produce results. Geometry is built on the definitions of a line and various shapes; of properties of certain triangles; and of figures such as rectangles, circles, spheres, cones, cylinders, and parabolas. Each of these is defined clearly, and hence, is an idea. They come through understanding. All of our counting, our accounting, our balancing bank accounts, or filling tax returns presuppose that we have understood and appropriated the basic ideas and concepts of mathematics.

Relations can define kinship such as cousins, in-laws, first cousins twice removed, blood relations, and marriage relations. Most societies have their own take on how to define these relations and what is the proper way of negotiating them. Relations can define space: longitude and latitude; north, south, east, and west, up and down; right and left; or here and there. Once we have the notion of place we can move on to the idea of movement, velocity, acceleration, direction, and the like. Relations can define time. A day we define as a rotation of the earth on its axis, a month as the revolution of the moon around the earth, and a year as the revolution of the earth around the sun. We take a regular pattern of our solar system and divide it into hours, days, months, and years. For our day, we simply subdivide the unit of the day into twenty-four hours, an hour into sixty minutes, and a minute into sixty seconds.

Causes are ideas. Aristotle thought of four causes as four different answers to four different questions. Formal cause answers, "What is it?" Material cause answers, "What is it made out of?" Efficient cause answers, "What made it to be?" And final cause answers, "What is it for?" If we can answer these questions about something, then we have a systematic knowledge about it. There are other causes such as instrumental, exemplary, and creator causes. We understand something only to the extent that we can answer these questions about them. The idea of cause permeates all of our discourse of questioning and answering. Whenever we ask such questions, we are looking for the relevant causes. When we answer correctly, we have found the cause. Without the idea of causality, our questions would be meaningless and our answers just as nonsensical. Can we see causes? Hume claimed that we can see sequences of sensations but cannot see causes. He concluded that causes are not real. I claim that we see sequences of events but understand the cause of the sequence. Causes are understood as the correct answer to intelligent questions; they are ideas produced by intelligence and not images produced by the senses. When we say that John caused an accident by speeding, we are presupposing our grasp of causes, laws, velocity, and the consequences of speeding.

Laws are ideas. All of the sciences of physics, chemistry, biology, botany, economics, and mathematics enunciate laws. The law of gravity is an understanding of how material bodies attract one another according to their mass and distance. It applies everywhere, from the smallest particle of an atom to clusters of galaxies. Newton's three laws of motion apply to all motion, from the smallest to the largest, from the atom to the galaxies. When we play billiards we are applying the laws of motion, as well as ideas of friction, momentum, force, spin, and center of gravity.

Distinctions between genera and species in the world of plants and animals are ideas. They involve definitions, boundary conditions, classification, identifying, and distinguishing. The sciences of biology and botany are largely classificatory. They define and divide animal, vegetable, and mineral in classes, orders, families, genera and species, subspecies and varieties. They are definitions produced by intelligence and not similarities based on sensible family resemblance. When we say, "This is a maple tree," we are presupposing the notion of genus and species, the principle of individuation, and the idea of universals. When we distinguish chalk from cheese we are similarly operating in terms of distinctions, genera and species, and universals, which have passed into the habitual texture of our minds. It is not common to talk about universals these days, but once we distinguish between a dog and a cat, mice and men, or trees and flowers, we are invoking the idea of universals, of genera and species.

Some contemporary philosophers look at human knowing and see something simple, direct, and immediate.[12] They feel justified in calling human knowing a direct intuition, an immediate perception, a simple contact between knower and known. I would reply that it sometimes looks simple because it has passed into the habitual texture of the mind. If we look closely we can see that it is not such a simple thing; we can recognize the five characteristics of insight—that it is discursive, mediated, active, passive, and involves ideas and images. If we examine more protracted experiences of human knowing, many of these characteristics and activities are clearly

---

12. For example, see Searle, *Seeing Things as They Are.*

and explicitly differentiated. We must attend not only to our present acts of understanding but to where and how this knowing started in the difficult process of discovery, learning, education, concentration, and the struggle to understand. The world of the adult is a world permeated with meaning: relations, distinctions, causes, laws, regularities, explanations, principles, and theory. They have passed into the habitual texture of the mind; we sometimes do not notice that they are there.

Conclusion

This chapter considered where ideas come from, what happens when we get an idea, and what difference ideas make. I conclude with some important points that I have arrived at on the basis of empirical examination of the experience of insight. (1) Innate ideas do not seem to function in any way when it comes to understanding and learning. The content of all ideas can be adequately accounted for once we recognize the ability of the mind to ask questions about what has been experienced in order to understand correctly. At most, innate ideas are redundant; worse still, there are further problems accounting for their existence in the first place. (2) It is clear that ideas are different from images, not just by being "faint," but in their origin and nature. Images emerge in connection with sense experience and are particular, concrete, and sensible. Ideas emerge as answers to intelligent questions; they are universal, abstract, and intelligible. (3) The act of human understanding can be adequately defined as an idea emerging from images in response to questioning. (4) The mind continues to depend on sensing and images in its further thinking, understanding, and development. (5) The mind is transformed by the accumulation of ideas, theories, principles, and causes which constitute the habitual context for further acts of understanding.

It has taken two chapters to identify the five characteristics of the basic structure of a human act of understanding. This account is complicated because the reality is a complex, integrated combination of sensing and understanding. It is tempting to simplify. That would have a short-term gain, but it would lead to mistakes and confusion in the end. Now we are in a position to study the development of understanding and different species of the basic act of understanding.

5

Developing Understanding

The Falling Man

In 1907, Einstein had produced his special theory of relativity but it did not apply to nonuniform motion and did not include gravity. Then one day:

> "I was sitting in a chair in the patent office at Bern when all of a sudden a thought occurred to me," he recalled. "If a person falls freely, he will not feel his own weight." That realization, which "startled" him, launched him on an arduous eight-year effort to generalize his special theory of relativity and "impelled me toward a theory of gravitation." Later, he would grandly call it "the happiest thought in my life."
>
> The tale of the falling man has become an iconic one, and in some accounts it actually involves a painter who fell from the roof of an apartment building near the patent office. Einstein refined his thought experiment so that the falling man was in an enclosed chamber, such as an elevator in free fall above the earth. In this falling chamber (at least until it crashed), the man would feel weightless. Any objects he emptied from his pocket and let loose would float alongside him.
>
> Looking at it another way, Einstein imagined a man in an enclosed chamber floating in deep space "far removed from stars and other appreciable masses." He would experience the very same perceptions of weightlessness. "Gravitation naturally does not exist for this observer. He must fasten himself with strings to the floor, otherwise the slightest impact against the floor will cause him to rise slowly towards the ceiling." [The man would not know whether he was falling freely in a gravitational field, or if he was in free floating weightlessly in a zero gravitational field.] . . .
>
> Einstein called this "the equivalence principle." The local effects of gravity and of acceleration are equivalent. This became a foundation

for his attempt to generalize his theory of relativity so that it was not restricted just to systems that moved with uniform velocity. The basic insight that he would develop over the next eight years was that "the effects we ascribe to gravity and the effects we ascribe to acceleration are both produced by one and the same structure."[1]

It took Einstein eight years to develop his field equations for general relativity. What was he doing for eight years after he got the basic insight?

Introduction

In the previous two chapters, I examined individual eureka moments and the steps involved in understanding. But what happens next when we have had a great insight? Perhaps it will be followed by a stream of other great insights, but more usually, understanding now develops in a quieter fashion. Understanding develops slowly, relentlessly, as we ask about the implications, the applications, the extension, the clarity, and the precision of our original insight. Much work still has to be done.

Einstein had the "happiest thought in his life" in 1907. He grasped the equivalence of weightlessness in deep space and weightlessness in a free-falling capsule. That is a relatively simple idea that most of us can understand. But to do the math, to work out the equations, to incorporate nonuniform motion, to be able to apply the theory to any motion, and to conceive gravity not as an attractive force but as curved space, took him eight years of concentrated effort. This chapter is about the processes involved in that kind of intellectual development. We pick out what seem to be the main vectors of development from single acts of understanding to a general formulation of a concept, law, or theory. My treatment is not by any means exhaustive. My focus continues to be on how the mind actually works and how the dynamism of desire impels these developments. What happens in your mind as we mull over the implications of an individual insight?

In talking about developments, I am focusing on a stream of individual insights that make up a process. It is intelligence in operation, but now I am moving from confusion to clear expression in language, from ideas to concepts, from particulars to general statements, from description to explanation, and from lower to higher viewpoints. Finally, I accept the limitations imposed on understanding by the degrees of intelligibility and unintelligibility in the universe we live in. My limited aim here is to identify the processes at work, to recognize that questioning is still the driving

1. Isaacson, *Einstein*, 145–47. See also Rothenberg, *Creativity and Madness*, chap. 2.

force, and to appreciate the extraordinary flexibility and creativity of human intelligence.

Development itself can be simply defined as a linked sequence of stages, from vague to clear, from simple to sophisticated, from undifferentiated to integrated, from descriptive to explanatory, from implicit to explicit. Humans develop physically, chemically, biologically, psychically, sensitively, intellectually, morally, religiously, and as whole integrated persons. Intellectual development takes place in this matrix, and I am identifying just some of the basic vectors of development. Understanding can become deeper, more comprehensive, more realistic, more practical, more unified, and more accurate. If we want to understand "understanding" we must identify this dynamism—that it is always changing and developing.

Formulating in Words

The use of language by human persons is in itself the result of many acts of understanding. Every child makes this breakthrough for him or herself. From listening, pointing, babbling, and interacting, the child finally grasps the connection between the dog and the oft-repeated sound "dog" that is spoken by the parent. It is a first simple insight into naming, identifying, and classifying. Later, the child will learn the alphabet and each letter is a triumph of understanding. Then, the child will learn words and sentences and so be able to express propositions in verbal form. Later, he or she will study literature, grammar, style, analogy, metaphor, poetry and prose, fact and fiction, and develop a flexibility and control over the use of words and expressions. Each of us has travelled this journey of mastering language as an expression of meaning.

Why are we obliged to express insights in words? Insights occur before we are able to express them. We know what a circle is, but it is difficult to define correctly. The process of formulating in words makes what is implicit become explicit; it makes a vague notion become a clear concept and pins down the insight so that we will not forget or lose it. We need to put it into words so that we can communicate with others and so that we can go further with the idea and introduce additions, qualifications, reservations, and exceptions.

Why is it so difficult to write a good article or paper? How many revisions might I go through in writing a paper for publication? First, I sketch a rough outline, followed by a detailed draft, and then a readable and almost complete presentation. Then the copy editor works on it, maybe a peer reviewer makes suggestions, and I rewrite it. Finally, some finishing touches, and it is ready. Why is it so painful and difficult? Because I am trying to be clear about my sources, evidence, and argument. I want to express this in a clear, orderly, and simple fashion so that the reader will easily understand and there will be no room for misunderstanding. Thinking is rewriting.

The development of understanding is mirrored in the development of language. The development of the child's language is an indication of the child's mental development. We judge students by their ability to express themselves easily and richly. Languages that are spoken by few people, have a short history, and have published a paucity of written texts are usually simple, limited, and poor. Other languages such as English have a long history, a literary tradition, and an abundance of classical writings in science, literature, and poetry. It is spoken in many countries and cultures, and is rich with nuance and meaning.

The creativity of intelligence is mirrored in the creativity of language. Many thousands of language systems have been invented and are now extinct. Contemporary languages are many and they continue to develop and change. New words are invented for new meanings; old words are given new meanings by common consent. A language will vary from one place to another according to local understanding and culture.

The flexibility of intelligence is mirrored in the flexibility of language. A language can be used to examine the limits of its own use; there is no need for a metalanguage to talk about language. We can understand "understanding"; we are using the word in two senses. In the first sense, it is the normal activity of understanding; in the second, "understanding" has become the object to be understood. We can use language and vocabulary in this reflexive way to understand language and vocabulary without having to invent a further language.

My aim here is not to give a complete account of a philosophy of language but to point out the obvious dependence of language on prior understanding. It is of course true that being enculturated into a given linguistic family will influence one's education, concepts, and worldview. However, in principle, understanding is the source of language, and thus, languages can be translated and humans can communicate by learning one another's language and forging a new meaning to old words. A parody of an educational system states that education is a process, where information passes from the notes of the professor to the notes of the student, without passing through the mind of either one. A correct definition of education would be the following: ideas passing from the mind of the professor through his spoken and written words, to the mind of the student through their written and verbal participation. A book is merely ink on paper; a text is meaningless unless we advert to the mind that produced it. Ideas exist not in books but in minds.

Generalizing

An essential characteristic of individual acts of understanding is that they pivot between the abstract and the concrete. One aspect or application of this characteristic is a pivoting between the general and the specific, the universal and the particular. We continue to describe simply and honestly what happens when we understand. We do not begin by saying what intelligence must do; we are looking at the activity of intelligence to discover what it is. We understand the nature of language from what it does. The next point is the fact that insight generalizes.

Helen Keller was afflicted by a disease at the age of eighteen months, which deprived her of sight and hearing.[2] At the age of six she still could not communicate and was unhappy, unruly, and wild. Her tutor taught her the alphabet by signing letters on her hand. The breakthrough came one day in the garden as she felt the flowing water with her left hand. At the same time her tutor was tracing the word w-a-t-e-r on the palm of her right hand. The insight was to understand how they were connected; she realized that the shapes formed on one hand referred to the experience she was having on the other hand: the substance was water. It was an insight of naming, an insight into the correct use of words. It involved grasping a relation between an arbitrary sign or sound and a datum of experience. Naming is the beginning of the expression of understanding in words.

Crucially, the word did not only refer to this one particular experience of running water; it referred to past experiences dimly remembered, and forward to future experiences. It referred to typical aspects of this experience, to the essentials not to the nonessentials, to the general and not to the particular. When she went to the house she was able to recognize that the liquid coming from the tap was the same as that in the garden. The liquid offered for drinking at the table had the same name; the substance she washed with was also in the same category. The insight was to see the sameness behind all these experiences. The same data are to be understood in the same way. Once one has understood one set of data, then any similar set of data will be understood in the same way. On the first occasion, the insight is difficult, but to repeat it is a matter of habit; it becomes easier and easier until it becomes so habitual that it is hard to recognize as an act of understanding.

Helen did not have to be taught how to generalize; it is one essential aspect of the insight of naming that it does generalize. It does not refer exclusively to this particular; rather, it places this particular in a general category. It pivots between the particular and the general. If the name "water"

2. Keller, *The Story of My Life*, 45.

referred only to what was experienced in the garden, then, what was later experienced in the water for drinking would have another name. Insight automatically begins to classify, to divide into categories, and to understand the particular in the light of the general. Further learning and later insights refine the first clumsy attempts at classification. Helen had still much to learn about liquids: alcohol, kerosene, ice, steam, etc. The limits of the categories had yet to be set. The justification for the insight had to be made more explicit. The experience of water could be very varied as in steam or ice or snow, yet it was the same substance. Naming is only the beginning of understanding, but it is an essential activity of generalizing.

Commonsense Generalizing

Commonsense generalizations tend to be made very easily, quickly, and loosely. In any discussion, we frequently jump from the particular to the general. This politician is corrupt; therefore, all politicians are corrupt. These Irishmen are drunk; therefore, all Irishmen are drunks. These workers are lazy; therefore, all the workers are lazy. The basic procedure is essentially valid, as it is the work of intelligence, a sign of understanding at work. But that does not mean that every generalization is justified or correct; counterexamples will often be invoked and so the arguments proceed. The activity of generalizing is ubiquitous: learning consists in understanding more and more the correct extension and application of words, namely, to what particulars these general terms can be applied. This is done in a loose way at the level of common sense but more precisely in the explanations of science.

There is a movement from the particular to the general, but there is also a reverse move from the general to the particular. Classifications are refined by reference back to concrete applications. A doctor can learn about malaria in his training from a textbook, but it may be twenty years before he is confronted by a particular patient with a certain range of symptoms. It may take him a while to make the connection, but then he gets it: this patient is suffering from malaria. So this is what malaria is like in the concrete! The general is applied to the particular. Diagnosis consists in recognizing that the general category described in the textbook is realized in this concrete particular.

We may see something coming down the road from a distance, but we do not yet know what. So we describe it in the most general category available: it is something. But as it comes nearer, we can refine the category and assert, "Oh! It is a truck." This is a narrower classification but still very general; there are many trucks in the world. As it comes nearer, we are able to recognize our neighbor coming with his truck to collect sand and exclaim:

"Oh! It is John." Finally, we have reached the particular. But we can only talk about the particular truck in terms of general categories, a something, a vehicle, a truck, a Ford, a tipper, and the like.

Proper names are given to people because it is important to recognize this particular person, John, as an individual in the class of human person. We can know particulars but only with a reference to the general category or classification by which we understand and name. We pivot easily between the general and the particular. They are complementary notions rather than being mutually exclusive.

Scientific Generalizing

At a more refined level, the scientist is engaged in the same process of generalization. Henry Cavendish (1731–1810) discovered that water could be formed by the combustion of hydrogen and oxygen. Antoine Lavoisier (1743–1794) confirmed this in 1785 by combining fixed amounts of hydrogen and oxygen to form water. It was an enormously important discovery given the importance and prevalence of water in our environment. They must have been very excited with such a basic discovery. Perhaps they repeated their respective experiments a few times to check. What they did not do was to attempt to demonstrate that *all* water was a combination of hydrogen and oxygen. That was taken for granted. It was not necessary to prove that English water was the same as French water, that hot water was the same as cold, or that tap water the same as river water. It was not necessary to repeat the experiment a month later to see if water was still made of hydrogen and oxygen. It was recognized that particular times and places were irrelevant to the correctness of the insight. The insight was precisely into an essential property of all water: to be water it must be a combination of hydrogen and oxygen. It was an insight involving generalization even though the experiment was only performed on a limited number of samples. But the nature of the insight was such that the conclusions could be applied to all water, hydrogen, and oxygen, regardless of time, place, or circumstances.

The principle at work here is that similars are similarly understood. If one set of data is grasped by an insight, then another set of data similar to the first will be grasped by the same kind of insight. One does not need a new kind of insight for each particular instance of water. Instances of water are sufficiently similar for the same insight to recur. One does not need to compose or decompose every instance of water to prove that water is a combination of hydrogen and oxygen. It is the very nature of insights to generalize.

To understand involves the ability to classify, categorize, define, and divide; it is to be able to assign the particular a place in the scheme of things. It means to have a set of general categories in the light of which one can identify new particulars, which are encountered for the first time. The advance of any science proceeds in this way. There was a time when only five subatomic particles were recognized and now there are thirty or forty. Research has revealed all sorts of new phenomena; the old categories are not sufficient. The new phenomena must be given a name, and the name enables researchers to determine its properties. But that might well lead to still further subdivisions. Advancing understanding involves finding more refined, sophisticated, and accurate classifications and generalizations.

Which data are similar to other data? Who decides that these data are similar to those? There is no simple set of rules that can be applied mechanically to give automatic, correct results. There is only the driving force of questions, understanding, and the search for better and more perfect understanding. Mistakes will be made, but they can be corrected. What is similar and what is different? What are the significant similarities and what are the significant differences? Which are descriptive similarities and which are explanatory? It is a matter of intelligence and insight to recognize significant similarities and differences. There is heavy water and light water. There are liquids that look like water, but are actually alcohol, sulfuric acid, or some other liquid.

"Induction" is a term used by logicians for a procedure that goes from a number of individual cases to a general conclusion. The opposite procedure by which we start with a general statement and apply it to particular cases is called "deduction." Logic concerns itself with the logical procedures and arguments involved in doing this correctly and identifying fallacies when incorrect procedures are used. Undoubtedly, logic is of great value when it clarifies these procedures, reveals unstated premises, uncovers fallacious arguments, or shows that conclusions do not follow from premises.

There is a legitimate and important function that the logic of induction has to perform. The generalizer tends to get out of control. The most common fallacy in ordinary conversation is jumping to conclusions from an insufficient number of cases. We do need Mill's rules as well as the fallacies and syllogisms of logic to keep things under control.[3] We use the logic of induction to introduce formalization, consistency, and coherence to our generalizations. But the crucial point is that the logic of induction helps us to generalize correctly; it cannot justify the process itself, which is simply intelligence at work.

There is also a logic of deduction. In fact, most logic tends to be deductive, namely, arguing from given premises to specific conclusions. We simply

3. Mill, *A System of Logic*, 448–503.

make the same point that we made as regards induction: the human mind pivots spontaneously from the general to the particular. However, the logic of the syllogism helps us to make correct deductions rather than fallacious ones. That is how we understand; that is how scientists proceed. Scientists do not need a course in formal logic to work from general principles to a particular conclusion.

Description to Explanation

Einstein developed abstract theoretical equations from a commonsense experience of the similarity between weightlessness when there is no gravity and weightlessness because of free fall. Physicists need the necessary equations when they apply the math to concrete problem, for instance, to understand the perihelion of Mercury. We are at home in the commonsense world of sensible experiences; however, we tend to struggle in the world of definitions, higher math, equations, and mysterious symbols. This is an example of the transition from description to explanation. History is replete with attempts to explain why there are these two worlds of common sense and theory.

Plato faced this problem by distinguishing two kinds of knowing: one of conjecture or belief and the other of understanding or knowledge. The first kind he dismissed as an illusion. How can someone have true knowledge of something that is always changing? But one can have knowledge of Ideas because they do not change. In the Renaissance, philosophers and scientists divided knowledge into that of primary qualities and secondary qualities. The five primary qualities—extension, figure, motion, number, and solidity—really belong to a body. Secondary qualities—color, taste, smell, sound, and temperature—are not true qualities of bodies, but powers in the body to produce these sensations. Kant introduced his distinction between the thing as it is perceived and the thing-in-itself. The various attempts to distinguish common sense and theory met with mixed success; none seem to have been fully comprehensive, critical, and acceptable. The tension between commonsense knowing and scientific knowing continues in much of philosophy of science today.

I deal with this problem in terms of distinguishing between descriptive knowing and explanatory knowing, both of which are legitimate and valid ways of knowing, but from different perspectives. In this section, I present a technical, precise meaning to the operations of describing and explaining. It turns out to be very enlightening, as it solves a problem that arises in all scientific and philosophical disciplines. It is just another way in which understanding develops by moving from descriptive to explanatory categories.

Describing

We do not seem to have much difficulty in describing things. When asked to describe a point, students will usually suggest words like a dot, a mark, a spot, a small stain, a little dot, and so forth. A line will usually be described in terms of a path, a long mark, a series of dots very close together, or an infinite series of dots. A circle can be described as a round ball, a wheel, or a regular curve. Even more easily, we can describe trees, tables, landscapes, and objects. Clearly, we have little difficulty describing, but what exactly are we doing when we are describing?

My definition of the activity of describing is that we relate things to ourselves. We assume that we are the center and that things are related to us. We relay how it seems to us, how it appears from our perspective. We do this by using our senses; thus, descriptive knowledge is dominated by how we see things, hear them, feel them, taste them, and smell them. To describe a table is to say what it looks like to us, how it feels and smells, how it presents itself to us. To describe a point or a line will be to say what it looks like to us, to use the words and images that can best be used to describe it. To describe the movement of the heavenly bodies is to say how they seem to be moving from our point of view, assuming that we are the point of reference.

The most obvious thing about description, then, is that it is relative to us. The point of reference is presumed to be ourselves. Terms like right/left, up/down, there/here, now/later, big/small, close/far, and the like all presume that we are speaking from our point of view. But they may be different for another observer, because he or she is relating things to his or her own experience and point of reference. Descriptions are conditioned by the point of reference of the observer. Consequently, ordinary descriptive knowledge will be relative to the observer; it will be ambiguous and approximate. One might report to the doctor, "I have a terrible fever," but the doctor will usually treat this with a little skepticism and check with a thermometer. One might say, "There was a huge crowd at the demonstration." That assessment may depend on whether one is for the cause or against it. It is rare that a chemistry textbook will say to add some concentrated acid, simmer for a while, and mix a pinch of this with a little of that. When we use works like large, heavy, warm, many, bright, far, fast, soon, sweet, or easy we are usually using descriptive terminology. Even though we may have a fair idea of what we mean by those terms, there is no guarantee that another person will have exactly the same idea.

Description is where all of our knowledge begins. The child relates everything to him or herself. Traditional cultures are predominantly descriptive; all cultures must begin at that level. The empirical sciences begin by describing the materials that they study.

Descriptions, despite their limitations, can be labeled correct or incorrect. If one is observing the movements of the heavenly bodies and says the stars are not moving, whereas another says that they are moving at random, and still another that they are moving from east to west, then, there is a problem. There comes a point when descriptions have to agree. If serious discrepancies occur, then we have to look for the source of misunderstanding. Are we looking at the same thing? What do we mean by movement? Do we include movements that can only be detected after hours of observation? Discrepancies are usually resolved when we look again more carefully, more intelligently, and more systematically. If two witnesses in court give quite different accounts of the same event, there comes a point when we can correctly conclude that one of them must be lying, misremembers, or that their vision was obscured.

In addition to ordinary description, there is also scientific description, namely, description as it prepares the way for explanation. Scientific description is controlled and guided by theoretical intelligence. Here description can become very sophisticated and refined. If one is looking at the heavenly bodies with the naked eye, then the observations are going to be very approximate and of little value. But as a person advances in the science of astronomy, refines his or her techniques of measuring, uses sophisticated telescopes, and directs his or her attention by way of theory to search for something specific, then the person is using scientific description. It is still description, because the person is still reporting what he or she sees and how it appears to the self, but it is no longer vague and approximate. Even though the individual is using a telescope, the description is still a reporting based on how and what he or she sees.

Returning to Plato, he had a problem of differing sense perceptions of warmth, sweetness, size, distance, and so on. Some say the weather is hot, some say it is cold. At the level of ordinary descriptive knowledge there is no definitive resolution to this ambiguity and disagreement. Because descriptive knowledge is relative to the perceiver, the element of relativity cannot be overcome. Plato solved this problem by discarding this kind of knowledge as intrinsically flawed and not real knowledge. I am of the opinion that it is true knowledge, even though it is only descriptive. To escape from the relativity of descriptive knowing, we have to shift our perspective, prescind from the observer, and jump to explanation. Plato asked the question: "Is the wind *really* cold? Is the food *really* sweet?" His answer was to escape into a noetic heaven where pure coldness, sweetness, oneness, being, and so on existed perfectly and permanently. We can ask the same question but find the answer in a slightly different direction. Even if we accept the limitations of descriptive knowledge, we can escape the relativity of this kind of knowing and get something which is more accurate, objective, and permanent. That is explanatory knowing.

Explaining: Measuring and Defining

To explain things is to relate things to one another, to prescind from the observer's point of view to the extent that that is possible. This usually involves a shift to a technical language, definition, and often measurement. It is a shift to a theoretical point of view, which will eventually return to the concrete by way of verification. It enables tremendous precision to be reached in measurement and calculation, as well as in the use of technical terms and definition. There seem to be two principal ways to move into an explanatory framework: by way of measurement or by way of definition. I will consider them in turn. My concern is still how intellectual development actually occurs in individual subjects who are in real historical situations.

The technique of explanatory measurement was discovered by ancient civilizations when descriptive categories proved to be inadequate. One could hardly build the pyramids on the basis of big stones, long ropes, slanting, and the like. Nor was it easy to divide out equal plots of land on the basis of large, small, pretty large, and so forth. Nor could one anticipate much progress in astronomy if scientists were confined to descriptive language such as over there, up there, far away, and very bright.

The basic breakthrough was to adopt a standard length, line up the object to be measured, and then see how many times the standard measure measures it off. This is one prime example of relating things to one another. Instead of relating things to an individual's perception of size, everybody can now agree on a standard measurement. If one desires to compare two distances, he or she can measure each of them in terms of the standard and then compare the measurements. Simple arithmetic can then be used to divide a field into five equal sections, to determine how many blocks of what size would be needed for a pyramid of a determinate size, and to discover how long it would take to complete various journeys. Geometry can also be utilized in the calculation of areas of fields of different shapes, and extended to capacities and volumes of containers.

The same technique can be used for weight. One adopts a standard weight, ensures everybody has the same standard, and uses it. Now the standard measure can weigh corn, tomatoes, or gold. The difficulty is to ensure that everybody recognized the standard and adhered to it. In biblical and

Greek times, people were aware of the danger of false weights which could favor the trader. It was the Scientific Revolution that would come to exploit the possibilities of explanatory measurement to the fullest.

One further advantage of explanatory measuring is in the precision that is possible in calculations. Once one has a standard, it can be subdivided into as many smaller units as desired. Similarly, it can be extended by multiplication to cover expansive distances as far as the circumference of the earth. With fractions and decimals and eventually calculus, one can deal with infinitely small areas and lengths. Now, the descriptions of big, small, or pretty large are replaced by 1.775 inches, three and a half miles, 175 meters, or 100 watts. Distance and weight can be specified to any degree of accuracy that one desires. Provided that everybody is following the same standard, there is no possibility of misinterpretation or ambiguity.

Once one has basic standards of distance, weight, time, and angles then he or she can extend the technique by the use of scales. How does one measure warmth? Is there a way of shifting to an explanatory framework? How does one relate things to something else in this case? Someone discovers that metals expand in a regular manner with an increase in heat. A metal like mercury, which is easy to handle, expands and contracts as it heats or cools. Once an objective property has been determined, the trick now is to fix the scale at the top and the bottom. Assume that the freezing point of water is zero and the boiling point of water is one hundred. Fix the scale from the freezing point to the boiling point. With the advent of the centigrade thermometer, one systematically relates the expansion of the volume of mercury with the increase or decrease in heat. The freezing point and boiling point of water provide reference points. Now it is possible to specify in degrees the exact temperature of a patient. The more accurate the instrument, the more accurate the measurements of temperature can become. We have shifted from describing how warm I feel, to an explanatory concept of temperature. The same happens in so many other fields where instruments are constructed to relate different factors and to measure the differential by means of a scale. A barometer measures air pressure in inches. Noise can be measured in decibels. Water density, viscosity, torque, wavelength, light intensity, and electricity can all be measured using similar kinds of techniques.

Measurement is a technique of marking off, but it is guided by concepts and definitions. The invariance of standards in scientific work resides, not in the physical bars or weights, but in the invariance of laws and concepts. All understanding involves some pivoting between the abstract and the concrete; this becomes explicit in the field of explanation. Standards of length, temperature, mass, specific gravity, the laws of motion, point, line, and circle are all abstract concepts. Ideas emerge from images; concepts are formulated ideas. We can feel heat, but we cannot feel temperature.

It may be surprising to realize that a yard or a meter is a concept. But just as a circle is a concept to which concrete visible circles approximate, so a yard is a concept to which various measures approximate. There can be no perfect coincidence between the concrete and the abstract. The stick of metal that is preserved at the same temperature and pressure is the closest the concrete can come to the abstract concept of a meter. But if someone asks, "Where is the precise end of the bar?" there is a problem, for the end of the bar is uneven. It may seem to be even to the naked eye, but a microscope reveals that what is concrete is always uneven. We have noted how the descriptions of the point, line, and circle are usually given in terms of visual images, like a dot, a path, or an even round figure. Euclid could not have developed his geometry on that basis. He needed definitions of point, line, circle, cone, and other geometric shapes. For him a point was a position without magnitude, and a straight line the shortest distance between two points. But a position without magnitude cannot be seen! It is a concept. Euclid used images to manipulate concepts. He used description to reach explanation.

When one moves from physics and chemistry to the biological sciences and especially when one comes to the human sciences, measurement loses its primacy. But that does not mean that these higher sciences cannot be explanatory. The way to explanation in the higher sciences is largely by way of explanatory definition, where the terms define the relations and the relations define the terms. Measurement, standards, and counting are not entirely replaced but yield in importance to the power of explanatory definition. Explanatory definition goes beyond descriptive definition, because it relates things to one another, rather than relating them to oneself.

Hence, we can get some idea of the importance of a system for explanatory definition. It is often not possible to define one element explanatorily in isolation from everything else—as Socrates found to his cost. Socrates was trying to define virtues individually in isolation from other basic concepts and principles and usually failed. Aristotle set up a system of basic terms and principles, then defined the virtues systematically in relation to vices of excess and defect. The context of explanatory definition usually involves a system of terms and relations, such that the relations fix the terms and the terms fix the relations. The periodic table in chemistry is a typical process of setting up such a system of terms and relations: arrange the known elements according to their atomic weight and note that they seem to fall into a pattern. Each element, given its place in the pattern, is defined in relation to the previous one. It is so systematic that a chemist could predict unknown elements even though they had not yet been discovered.

Technical terminology is part of the process of moving from description to explanation. In description, terms are usually vague, nontechnical, and expressed in visual images or image language. "Form" and "matter" were words with a commonsense meaning at the time of Aristotle, and sometimes he used them in that way. But he also assigned a technical meaning to those words, which became part of his explanatory system with defined ranges of meaning. Sometimes new words have to be invented for the new system, but more commonly, ordinary words are used and assigned a technical meaning within a context of definitions and postulates. It is normal for a discipline to move from vague, descriptive categories to precise, technical, explanatory categories and terminology. The person of common sense should not expect to understand such terminology unless he or she has been initiated through an appropriate education.

Description and explanation are complementary procedures. They are both valid forms of human knowing. All one has to do to avoid confusion is to continually add the proviso, from the point of view of description, or from the point of view of explanation. Does the sun rise in the east and set in the west? From the viewpoint of description, it is certainly true. Anyone who reports that he or she sees the sun rising in the west and setting in the east needs to have his or her coordinates straightened out. Does that mean that we disagree with Copernicus? No, because Copernicus is looking at the solar system from the point of view of explanation. If we prescind from the observer and relate the movements of the planets and the sun to one another, then, the earth is rotating on its axis and revolving around the sun. They are two different valid points of view. All we have to do in order to avoid confusion is to be clear whether we are adopting a descriptive or an explanatory point of view. Nothing but confusion can and does ensue when these points of view are not distinguished. Any problems between common sense and theory can be solved by distinguishing describing and explaining. In principle the two points of view are complementary and not in conflict.

The so-called rift between common sense and theory is not a problem. I have identified a natural movement from common sense to theory and back to common sense using a multitude of examples. There are not two worlds that are separate and apart, competing, or mutually excluding one another. There are two perspectives in the development of understanding: insight as descriptive and relating to us and insight as explanatory and relating things to one another. We have identified these and can move seamlessly from one to the other. Both have an indispensable place in the development of understanding. This ability is necessary in all areas of human knowing and professional expertise—and especially in philosophy.

Verifiable and Nonverifiable Images

Images play different roles in description and in explanation. When one describes something, the person is relating how the object is perceived, how it looks, sounds, tastes, smells, and feels. Things are related back to the individual by way of sensible properties. If there is a disagreement with someone, then, the two of them can go back to the data and the images. The disagreement might be over whether a certain star is twinkling; whether a wall is white, cream, or gray; or whether the weather is cold or cool. How do they solve such disagreements? They go back to the data, look again more carefully, more attentively, and more honestly. They define their terms. In description there is always a sensible image and the description must be in conformity with the image as sensed. There is a verifiable image, and one can verify the descriptive affirmation by reference back to the senses, the imagination, or memory.

Explaining something involves relating things to one another and setting up a framework of concepts. It requires that one prescind from the perspective of the observer. Explanatory concepts are leaps into the world of relations between things themselves. At the level of explanation there are no verifiable representative images: one cannot resolve disputes by going back to describing the data. We can have an image of warmth, but we do not have an image of temperature; we have an image of weight but we have no image of mass. Theory, system, explanation, definition, and measurement go beyond the field of representative images, because by definition they are relating things to one another.

On the other hand, we cannot think or know without images. So what do we do? In the field of explanation we construct useful, heuristic, and symbolic images to help us to think clearly and further our understanding. Euclidean geometry uses the images of points, lines, circles, and triangles to explore the concepts and necessary properties of these figures. Niels Bohr suggested a very successful image of the atom. He gave us a picture of the atom with its nucleus of protons and neutrons at the center, with layers of electrons spinning around in fixed orbits much like the planetary system. It was an image that embodied all that had been learned about the atom up to that time. It suggested fruitful questions as to the relations between the subatomic particles; it was helpful in studying the relations between elements and suggested possible explanations of how elements bond together to form molecules. But it is not, and was not, what atoms look like in reality. It is a constructed, pedagogical image. It is not verifiable as an image. To verify an image as an image, one must have the corresponding sensation. To see what atoms look like in reality, one must be able to see them. At the moment it is not possible to see individual atoms, although it may eventually be possible to construct a microscope to produce a visual image of the atom. Bohr would not be surprised, if it did not look like his constructed image. Others might be disappointed. The unfortunate thing is that we often confuse the constructed, symbolic images of explanation with representative verifiable images of description.

Every scientific discipline moves from description into explanation. Hence every discipline moves from the verifiable representative images of description to the nonverifiable, heuristic, constructed, pedagogical images of explanation. The role of images is quite different in the two realms of knowing. Endless confusion arises when these two realms are not clearly distinguished. Scientists often confuse the verifiable images of description with the unverifiable, symbolic images of explanation. Instead of telling us what has been verified, they give us a picture of what scientific reality really looks like. Is light a wave or a particle? Both "wave" and "particle" are images. We use the image of wave to explain certain elements of the properties of light. We use the image of a particle to explain other properties. In this case, the images of wave and particle are not images of description, which can be verified by looking more closely. They are images of explanation and hence nonverifiable as images; they are symbolic and heuristic. We use them if they help us to understand; we abandon them if they are not helpful in understanding.

We tend to be more at home in the world of description and verifiable images. To move into the world of theory and concepts that relate things to one another and have verifiable relations demands an intellectual asceticism, which is difficult to sustain. Yet it is clear that this distinction between describing and explaining must be made and that it is of fundamental and universal relevance.

It is hard to define justice in isolation: Aristotle constructed a table of virtues flanked by the vices by excess and defect, in order to define the individual virtues, with justice being just one of the moral virtues. Einstein did not find the essence of gravity by gazing at it, but by manipulating the concepts of space, time, motion, the speed of light, acceleration, and free fall, combined with complicated mathematics. Crick and Watson did not find the essence of the DNA molecule by looking, or describing, but by identifying the chemical components, determining what requirements had to be fulfilled, and using their imagination to suggest possible structures. A phenomenological method of description has to be complemented with a jump to explanation and concepts.

Higher Viewpoints

The process of human knowing is dynamic; the operating force behind this dynamism is questioning. We have outlined the heuristic structure by which we proceed from questions to correct answers. By this means we arrive at an answer to one particular, limited, specific question, but further questions automatically arise by which we seek deeper understanding or move on to related topics. If we are aiming at a deeper understanding, we are usually aiming at a higher viewpoint. Our knowing is progressive and cumulative. Insights pass into the habitual texture of the mind, but then they become the material for further insights at a higher level of generality. A higher viewpoint presupposes a set of insights at a lower level of generality. We question, study, and eventually more clearly understand some particular matter or data. Ideas accumulate, and similarities are noted.

But at a certain point the question will arise as to how this aggregate of lower insights relate together. Is there an organizing act of intelligence that can grasp how they fit together? At this stage the data for the further insight are precisely the set of earlier insights that have already occurred. What is sought is a principle of unification, which will establish what these insights have in common and how they differ. What is sought is an insight into insight, or more precisely, a higher viewpoint.

Finally, there comes the emergence of the higher viewpoint. There is discovered a law, a principle, and a new set of postulates, definitions, and conclusions. The validity of the original individual insights remains intact; but they are swept up into a new unity, framework, or schema. The higher viewpoint is characterized by its generality, its simplicity, its greater exactitude, and its precision. Consider a series of examples to see how this works:

The transition from elementary arithmetic to algebra provides one example. The first painful steps in learning arithmetic are usually taken in counting. Each number has to be identified by its symbol, and this has to be associated with a sensible experience of quantity. Children learn to count from one to ten, write down the numbers from one to ten, and are able to count out ten oranges or ten pencils. Each number and each operation successfully mastered is an individual insight, a breakthrough, a little flash of light. As familiarity increases with repetition, the operations of addition and subtraction are added. Mostly this is done in the context of sensible objects like oranges, cookies, or pencils. But the operations can be generalized by learning the addition tables and learning the rules for subtraction. Multiplication and division are another breakthrough, another intellectual triumph, which are not totally unrelated to the previous operations yet go beyond them by generalizing. Multiplication is simply the addition of a certain number to itself so many times.

A crisis point might occur at this point when numbers appear in the operations that cannot be verified in sensible experience. Subtracting a larger number from a smaller yields a negative number. How can one represent a negative number sensibly? Dividing prime numbers results in fractions; they do not go in evenly. How are fractions multiplied or divided? How does one relate square roots with negative quantities to concrete reality? Are these operations valid, if there is no corresponding sensible experience with oranges or cookies?

The trick is to break free from the constraints of sensible experience. Numbers can be defined as the result of operations that are performed according to rules. Then mathematics is free to develop in all sorts of operations with strange kinds of numbers. These operations are generalized in algebra, whose symbols allow further operations to be conceived and executed. Algebra is a higher viewpoint from arithmetic, because it generalizes the operations that are performed on sensible quantities; it goes beyond the limits imposed by immediate sensible quantities. It is a set of insights that presupposes the validity of all the different insights of arithmetic but systematizes, relates, and generalizes these operations in a particularly expeditious way.

In chess, one can distinguish between a beginner, average club player, international master, grand master, and world champion. The beginner learns how the pieces move, is taught the rules of the game, but understands little else. The average club player knows the rules and how the pieces move but applies these rules in a context of strategic and tactical understanding. The international master will presume all of this basic understanding of the game but adds to it an understanding of the history of chess, memories of great openings and games, better judgment, and experience about positions and material. The grandmaster presumes all of this but adds individual ability; a mastery of openings, middle games, and end games; an exquisite ability to defend and to attack; and superior competence. The candidates for world champion presume everything that has been previously stated but bring the game to a yet higher level of total competence and innovation. Each of these levels represents a successive higher viewpoint. These are different levels of understanding of the same rules, the same pieces, and the same board. However, the mentality, competence, challenges, and novelties are different at each stage of the progression from novice to world champion, from lower to higher viewpoint.

Perhaps another example can be seen in the relation between the empirical sciences and philosophy. Each of the individual sciences develops its own methods, theories, concepts, and definitions. It progresses in understanding its own particular area of matter assigned to it. Each science has its domain, its territory, and its limitations. But questions arise that go beyond the domain of the individual sciences. Who laid down these domains? How are the sciences related to one another? Is there anything that they leave out? Who criticizes and evaluates the scientific method itself? Is matter the ultimate reality of the universe? There is a felt need for some higher principle of unification that organizes the sciences, their methods, and their conclusions. Philosophy emerges as the needed higher viewpoint, a total worldview that encompasses everything. It does not invalidate the conclusions of the sciences; rather, it sweeps the multitude of conclusions into a higher unity and synthesis, namely, a higher viewpoint. A materialist reductionist philosophy would claim that there is only one science, namely, physics and all the other sciences can and will be absorbed into physics. A constructionist philosophy would claim that the relation between the sciences is an arbitrary construction, that there is no rational basis or systematic principle for relating the sciences to one another. I would hold that there are such principles and that the sciences can be related in an orderly, systematic way. Each of these philosophical positions are higher viewpoints; but not all higher viewpoints are correct.

Finally, there are a multitude of competing philosophies. In history there have been a succession of philosophies, which have contradicted one another, criticized one another, or supplemented and complemented one another. These are all individual attempts to understand the world, man, God, knowledge, and truth. But how are all of these attempts to be related together? Is philosophy just going nowhere? Is it a waste of time? Or can all of these efforts be used as data for a new understanding of understanding, a philosophy of philosophies? My effort is to shift from the content understood to the activity of understanding itself, thus, providing the basis for a new higher viewpoint in philosophy. If we can pin down an invariant structure of the knowing subject, then we can indirectly pin down the content of all that is to be known. If we can understand what it is to understand, then we will indirectly be able to understand any philosophy, any science, and any branch of human knowing. Conversely, if we can also understand the process of misunderstanding, then we can also grasp the secret of decline, error, and falsehood. If we can grasp the dynamics of understanding and misunderstanding we will have the key, the fixed base, and the invariant pattern that opens upon all further acts of understanding. This can provide the means to a universal viewpoint.

Higher viewpoints are not just new theories, paradigm shifts, or revolutions in thinking. They are a special kind of insight that presuppose an aggregate of individual insights but sweeps them up into a new unity that confers a new significance. They represent a new unity, a deeper synthesis, a higher integration. The advantage of the higher viewpoint is its generality, its simplicity, and the speed with which it gets to the point. It is part of the normal process of developing intelligence.

Probabilities and Chance

Can we understand nonsense, random sequences, chance occurrences, irrational numbers, probabilities, the insignificant, the meaningless, the irrelevant, or the sensible as sensible? Are there limits to the development of our understanding? How can we talk about nonsense, or probabilities, if we do not have some intellectual grasp of what we are talking about? I defined abstraction as focusing on the important, the significant, and the relevant data while leaving aside the unimportant, the insignificant, and the irrelevant. But can we simply ignore and abandon data which from one point of view happens to be unimportant, insignificant, or irrelevant? It is important to consider the possibility of some useful understanding of data, which cannot be understood in terms of direct insights. In this section, I will introduce the notion of inverse insights to complement the account of direct insights.

For the most part, in this and previous chapters, I have been talking about direct insights, which grasp a law, a regularity, a pattern, a correlation, or a link between cause and effect that is enormously positive, satisfying, and helpful. The insights cited from Archimedes, Helen Keller, Crick and Watson, and Einstein are of that sort. This was the kind of insight sought in the Scientific Revolution, which can be called the era of classical science and classical method. Typical of the laws discovered in this period were the heliocentrism of Copernicus, Galileo's law of uniform acceleration, Kepler's laws of planetary motion, Newton's three laws of motion, and Einstein's famous equation that energy equals mass multiplied by the speed of light squared. These laws are direct insights into a regularity discovered in the data. They are extremely satisfying, as they illuminate a vast array of data from the past, the present, and the future and can usually be applied across the board. The laws of motion apply wherever and whenever anything in the universe moves, from the motion of subatomic particles, to the motions of the planets, to the swirling of the galaxies. Einstein's law applies to all mass and to all energy from the microscopic to the macrocosm.

In the case of classical laws such as these, the law is an abstract formulation of a concept, whereas the data is concrete and diverse. Does the law exhaust the intelligibility of this data? Galileo formulated the law of falling bodies: velocity equals distance multiplied by time squared. He noticed that the more perfect his equipment and the better he could measure the time, then the nearer the data came to coincide with his law. But how could he have perfect equipment? How could he eliminate friction and air resistance in order to get a perfect measurement of time? He could improve on all three, but there was no way he could totally eliminate experimental error. He just had to make allowances. The abstract laws never perfectly coincide with the concrete data. The abstract can never perfectly coincide with the concrete. There is always an experimental error, even if the error is minuscule and for practical purposes can be ignored.

These were the kinds of laws and the kinds of regularities, which were sought in the Scientific Revolution in astronomy, chemistry, physics, biology, botany, geology, and atomic physics. The presumption was that all scientific laws were of this type and this was the only intelligibility worth having. But scientists who articulated these laws blithely ignored the gap between the abstract and the concrete and the fact that they always had to allow for experimental error. They presupposed a deterministic universe and claimed that once all the laws were discovered, then we would have a complete understanding of the universe and could accurately predict and control everything. It was the vision of a clockwork, deterministic universe working exclusively according to these classical laws of science.

History would provide an antidote to that illusion. Malthus and Darwin were already using a method of probabilities in population studies (e.g., *Essay on the Principle of Population*) and in the diversification of species (e.g., *The Origin of the Species*), respectively. The sociological studies of Durkheim relied heavily on averages, statistics, and probabilities. The dagger blow to the clockwork universe came with quantum mechanics and Heisenberg's uncertainty principle. Quantum physics, as I understand it, deals with probabilities rather than certainties. It places probabilities at the center of scientific understanding. This was a complete change to the expectations of previous classical science and was rejected by Einstein to the end of his life: he famously declared, "I, in any case, am convinced that He does not play dice with the universe."[4]

Thus, it began to be realized that in addition to scientific laws of the classical type, which grasped a direct intelligibility, there were other laws that, although they did not give such satisfaction, were part of our scientific understanding of the universe. These were statistical laws, which dealt with probabilities, averages, rates, frequencies, and occurrences. These kinds of laws, however imperfect, were necessary in every area of science and in every application of the abstract to the concrete.

4. Born, *The Born-Einstein Letters,* 88.

This new kind of understanding can be called an "inverse insight." It accepts that all data has to be understood but cannot necessarily be understood in terms of a direct insight of the classical type. It is inverse as it focuses on the data which direct insight cannot cope with. It can be defined as an "insight into the absence of an expected intelligibility."[5] We expect everything to be explicable in terms of classical laws. We are shocked when probabilities and averages are not amenable to such laws.

How do we understand a random sequence of numbers from the spinning of a roulette wheel? The sequence is only intelligible in terms of averages and probabilities. The probabilities operative in one roll of the wheel do not change for the next roll of the wheel. It would be a mistake for a gambler to think that because a certain number has not turned up for many rolls, then it is more likely to turn up at the next roll. The law of averages is a statistical law not a classical law; it states how often a number is expected to appear in the long run. We are inclined to think that if a number fails to appear over numerous rolls, then it is more likely to appear in the next occasion in order to satisfy the law of averages. A law is a law and so we expect it to be a classical law, from which we can predict and control future events. But the law of averages is in a different realm. It is an insight, but it is an insight of an absence, a lack, a nonsense, an irregularity, an irrational element. It is not a direct insight, but an inverse insight. It is not a misunderstanding; it is not a correction of a previous insight. It is not a mistake; it must be either true or false. There is positive data that is questioned for understanding—the actual sequences of numbers in a roulette wheel are positive data. There is something to be understood. We spontaneously expect a direct insight. We normally expect that a law of mathematics must be obeyed in all cases. We expect the sequence to be regular, lawful, and directly intelligible. An average is intelligible but not in the way we expected. We can apply laws of averages to the sequence, but the laws do not specify a uniform regularity but, rather, the absence of such a regularity, and instead, the presence of irregularity and a law of probability. These provide a lesser kind of intelligibility.

One can formulate probabilities and averages precisely and correctly: the meteorologist might say that there is a 90% probability of rain tomorrow, a professor may tell a student that his or her work is only average, or a doctor may tell a patient that he or she probably has about four months to live. These statements are to be understood as statements of probabilities: they are not certain but probable. The key to understanding these kinds of laws is that what actually happens diverges nonsystematically from the stated law of probability. Let us suppose that a certain locality has an

5. Lonergan, *Insight*, 44.

average annual rainfall of fifty inches a year. That does not mean that every year the area will get fifty inches of rain. In one year, the region might get seventy inches, in another year thirty, and in another forty. One should expect a divergence. However, the divergence is nonsystematic; it goes up and down in a random manner. There is no law that governs what will happen in a particular year. If there is a systematic divergence, then the average is wrong; if the rainfall is regularly above the stated average, or below the stated average, then the average is wrong and has to be adjusted. In short, each particular year one should expect a nonsystematic divergence from the average; however, in the long run, one should expect the figures to converge on the stated average. This is the kind of intelligibility expressed in statistical laws.

To understand any concrete event or occurrence one has to invoke both classical and statistical laws. In the end, although classical laws are abstract, to be useful they have to be applied in concrete situations. For example, to apply Newton's laws of motion to playing snooker, one needs to determine which law applies, in what priority, to what degree of accuracy, and to what degree of experimental error. A very good player can occasionally get a perfect score of 147 points. But why can the expert player not do it all the time? Because of small degrees of miscalculation of the force needed, inaccuracy in striking the ball, and imperfections in the cue, the ball, and the surface, the player can only do it perhaps once in a hundred times—which is a reference to statistical laws. In engineering, in medicine, in particle physics, in politics, in chemistry, and in all areas one can identify this combination of the classical and statistical methods.

We are now in an advantageous position to define "chance." Chance is simply the nonsystematic divergence of the actual from the ideal. If the average rainfall is fifty inches a year and the region gets sixty inches, then the element of chance involved is the ten extra inches above the average. Chance, then, is an element in applying laws to the concrete, and thus, statistics will always play a part in analyzing concrete situations. It is a minor element because it is circumscribed and limited by the application of both classical and statistical laws. It represents a minor deviation, a minor nuance in the application of these laws. Wherever classical laws are applied in a concrete situation, one must also invoke probabilities, and hence, an element of chance. There is an element of chance in just about everything in our lives—health, career, relationships, finance, education, disease, climate change, agriculture, and so on.

Classical science is inclined to lead to a determinist philosophy, namely, that the universe is a giant clockwork machine, where in principle, everything could be controlled and predicted once we know all of the laws.

Statistical thinking is inclined to lead to a philosophy of indeterminism, which holds that everything happens by chance. But there is no need to abandon one mistaken background assumption (e.g., determinism) for another mistaken background assumption (e.g., indeterminism). The widespread acceptance of statistical method, which acknowledges that there is an element of chance operating in our universe, has encouraged this notion of total indeterminism. The notion of chance and statistical method I have presented here admits that there is a chance element operating but only in complementarity with classical scientific laws. Both determinism and indeterminism are at work.

Is there any data or aspect of data which simply cannot be understood in any way? As I have explained in detail, to understand means to grasp an idea from an image, to draw meaning from what is meaningless, to ascertain the significant from the insignificant, and to reveal the intelligible in the sensible. Sensing intends the sensible; intelligence intends the intelligible. The sensible simply as sensible can be sensed, but it cannot be understood, by definition. The ultimate significance of the sensible is that it is the fruitful field in which intelligence can operate. The empirical residue is that element of the sensible that can be sensed but cannot be understood; it cannot be brought under law. Ultimately there is no perfect coincidence between the intelligible and the sensible.

Therefore, a direct insight will always grasp what is intelligible, significant, regular, systematic, relevant, and meaningful. The inverse insight confronts us with the reality of a lack of intelligibility. While there are degrees and kinds of intelligibility attainable in the universe, there is also an element of chance operating. The universe and all that happens in it can only be understood comprehensively and correctly by a combination of direct and inverse insights.

Conclusion

We can now put together the elements I have analyzed and construct a coherent picture of holistic intellectual development. I have shown that understanding expresses itself in language and that the development of understanding parallels the development of language. I have elucidated how we generalize and that this is a legitimate, normal development of intelligence. I have shown how a science normally starts with describing the phenomena in its domain, but it usually moves on to explanation through the process of measuring and definition. I have considered how a series of individual insights coalesce into a higher viewpoint, which, in turn, provides the data for a higher synthesis or understanding. Chance presents itself as a roadblock, given that it is irregular, nonsystematic, and unintelligible. The universe is nuanced and there are degrees of intelligibility. Thus, I demonstrated the need for a statistical method, which complements the classical method.

Perhaps, we now have a better sense of what Einstein was doing for those eight years between his original insight and his formulation of the equations of the general theory of relativity. He was formulating appropriate concepts. He was generalizing from seeing a painter fall off a ladder to a general theory of motion. He was doing the mathematics and moving into the world of theory and explanation. He was certainly reaching a higher viewpoint, a new synthesis of previous insights into space, time, motion, and gravity. He was doing experiments, even if they were mostly in his imagination. He never seems to have accepted that probability or chance was a constitutive element in the working of the universe. Life is not just a stream of happy eureka insights, but rather, it includes the drudgery of correct formulation, the expansion of generalizing, the struggle to explain, the reach for higher viewpoints, and the final encounter with the limits imposed on our human understanding of the world.

6

certain (handwritten)

How Understanding Becomes Knowledge

GUILTY OR NOT GUILTY

Hollywood loves the drama of a court case, with evidence and counterevidence, arguments and counterarguments weaving their complex way through the story to the dramatic conclusion. Imagine that we are called upon for jury duty. We are asked only one question and can give only one answer: guilty or not guilty. Presuming that we are responsible citizens, how should we conduct ourselves during the trial and the jury deliberation?

Our first minimum duties surely would be to pay attention; listen to the witnesses, the lawyers, and the judge; understand the forensic evidence; remember what was said; and try not to be distracted or to fall asleep.

But then we need to understand the arguments, the interpretation of the law, the timeline of the crime, the evidence, the alibis, and the motive. We will have to pass an individual judgment on each of the witnesses: are they honest, trustworthy, coherent, and convincing? We must pass judgment on the evidence: is it circumstantial? Does it put the accused at the scene of the crime? Does it implicate the accused to the exclusion of anybody else?

We will judge the arguments of the prosecutor and the defense attorney. The prosecutor will weave an argument incorporating all of the evidence and witnesses in order to point to the guilt of the accused. The defense lawyer will try to pick holes in this story, point out inconsistencies, remind the jury of counterevidence, and construct a story indicating the innocence of the accused and the possibility that the crime could have been perpetrated by somebody else.

In the jury room, the thought processes of each individual juror will be expressed openly. The evidence will be recalled, each part will be analyzed, each witness will be evaluated, and each argument will be critically examined. An individual juror may have missed something, so we learn from one another. There is an opportunity to ask questions and clarify arguments and conclusions. A majority view seems to be emerging. All of the arguments and evidence seem to be pointing in one direction. Is the defendant guilty or not guilty beyond a reasonable doubt? We do not need to be certain, but to judge beyond a reasonable doubt. A consensus emerges.

Is the defendant guilty or not guilty?

Guilty, your Honor.

From Thinking to Knowing

I have already devoted five chapters to discussing the various characteristics of the act of human understanding; I have examined how understanding develops and how there are direct and inverse insights, as well as higher viewpoints. Despite all of this work, we have not yet reached knowledge! We are still in the world of ideas and hypotheses. Thus far, I have examined thinking but not knowing. Now is the time to introduce the critical question of truth into the discourse. Now is the time to make the transition from clear and distinct ideas, to true affirmations about what is true and real. All of the previous work serves as a preparation for this moment. I believe we are well-situated to make this shift if we continue to use the method of self-appropriation.

In the interests of doing one thing at a time, I have focused on direct insight into possibilities. I have bracketed the process by which we evaluate the possibilities to find the correct solution. In most of our thinking, we are not just brainstorming and fantasizing, we are actually looking for correct solutions. Archimedes probably had many insights in his laboratory as he experimented with gold and silver, weighing, mixing, making prototypes, and getting volumes. However, none of the ideas worked and were rejected: they did not solve the problem at hand. He was not looking for any idea at all but for one that would work. He continued to reject possible ideas until in the baths he found the correct idea and procedure. Crick and Watson were looking at many possible structures for the DNA molecule; however, the initial possible structures did not work, as they conflicted with the requirements of current data. They rejected these unsatisfactory possibilities and kept looking until that Sunday morning when they found the correct structure. Aquinas was not looking for any old argument against the Manichees; I am sure he was familiar with many possible rebuttals. He wanted a valid, solid, unassailable argument that would shake the very foundations of their beliefs and knock them flat. There is a very specific process for getting ideas, and there is a different specific process for getting correct ideas. They normally work in tandem; often it is not easy to differentiate between them. But if we examine the simple process of solving a puzzle, doing a crossword, or devising an outline for an essay, we find a process that involves developing a stream of ideas that are quickly rejected or accepted until we arrive at a satisfactory outcome. The process of getting ideas is different from the process of sorting out the ideas into true and false, correct and incorrect, or what will work or will not work. The first process gives us possible hypotheses. The second process gives us true human knowledge. There is a constant pivoting from one process to the other. That is the distinction I will identify in this chapter.

We can learn a cautionary lesson from René Descartes. His clear and distinct ideas have much in common with what I have called direct insights. However, his first and favorite clear and distinct idea was: "I think, therefore I am." It is a fundamental point for him, because he considers it undoubtedly true and irrefutable. Then, he goes a step further and asserts: "And consequently it seems to me that I can already establish as a general rule that all things we conceive very clearly and distinctly are true."[1] He states this three times in his *Meditations*. He explicitly affirms that all clear and distinct ideas are completely true; he takes this as a general rule. Unfortunately, he conflates the insight into possible ideas with the insight into the truth or falsity of ideas. By conflating, I mean that he puts together as one thing what he should distinguish into two questions and two processes of understanding. If Descartes performed some self-appropriation he would have noticed how many bright ideas he got but rejected as irrelevant or plain wrong. If the question of truth is absorbed into the question of direct understanding, then it disappears as an explicit philosophical issue, which results in drastic consequences for subsequent philosophy.

Thus, we need to differentiate explicitly between two levels of cognitional process. What I have been examining until now has been the simple, basic act of human understanding. There were three basic steps in that process: the question of intelligence applied to data, the occurrence of insight, and the formulation or development of the insight. Now I am moving into a critical mode, which involves (1) asking a new critical question, (2) looking for a reflective act of human understanding, (3) and concluding in a judgment of truth. This is a parallel process, but whereas the first process

---

1. Descartes, *Discourse on Method and the Meditations,* 54; see also 58, 113.

concludes with a formulated hypothesis, the second concludes with a judgment of truth. (It might help to look at the diagram in chapter 8.)   *p. 189*

1. *The New Question.* The questions regarding intelligence look for more information, explanation, and documentation with the goal of satisfying understanding. But now the critical question becomes: "Is that understanding correct or incorrect?" Ideas are ideas, but are these ideas true and correct? Do they belong to the real world, can they be verified, and does this solution work? In this critical mode, just any old answer will not do.

2. *The New Insight.* Direct insight gives us clear and distinct ideas as in Descartes. But now we are looking for a reflective act of understanding. What do we need to do in order to verify our hypothesis or idea? We have to assemble evidence and show that the evidence entails the conclusion. It is a reflective act of understanding that grasps the sufficiency of the evidence and the connection between the evidence and the conclusion.

3. *The New Product.* Acts of direct understanding issue in formulations. We get an insight and express it in clear terminology, definitions, concepts, theories, and explanations. Reflective insights, by contrast, produce judgments, which are statements of true or false, affirmations or denials, or verifications or rejections.

In this chapter I will deal in sequence with this new critical question, this new insight, and this new product of a judgment. It is helpful to note the parallel between these three new topics and the previous questions, understandings, and formulations. But the turn to making a judgment places us in a completely different mode—the critical mode. I use the terms "reflective insight" and "reflection" to identify the critical mode. "Reflection" is often used in a neutral sense of just thinking about something. In this text, it is always used in the sense of answering the critical question: is it true? I usually use the term "intelligence" to refer to activities of understanding possibilities and "reason" when referring to activities of understanding truth or falsehood.

It is hard to overemphasize the importance of identifying the process of moving from direct insights, which are a dime a dozen, to the act of reflective understanding, which grasps truth, correctness, and usable solutions. I started with the example of the jury and what they must do in order to fulfill their civic duty. The jury provides a good model of what must be done when asking a question about the truth, namely, assembling evidence and witnesses, evaluating arguments, and coming to a definitive conclusion. It can be a matter of life or death. There is a right way to proceed to reach a verdict: paying attention, being objective, analyzing arguments, evaluating evidence, and passing judgments on witnesses. There is also a wrong way: relaxing, daydreaming, being biased, not thinking about evidence, and making rash judgments. My goal is to identify this right way. What do we need to do in order to affirm our judgments as true or false? We are not just playing with ideas; we are dealing with the real world, of what is and what is not, of life and death.

The Critical Question Arises

We can distinguish, then, *questions for intelligence* and *questions for reflection*. Questions for intelligence are questions asking for further information, questions seeking a clearer understanding or distinction, or questions that are looking for further content. Questions for intelligence often take the following forms: When? Why? How many? How often? What is the weight? What is the distance? What is the cause? What is the required correlation? What is the required word? What is the formula? What is the definition? These questions cannot be answered with a yes or no; they are looking for more data, more content, clarifications, further relevant information, and further direct understanding of possibilities.

The question for reflection is the critical question. Is this true? Is this useful? Is this direct understanding correct? Is it so? Is it real? Does it exist? Is he really sick? Does he really have cancer? Did he really do that? Can this hypothesis be confirmed and raised to the status of a verified explanation? A series of critical questions arise, which are different in intention and tone from mere brainstorming. These questions anticipate a different type of answer, namely, a yes or no answer. They are not looking for further information or further understanding; they are looking for an affirmation or denial. A question already specifies the kind of answer that will satisfy it. If I ask, "What is that?" and you answer "Yes," you have not been much help. If I ask, "Is it really true?" and you answer, "Five o'clock," then again something is wrong. So the first characteristic of the critical question is that it is asking a fundamentally different kind of question than the question for direct insight.

Direct insight must precede reflective insight. To ask, "Is it so?" presupposes that we have understood what "it" stands for. Direct understanding presents the content for the question for reflection. If the direct understanding is vague, confused, or ambiguous, then the judgment will be similarly ambiguous. Many a philosophy discussion hinges on the phrase, "Well, it depends on what you mean." Further clarifications, definitions, or divisions bring us back to the level of direct understanding. But again the question will eventually recur, "Is it true?" We are back to the critical level of judgment.

The answer to the question for reflection can be an affirmation, denial, or anything in between, such as, probably, possibly, very likely, and so on. There are very few judgments of which we can be absolutely, unequivocally, and eternally certain. There is a wide range of probabilities from the highest probability, which we can consider as virtually certain, to the lowest range bordering on the merely possible. But all of these are legitimate and coherent answers to the question for reflection. Probabilities are judgments or affirmations, and thus, are either true or false. We can also answer: "I do not know. I am not sure. I do not have sufficient evidence for that." These are reasonable answers to the question for reflection and invite the search for more information so as to answer the question correctly.

The question for reflection arises in slightly different forms depending on the context. It seems to arise spontaneously. It arises in children; children are said to reach the age of reason at about seven years of age. About that time the child begins to evaluate the stories they are being told by adults. Fairy tales, Santa Claus, tooth fairies, nursery tales, myth and magic, and stories about monsters that eat people are slowly examined and found wanting. There is no evidence for them, all the available evidence is against them, they do not stand up to criticism. Children do not need to be taught to ask the critical question. Even children can and do ask Plato's question, "Is it really real?"

Slowly, there emerges the principle of sufficient reason: the person needs reasons to accept something as true. I interpret this not as a law of logic but as a norm that is immanent and operative in the unfolding of the desire to know. It is what it means to be reasonable. Knowledge is knowledge of the real world. Slowly, the process of education reveals to us the difference between legend and history, between alchemy and chemistry, between magic and science, or between astrology and astronomy. Across the board the principle of sufficient reason is telling us that we cannot assert something as true unless there is evidence and argument in its favor; it is hazardous and silly to believe something for which there is no evidence whatsoever. The process and the criterion become clearer and more explicit, the more we advance in education and reflection on the process of knowing.

The most general form of the critical question is simply, "Have I understood correctly?" The first bright idea is not necessarily the best. Solving mathematical or word puzzles involve a constant shifting from grasping possibilities to judgments as to whether these possibilities are correct or not. Solving a crossword puzzle is a clear example of the process of looking for possibilities, rejecting ones that do not fit, and finally, finding the correct word. The desire to know is not a desire for possible ideas but a desire to correctly understand and to reach verified knowledge. There is something very fundamental about this constant shifting from possibilities to reflection; it is a kind of hypothetical-deductive method in the sense of constantly throwing up hypotheses only to sort them out and reject many of them, because they do not satisfy the criteria set in the question. Thinking is a constant stream of ideas, images, examples, direct insights, and inverse insights. Intermingled, we find questions for reflection, which select and reject in the critical mode in order to work toward a correct understanding.

There are certain limited contexts where questions for reflection do not arise, such as when we are writing novels, composing poetry, creating a work of art or comedy, brainstorming, playing games, producing movies, and storytelling. However, in the real world, we are obliged to constantly ask the critical questions, "Is it true? Is it real?" In scholarship, science, engineering, history, or any of the areas of knowing, it arises spontaneously and we normally are not satisfied until we reach what we consider to be true answers. Our questioning is purposive; we are seeking knowledge, the true and correct solution. If we jump to conclusions on the basis of insufficient evidence, we realize that our colleagues will reveal the shortcomings of our research and show that we are wrong. The strength of the scientific method is this emphasis on the critical question, the need to verify conclusions in a way that the verification process is open, repeatable, and transparent.

Our criminal justice system depends on the proper functioning of the jury system. The jury system presumes that ordinary citizens are capable and responsible in distinguishing guilty from not guilty, true from false. Doctors are normally capable and responsible in diagnosing a patient and prescribing appropriate treatment; they ask the critical question, "Is this really cancer?" They assemble evidence, examine blood slides, consult with specialists, and reach a judgment and treatment. We hold them responsible for their mistakes in judgment. Engineers are normally capable and responsible in designing bridges that will not collapse and cars with steering mechanisms that will not disintegrate in the event of hitting a pothole. All of the sciences and disciplines are constrained by the obligation of living in the real world, understanding and applying the laws of nature, and correctly reaching true judgments in their area of expertise. The truth, correctness, or reality of a proposition arises in all of these disciplines as a constituent component of their competence.

We instinctively revolt against blatant contradictions. If two witnesses at a trial give a totally different account of the defendant's actions, then this contradiction has to be resolved in some manner. One is probably lying and the other is telling the truth. Two economists can give two contradictory interpretations of the same event, for instance the financial collapse of 2008. They cannot both be entirely true. Either they are both partially true, both wrong, or one is wrong and the other right. If one doctor concludes that a patient has malignant cancer and a second opinion concludes that the mass is benign, one of them is wrong.

Does the critical question arise in philosophy? Must a particular philosophical assertion be accepted as true or rejected as false? It is very common to hear the view that philosophical opinions are a matter of choice and that there is no reasonable basis on which we can distinguish between true and false philosophies. But that is a rather extraordinary position, even if it is politically correct. If we accept that view, we are relegating philosophy to the same category as fiction, or comedy, or perhaps tragi-comedy. To me, there is no point in doing philosophy if it is just fiction or an endless conversation that is going nowhere. Philosophy is about correctly understanding the real universe and our place in that universe. Just as physicists, doctors and historians are constrained by the facts, so are philosophers constrained by the facts about human knowing. Sadly, many postmodern philosophers do not feel constrained by evidence, arguments, or truth; rather, they feel free to choose ideas and theories on the grounds that they are original, novel, interesting, outlandish, or obscure. A correct account of human knowing must look at the evidence in the data of consciousness, understand the activities, organize them in a sequence, and show how the whole process works. There is one process of knowing, there is only one fully correct description and explanation of that process; all other explanations are either defective, one-sided, incomplete, or plain wrong. Even philosophers must distinguish between true and false.

Reflective Insight into Truth

I have explained what is meant by a critical question; now I proceed to the next step to outline the structure of the reflective insight, which will produce the correct answer in a true judgment. How can we be sure that our understanding is correct? How can we be sure that our judgments are correct? The special act of reflective understanding passes judgment on direct insights and declares them to be correct or incorrect, to be worth affirming or denying.

What are the grounds for uttering a judgment? It is easy to affirm conclusions, to have strong opinions about anything and everything; but are they informed opinions or random, biased, and arbitrary prejudgments? Arguing presumes there is a rational basis for conclusions. The challenge here is to uncover this rational process as it actually operates and to show that arbitrary choice is not a basis for judgments of truth.

In studying direct insight the actual moment of illumination is followed later by the expression of the insight in terms of a definition or formulation. First, the idea is grasped; then, concepts are formulated, made explicit, put into words, expressed in a definition, written down, and explained to others. Similarly, at the level of reflection, one first grasps the connection between the evidence and the conclusion, which is then expressed in a judgment. There is a parallel between the process from direct insight to the formulation and the process from reflective insight to judgment. Both are discursive processes moving from a question through a series of individual activities, and eventually reaching an answer.

I already noted the heuristic structure by which the mind proceeds from the question to the answer, from the known/unknown to the known, from a puzzle to a solution. The same heuristic is operating here while we examine how the reflective insight produces a judgment. If we have no evidence for something, we are merely guessing. If we have sufficient evidence for a judgment, it is silly not to make the judgment. In between silliness and guessing we have the process of weighing the evidence for making a reasonable judgment. But weighing the evidence is a metaphor borrowed from physical procedures of using scales and measuring weights. We need to go somewhat beyond vague metaphors to identify precisely and in explanatory terms what is the basic structure of all reflective insights.

In the general case, reflective understanding is a review, a looking back at the processes involved in direct insight to check whether proper procedures have been followed and whether anything has been left out. It is a kind of critical review as to whether the conclusion is warranted; it is a reflection on the sufficiency of the evidence for the conclusion. It involves checking whether the question has been answered and whether the criteria set in the question have been satisfactorily met. The reflective insight is a single insight that gathers together a multiplicity of data, insights, propositions, and hypotheses and then grasps the rational necessity of positing a judgment. A jury might be dealing with a trial that lasts for four weeks. Eight witnesses have testified, three forensic scientists gave evidence, and all were cross-examined. The lawyers proposed dozens of arguments, possibilities, and timelines. All of this material has to be digested, evaluated, put together, sifted through, discussed, and put into a coherent account that finally issues in the one simple judgment of guilty or not guilty.

We can identify in ourselves this process of checking, which spontaneously takes place yet is difficult to identify and isolate. Not any old answer will do. We automatically discard answers that do not satisfy the demands of the question. We want to be right, but how do we know that we are right? Review the conditions set by the question and ask whether they fulfilled by the answer. Is there any other answer that would satisfy? Has any data or condition been forgotten? Were the calculations correct? Mathematicians are taught to check their answers by working backward from the answer through their calculations to the question that was posed. In earlier chapters,

I discussed various examples to identify direct insights; now I will use similar examples to identify a reflective insight that issues in a judgment.

There is an imperative that is immanent and operative in this procedure. There are norms that are operating that do not come from outside. They are not imposed on us by law, authority, or logical rules: they are already there. We should not affirm something for which there is insufficient evidence; we should not withhold judgment when there is sufficient evidence. That is not just a logical rule; it is more than that. The desire to understand is purposive; once understanding is reached, we spontaneously ask whether the understanding is correct and true? This imperative constitutes an obligation to be reasonable, which I will examine later in detail.

Description of Reflective Insight

Because it is an act of understanding, the process of reflective insight includes all of the five characteristics of direct insight, which I have already detailed. The scope and depth of reflective insights will depend on five characteristics. (1) We experience the tension of inquiry. Do we ask the relevant questions? Are we serious enough to do the research? Are we concentrating on the problem? (2) Upon gathering materials, we arrange them in order and work on possible solutions. (3) The insight will come suddenly and unexpectedly, while we are to some extent passive; it may not be as dramatic as the direct insight. (4) The insight will pivot between the abstract and the concrete; we verify our judgments by reference to the concrete evidence. Reflective insight is intelligence at work; it is grasping a relationship, a unity, and a connection of necessity between the evidence and the conclusion. (5) It passes into the habitual texture of the mind: our judgments constitute who we are as knowing human persons, what we stand for, and set the context for further questions and answers.

The reflective insight is, however, more complicated than the direct insight. Direct insights are included in a reflective insight as part of the content. Reflective insight reviews the whole ensemble of data, images, ideas, concepts, propositions, connections, and relations to pass judgment on the whole intellectual process. Reflective insight gathers into a unity a vast multiplicity of factors; however, it focuses on one aspect, namely, the sufficiency of the evidence for the utterance of a correct judgment. It is because so many factors are involved that it is difficult to identify and appropriate the procedure of reflective understanding. We tend not to see the wood for the trees; there are so many factors involved in the evidence or argument that we fail to see the unity grasped by reflective understanding. Remember the jury that has so much evidence but only one judgment: guilty or not guilty.

The process begins when we have a bright idea, or a possible hypothesis, a complicated theory. But is it true? With this critical question, we begin to review all of the evidence from the very beginning; to be clear about the arguments; to check on the data; and to look for counterexamples, loopholes, mistakes, and confusions. If satisfied, we have grasped the sufficiency of the evidence and prepare for the expression of the judgment. Reflection means reviewing the process of knowing from the sense data, to the understanding, to the judgment. All of these activities are conscious, and so we can notice whether anything has been left out, whether proper procedures were followed, and so forth. In this way, we can reflect back upon the activities of knowing.

The unity that is grasped in this multiplicity is how the data, calculations, and observations constitute evidence for the conclusion. Reflective understanding must establish the relation between the evidence and the conclusion. No matter how complicated the evidence, the only interest of reflective understanding is the connection between, on the one hand, the data, the witnesses, and the evidence, and on the other hand, the arguments that link these to the conclusion. That is the unity expressed simply by the yes or no of the judgment.

The connection between the evidence and the conclusion may not be certain or necessary. It will often be given in the form of probabilities, from highly probable to barely possible. Reflective insight preserves the correct proportion between the evidence and the conclusion. If it is a theorem from Euclid, if the principles are accepted, then the theorem follows certainly and necessarily and must be posited as such. If it is a law of classical science that has been verified over and over again, then it must be posited as so highly probable as to be almost certain. If it is a statement of average life expectancy based on data from a census, which has been carried out carefully, then the conclusion can be affirmed, even though it is only expressing a probability. If there is not sufficient evidence to reach a conclusion, reflective insight can only issue in an, "I do not yet know" answer.

There are many extraneous influences that push toward either an affirmation or a denial. Temperament and feelings as well as prejudice and self-interest may push us very strongly in one direction or another. Some persons are temperamentally prone to jump to conclusions, which are rash judgments. Others are careful, do not want to commit themselves, or are afraid of making a mistake. These individuals hesitate to pass a judgment even though the evidence is overwhelming; they are indecisive or timid. The criterion that should be operative in the passing of a judgment is the reflective grasp of the connection between the evidence and the conclusion;

extraneous interferences should be put aside. That connection is grasped by intelligence and not by imagination, feeling, desire, or sense.

In the reflective mode, conclusions are verified by working backward through the calculations, reasoning, and arguments to the data on which they are based. Everything is criticized and evaluated. Were the samples pure? Is the calculator working properly? Were the interviews carried out by competent persons? Is there a possibility of crosschecking? Are there counterexamples? Are there exceptions? These questions are motivated by the question for reflection and are ultimately in view of the yes or no of the final judgment. In the normal process of thinking out a solution, we move very quickly from suggesting possibilities, to evaluating and rejecting them, and to looking for further possibilities. We move from direct insights to reflective insights and back again; that is the nature of discursive movement toward a correct solution.

Structure of Reflective Insight

Having described some of the qualities of reflective understanding, I now define it as *an act of understanding that grasps the sufficiency of the evidence and the validity of the arguments, thus, inferring a prospective judgment.* It is a single intellectual grasp or insight; the single insight encompasses the totality of the evidence and the validity of the arguments that link with the conclusion. The prosecutor and the defense attorney will use arguments linking the evidence to a guilty or not guilty verdict. The judgment is at first prospective because it can be affirmed as a true judgment only as a conclusion.

The question now is whether there is a general form or structure of the reflective insight. I defined the structure of direct insights as grasping ideas that emerge from images. What is the precise structure of reflective insight? Is the same kind of reflective insight present in commonsense examples, in the natural sciences, in statistical method, in medicine, and in mathematics? If it is the same in all of these different cases, then what is its general form? Can we outline a general case and then apply that to all the particular examples? Is there an explicit, universal form or structure to the reflective insight as such?

It seems that there is. To elaborate on this I will start with a general schema of terms and relations and later apply it to particular examples.[2] I propose the following as the basic structure of the reflective insight:

---

2. Lonergan, *Insight*, 305–6. I find the terminology of "conditioned, conditions, virtually unconditioned" that Lonergan uses cumbersome. It might give the impression that reflective insight is a matter of logic, which is far from the case. The term "virtually

1. A prospective judgment or a hypothesis;

2. A link between the hypothesis and its conditions;

3. The fulfillment of the conditions;

4. The verified contingent judgment.

1. *Any prospective judgment is a hypothesis.* We start with a bright idea, a possibility, but we know that it is not necessarily true. The only necessary truth by definition is God, who, if God exists, exists necessarily. Every other truth is contingent; it depends on conditions being fulfilled. But if the conditions are fulfilled, then it will be true. It is a contingent truth. This represents the question for reflection. Is this person suffering from cancer? Is the accused guilty of murder? Possibly, but we need to establish the evidence and whether the evidence entails the conclusion.

2. *A link between the hypothesis and its conditions.* In order to show that a hypothesis is true, we have to look for evidence that will entail the conclusion. What link is needed between the evidence and the conclusion? There is a process of inferring, entailing, justifying, and necessitating going on here. A detective knows that he or she cannot arrest a suspect unless there is evidence that will link the suspect to the crime. The link might be a witness who saw the suspect in the house, a DNA sample, or fingerprints at the scene. Indirect, circumstantial evidence does not necessarily link with the crime scene.

3. *The conditions are fulfilled.* The evidence is found, and it is sufficient and convincing. The detective finds the suspect's DNA at the scene of the crime, the fingerprints of the suspect are on the murder weapon, and there is a motive. Eddington travelled to the island of Principe to photograph an eclipse of the sun in order to gather evidence to prove Einstein's general theory of relativity. He deemed the photographs sufficient proof of the theory.

4. *The hypothesis has now been verified.* A prospective judgment has been transformed into a verified judgment. The detective has sufficient evidence to link the suspect to the murder and an arrest can be made, the suspect tried, and the final judgment given by a jury.

This is a universal structure of reflective insight; this is how we proceed to answer the critical question. It makes explicit the conditions on which the prospective judgment depends in order to be affirmed as true. Spontaneously, when we have a question for reflection, we ask what kind of evidence would be needed to show that it is true; then, we check to see if that evidence or data exists. If the evidence is sufficient and is linked to the conclusion, we

---

unconditioned" is particularly open to misinterpretation. The term "virtual" has come to have a wide variety of meanings, which are certainly not what Lonergan had in mind. I have replaced the term "virtually unconditioned" with "actually verified."

answer the question in the affirmative. We are objectivizing the spontaneous activities of critical inquiry in a precise terminology and formal structure.

Note also how the above is paralleled in the hypothetical syllogism. All forms of syllogistic argument can be reduced to the hypothetical form.[3] If A and B represent any number or kind of propositions or data, we can present the hypothetical syllogism thus:

> The Hypothesis: B.
>
> Major premise: If A, then B.
>
> Minor Premise: But A.
>
> Conclusion: Therefore B.

The hypothesis represents a possible answer to the critical question. The major premise represents the evidence as linked to the conclusion by a process of inferring, entailing, or arguing. The minor premise represents the sufficiency of the conditions that are actually fulfilled.

The reflective insight grasps that the evidence is sufficient and from it one can validly infer the conclusion.

Application to Typical Cases

The same structure that I identified above is present and operative in all reflective insights that produce a judgment: in commonsense descriptive judgments, in inductive arguments, in deductive arguments, in classical science, in statistical science, in practical and theoretical judgments, in mathematics, in philosophy, and in any other discipline that produces judgments of truth. In this section I will use some examples to illustrate and justify that contention. I am trying to show that the human mind is structured in such a way as to produce judgments of truth.

Suppose I am walking through the woods and I remark to my friend, "Oh! Look, there is an oak tree." My friend questions my judgment and asserts, "No! It is an elm tree." How do I proceed to prove my assertion that it is in fact an oak tree? Presumably I would look closer, examine some leaves, collect acorns that have fallen from the tree, and note the general shape of the trunk and branches. I assert that in my experience all of these are characteristics of an oak tree. If my friend is still not convinced, there seems to be no alternative but to consult a tree catalogue and show how the characteristics of the tree line up with the characteristics that are clearly defined in the catalogue. What is the reasoning involved? We see the tree but

---

3. Lonergan, *Collection*, chap. 1.

seeing is not knowing. We see data, but we affirm facts. The seeing provokes a question: what is this tree? We consider possible answers such as oak, elm, chestnut, beech, and the like. Most people acquire an elementary knowledge of the most common species of trees and will recognize the basic types. I have a better general knowledge than my friend. I press my case. If the tree has leaves of a certain shape, if the tree produces acorns, if it is deciduous, if it has the characteristic size and structure of an oak tree, I eventually conclude: it is an oak tree. Major premise: if it has certain characteristics, it is an oak tree. Minor premise: it has those characteristics. Conclusion: it is an oak tree. If it walks like a duck, quacks like a duck, looks like a duck, and swims like a duck, at a certain stage one is entitled to affirm that: yes, it is a duck.

Each act of knowledge of concrete reality involves seeing, questioning, understanding, critically reflecting, and concluding. It is not seeing alone, understanding alone, or judging alone. It is the reflective insight that grasps the unity between the distinct elements, which ground the judgment. Einstein's theory of general relativity would hardly be classified as rudimentary. Yet the crucial verification was performed by taking photographs from a camera attached to a telescope focused at the apparent position of a star during a solar eclipse. The seeing in this case was guided by high-precision instruments, extremely accurate calculations of where the star should be on Newtonian principles, and calculations of how the sun might deflect the light as postulated by Einstein's theory. For all the acumen and sophistication, without the seeing—the looking through the telescope—there would have been no evidence for the verification.

We make many commonsense judgments every day as a matter of course. Because they belong to the field of common sense, they are full of analogies and metaphors, undefined terms, and vague generalizations. Arguments in the context of common sense can go on forever. Evidence is presented in bits and pieces; valid arguments intermingle with dubious inferences. Who shouts the loudest or the last usually wins. Commonsense procedures are spontaneous but confused. Usually they are approximately correct: they work for the most part and are successful. There is a body of experience and custom built up over years that we rely on. But the underlying spontaneous procedure of common sense is to seek evidence, to look for a link between the evidence and the conclusion, and to be reasonable in positing a conclusion based on the available evidence.

I have outlined the process of human knowing as questioning, experiencing, understanding, and judging. This can be translated simply and clearly into a method for the sciences. The scientific method can be defined as *theories verified in instances*. The basic structure of human knowing is, not surprisingly, reflected in a theory of scientific method. Hence scientific method will follow this presentation in terms of the conditioned, the link between the conditions and the conditioned, and the fulfillment of the conditions leading to the actually unconditioned. Scientists ask questions about their area of expertise; they do not know the answer but they do have a hypothesis. They have an idea, which is the conditioned. Now how does one judge whether the hypothesis is true or not? In many cases a crucial experiment is implemented.

We might consider and reconstruct the thinking of Galileo as he tried to figure out how things fall, gravity, or the law of uniform acceleration. Galileo was convinced that Aristotle was wrong—wrong that the heavier the body is the faster it will fall and wrong that a body falls faster and faster because it is getting nearer to its natural place of rest. But it is not enough to say that somebody is wrong. One must produce evidence. Again, there is the issue of correct judgment, and there are consequences one way or the other. Galileo had many enemies and he knew that his findings would be carefully scrutinized. He was motivated to very carefully check each step of the way, because if he issued hasty or wrong conclusions, he would soon be exposed.

One can imagine the care he took. Galileo was influenced by Renaissance thinking. He also used thought-experiments—as did Einstein. But in the end he was an experimentalist. That is the side that I present here.[4] He set up an inclined plane and used balls of various sizes and weights to measure the time and distance of falling. The critical reflective mode operative in Galileo's work from the beginning and influences all of his experiments and activities up to the conclusion. He carefully thought out his methods. He used pendulums as well as inclined planes. He took all possible care with his apparatus, his measuring, his timing, and his calculations. He repeated the experiments again and again. He changed the length and measured the time; he changed the time and measured the length. He pushed the apparatus to its maximum length. He tried different inclines of the plane. He tried different ways of measuring the time. At one stage he used his pulse; he also used a sand clock. He worked with a bucket of water with a small tap that could be turned on and off; the time was measured by the amount of water that flowed while the tap was open. He tried the experiment with different materials. He worked on the tables of correlations and always found that the distances were always proportionate to the time squared. He considered other possibilities. Eventually the further questions were exhausted; there was sufficient evidence. The matter was closed; it was time to publish and move on to other areas of research. Experiments have continuously

4. For a discussion on Galileo's experimentalism I relied on Butterfield, *The Origins of Modern Science*, chaps. 4–5; and Burtt, *The Metaphysical Foundations of Modern Science*, chap. 3.

confirmed this law. Concrete results have continued to verify the abstract law. The more sophisticated the equipment, the more accurate the measurements. The more extraneous influences are excluded, the closer actual measurements converge on the requirements of the law.

Judgments that express probabilities are still judgments and can be classified as true or false. Meteorologists express their forecasts in terms of probability and will often give a figure such as a 90% or 50% probability of snow. The basis for this judgment is the evidence pouring in from surrounding areas on wind direction, temperature, humidity; on the principles of how high pressure and low pressure systems tend to move; and a myriad of other factors. Extraneous factors cannot be completely excluded, so predictions can only be given in terms of probabilities. Will there be a perfect storm? There will be a perfect storm if two low pressure systems from different directions with warm and cold air converge on a hurricane carrying warm, moist air. Indeed, there is a hurricane approaching, and there are two low pressure systems moving in from different directions. There will probably be a perfect storm. The conclusion can only be stated as a probability, as any of the systems might change direction due to other factors; or, they might change in density, humidity, or energy.

The judgment of probability is either true or false, accurate or inaccurate, correct or incorrect. What actually happens one day later does not determine the truth or falsity of the probability. A forecast is accurate to the extent that it considers all of the relevant data; understands all of the forces and laws of meteorology; and correctly grasps the link between the data, the laws, and the conclusion expressed in the forecast. A meteorologist might correctly forecast a 90% probability of a storm; if the storm does not happen, it does not mean that he was mistaken. It means that some extraneous factor, which could not be predicted, interfered. What actually happens will diverge nonsystematically from the probability. The competence of a meteorologist is judged not on the basis of one prediction but on the average accuracy of predictions over a long period.

Every area of human knowing involves an imperative to ask pertinent questions, to gather relevant materials, to understand laws applying to the subject area, and to reach conclusions based on the sufficiency of the evidence and the link between the evidence and the conclusion. This applies in all areas: an engineer designing a bridge, a doctor diagnosing a patient, a jury deliberating, a historian describing a battle, an economist predicting a slump, a particle physicist identifying a new particle, an astronomer examining background radiation, a sociologist conducting a survey, a philosopher developing a theory of knowing, and on and on. In the whole spectrum of human knowing and doing, there are few areas exempt from the obligation of fitting conclusions with the available evidence. When we seek relief from these constraints, we watch television, read novels, laugh at comedians, or enjoy poetry.

Characteristics of a Judgment of Truth

In this chapter, I started with the critical question for reflection and moved on to an analysis of the reflective insight that produces the judgment. I have outlined the universal process of reasoning that underlies and produces all judgments. It was presented in the terminology of the hypothesis, the link between the conditions and its conditions, the fulfilment of the conditions, and the conclusion that follows. Now the task is to identify the characteristics of the judgment—the product of the whole process. I have finally turned from possible ideas to true knowledge. The difficulty is that judgments are invisible; it is only by self-appropriation that we can distinguish between propositions entertained as possibilities and the same proposition affirmed as a personal commitment.

It is easy enough to make judgments; we make them every day. They can be simple judgments: the bus is late, it is raining, the computer is down, Fred is not in the office. Or they can be more complicated: there is a mistake in this calculation, this witness is lying, the economy is coming out of a recession, and the like. What is difficult is objectifying the process of making true judgments. It seems to be a neglected topic and yet it is central to any account of knowing. There are very few epistemologies who differentiate between the understanding mode and the critical mode, between formulation and judgment. Descartes, as we noted, compacted clear and distinct ideas with true ideas. Linguistic analysts do not consider mental activities as a fit topic, and hence, have difficulty distinguishing hypothesis from judgment. Kant talked a lot about judgment, but I am not sure if he adverted to the actual experience of making judgments; he emphasized judgment as a synthesis of terms rather than a personal affirmation. So often philosophers have offered theories about what knowing should be, rather than an appropriation of what knowing actually is. Surely, if we want to know about judgments, we should start with the experience of making a judgment, start with the data and move on to the explanation. The key to our procedure is this appeal to our own experience, to identify and verify everything we say about judgment.

To prevent misunderstanding allow me to briefly indicate what I do not mean by a judgment. "Judgment" is not being used in the sense of a moral judgment. The word often has the sense of the Last Judgment, a moral judgment of good or bad, the judgment of history, and so forth. There are, indeed, value judgments but these will be dealt in the next chapter. I am using the word "judgment" in a morally neutral sense as an affirmation or denial, of what is simply true or false.

By judgment, I do not mean aesthetic judgment. In aesthetics, judgments can be passed on paintings, poetry, literature, sculpture, and the like. But I am concerned with the intellectual pattern of experience that is operative in common sense, theoretical science, applied science, human science, and philosophy. There is an analogous truth in the field of aesthetics, where one might refer to an authentic poem, a true picture, and the like. To say that a poem is true is to be in the aesthetic pattern of experience; to say that a proposition is true is to shift to the intellectual sphere. In philosophy, we are in the intellectual pattern of experience where the operative criterion is truth; in aesthetics the operative criterion is beauty of some sort.

By judgment, I do not mean the phrase, "justified true belief." The phrase derives from Plato but was actually rejected by him. It is usually expounded in the analytic tradition nowadays in terms of logic. My focus is on how knowledge actually occurs and not how it might occur if logical laws are followed. I use the term "belief" in the sense of accepting as true on the basis of a source that we trust: I believe the professor, I believe what is asserted in the textbook, and the like. "Belief" in this account is not mere opinion or a dubious kind of knowledge. Belief can be quite certain, while knowledge can be merely probable.

There are two ways to the truth. One is by immanently-generated knowledge, meaning that we experience for ourselves, we work it out for ourselves, and we judge it to be true on the basis of what we have seen and understood. But there is a shorter way to the truth by belief in which we accept something as true on the basis of trust in a source such as a parent, a teacher, an author, a newspaper, or a television channel. In this text, I am mostly concerned with the first way and my analysis is explicitly about immanently-generated knowledge. However, much of our knowledge is actually of the second kind, namely, belief. We do not have the time or the energy or the resources to be able to prove everything for ourselves. We cannot possibly be expected to repeat all the research, the experiments, and the observations that have given us the body of knowledge of history, geography, physics, chemistry, biology, botany, and all of the other areas of human knowing. Belief is a collaboration with the rest of humanity in the search for further knowledge and understanding in all fields of inquiry. To reject such collaboration and trust would be to condemn ourselves to primitive ignorance. So it is reasonable to believe what we read in textbooks, what professors teach us, and what our tradition and culture hand down to us. Even in the sciences we rely on belief, as it is impossible to repeat all the crucial historical experiments and calculations on one's own. However, there is a critique of beliefs just as there is a critique of immanently-generated knowledge. We do not believe everything we hear and read. We rely on trustworthy sources, we look for competent people, and we are wary of those who have an ax to grind or a hidden agenda. We check things out for ourselves, if at all possible.

I will identify four characteristics of a judgment, namely that (1) a judgment adds no further content, (2) a judgment simply affirms or denies, (3) a judgment involves us in taking a personal stand, and (4) in a judgment knowing comes to term.

A Judgment Adds No Further Content

I have distinguished the question for intelligence from the question for reflection; the former adds further content in order to supply an answer, whereas the latter does not add any further content to the prospective judgment (other than the affirmation or denial). If one asks, "Is John sick?" I may answer, "Yes, he is sick," or, "No, he is not sick." In neither answer am I adding content to the question, yet I have answered the question with a judgment. The jury members are asked one question: is the accused guilty or not guilty? They are inundated with testimony, evidence, arguments, and data. They spend weeks attending the trial and a few days in jury deliberation. Yet their answer after all of this deliberation is a simple guilty or not guilty verdict. They have not added any material to what was presented in the trial. At the beginning, they did not know whether the person was guilty or not guilty. At the end they have knowledge; they have passed judgment beyond a reasonable doubt. It is the reflective insight that enables them to experience the presented evidence, to understand the implications of evidence, and to grasp the sufficiency of the evidence to infer the conclusion.

A Judgment Affirms or Denies

The essential characteristic of the judgment is this quality of personal affirmation or denial. There is a fundamental difference between considering a hypothesis as a possibility and uttering it as a personal conviction. It is an act of direct understanding that produces the hypothesis and an act of reflective understanding that produces the judgment. This happens within human minds; it is invisible. If we do not attend to our own mental activities, we will never know the difference between a proposition entertained as a possibility and a proposition affirmed as true. The data to justify this distinction are the data of consciousness, not the data of sense.

A proposition is a statement or a definition. A proposition can be a mere object of thought or it can be the content of a judgment. One could teach the philosophy of Kant merely as an object of thought. A teacher could go to great pains to clearly and accurately explain the whole of Kant's *Critique of Pure Reason*. But the professor may surprise the students at the end of the semester by saying that he or she thinks that Kant's account of knowing is wrong. In the context of teaching the history of philosophy, Kant's philosophy is simply an object of thought, a complicated system of terms and ideas that need to be explained. But it is not necessarily affirmed as a personal conviction by the teacher. A Kantian, on the other hand, not only teaches what Kant taught but also identifies with this position; for this educator, Kant is not only an object of thought but also an object of personal affirmation and conviction. Kant's views are affirmed as true.

A proposition can be a mere supposition, a definition, an object of thought, a synthesis of concepts, a consideration, or a hypothesis. Direct insight yields possibly-relevant hypotheses, which can be produced at will by the simple act of defining or supposing. Logicians often deal with propositions such as, "Socrates is sick," "all Irishmen eat porridge," or "Louis the fourteenth is the king of France." These are mere objects of thought. Sometimes, for the purposes of the argument they are supposed to be true. If they are considered to be true, then certain conclusions follow. If they are considered to be false, different conclusions follow. But in logic such propositions are not usually affirmed personally to be really true. Mere objects of thought are neither true nor false; the categories do not apply. Ideas are products of direct understanding; they can be brilliant, new, inspiring, appropriate, complicated, or crude. But the question, "Is it true?" only arises in the context of reflection on whether they are true or false.

The judgment adds only an affirmation or denial. But that is no small thing. From being a mere object of thought, a proposition becomes an affirmed content of knowledge. In this transition, we no longer merely think or suppose; we know what is and what is not. This is what divides fact from fiction, the real world from the world of fantasy, chemistry from alchemy, astronomy from astrology. This element is crucial. What could be more important than whether something is true or false, fact or fiction?

A book is a whole series of words and sentences that expresses propositions. One can read the book and understand the propositions without passing judgment on their truth or falsity. The ideas, suggestions, arguments, evidence, and conclusions of the book can be entertained as simply interesting. It is a further step and a big one to take sides for or against the conclusions. Then, we either agree or disagree. That is a judgment.

Marks on paper can represent and express the judgments of individuals, but the event, the happening, occurs only in a mind. While listening to a person speaking, we may not know whether the individual is telling the truth or lying, or whether the speaker is serious or joking. We have no immediate access to what is going on in his or her mind. But we do have access to these affirmations and denials in our own minds. We know when we are affirming and when we are merely supposing. We know when we are telling the truth or lying. Supposing and judging are quite different from one another. We must examine the data of consciousness in order to be able to distinguish possibilities from affirmations. Those who pay no attention to mental activities can never know the difference between a hypothesis and a judgment.

Judgments Involve Taking a Personal Stand

There is an element of personal responsibility that enters with the judgment, which is not there when we are merely considering or supposing. As long as we are merely thinking of possibilities, we are still sitting on the fence and can go either way. But once we have made the judgment, we have come down on one side or the other and are committed to the judgment. Our judgments make us what we are as reasonable human beings. The whole person is involved from the first activities of questioning, to manipulating the data, to the activities of understanding, to the activities of reflective understanding, and to issuing a judgment.

We complain about our bad memory, but we do not complain about our bad judgments. We feel that we are not responsible for our memory; either we have a good memory or a bad memory. We are embarrassed if we forget someone's name, but we use our bad memory as an excuse. But we take personal responsibility for a judgment, because it is a commitment. We made the judgment on the basis of the evidence. We could have looked for more information, could have asked for clearer definitions, could have asked further relevant questions, or could have introduced appropriate qualifications and reservations. We could have refrained from judging, if there was not sufficient evidence. We excuse our bad memories, but we are responsible for our judgments.

We cannot be excused for affirming the truth of a falsehood; we are held responsible. A meteorologist is expected to know his field of study, and his or her judgments are expected to be accurate within a given degree of probability. If there is not sufficient evidence, the meteorologist should say, "I do not know." Doctors, engineers, astronomers, teachers, researchers, historians, reporters, and the like are all held to be responsible for their judgments. We are responsible for assessing the evidence and enunciating a judgment, which correctly mirrors the weight of the evidence as probable, highly probable, or certain.

Strangely enough, we cannot avoid making judgments; we have to take a stand. Paradoxically, even sitting on the fence involves taking a stand. Consider the philosopher who says, "Judgments are not important; we can do without them." In the very act the philosopher is making a judgment. Or consider the skeptic who says, "I know nothing," yet in making such a statement, the skeptic is positing a judgment. Then, there is the relativist claim, "Everything is relative"—except this particular statement that everything is relative. Judgments are inescapable; we have to take a stand—even if our stand is to run away!

In a Judgment, Knowing Comes to Term

When positing an affirmation, the entire series of activities involved in the knowing process reaches its terminus. When we have solved and checked a mathematical puzzle or have finished a sudoku, we know that the solution is correct and simply move on to other matters. The problem has been exhausted and no longer retains our interest. It is no longer challenging; it is, in fact, boring. All of the activities of questioning, searching for images, looking, drawing, considering, remembering, defining, exploring, testing, checking, reviewing, and reflecting come to a full stop when we pass the judgment; we recognize the experience of closure and can move on. The judgment sweeps everything into one affirmation or negation. A unit of knowledge is added to our habitual store and we move on to other matters. A jury reaches a verdict of guilty or not guilty; the matter is closed and the judge moves on to the next case. A scholar finishes writing an article, has reached a conclusion, sends it off to a journal, and moves on to researching the next article. A doctor diagnoses a patient, prescribes appropriate medicine, and calls for the next patient.

Judgments occur in developing minds and within a context of many other judgments on which they depend in various ways. I identified one of the characteristics of insight in that it passes into the habitual texture of our minds. The same thing happens with judgments. A judgment can rarely stand in glorious isolation. The context might be descriptive, common sense, or theoretical and explanatory. If we do not distinguish the two contexts, endless confusion can follow. Higher viewpoints will depend on a previous context of lower judgments. Our own individual judgments today depend on our previous judgments and on the entire context of questions, insights, formulations, and the like that is our intellectual history. The expert in any subject is the one who has set up such a context of knowledge and experience so that he or she can deal expeditiously and immediately with any new problem or question within the field. Habits of inquiry and research are built up over years and the competent person immediately knows how to cope. Our judgments also look to the future. We realize how little we understand and how much remains to be done. Our knowing is dynamic: a restless devotion to the task of adding increments to a merely habitual knowledge.

The Criterion of Truth

My approach to the question of truth is not by declaiming dogmatically from the housetops what it is; rather, it is by observing how we are in fact bound by the imperatives of attention, intelligence, and reason. At the level of experiencing we get data or presentations. At the level of understanding we get a possible hypothesis. It is only in correct judgment that we attain the truth. An operational definition of truth would be: truth is what we reach when we utter a correct judgment. But how do we know that we have reached a correct judgment? In answering this question, I will distinguish between a proximate and a remote criterion of truth.

The proximate criterion of truth refers to the particular judgment and the sufficiency or insufficiency of evidence required for that conclusion. Truth is only attained in a correct judgment, which is generated by a reflective grasp of the evidence that infers the judgment. The immediate criterion of truth, then, is reflective understanding, as it grasps the sufficiency of the evidence; the link between the evidence and the conclusion; and the rational necessity of positing the conclusion as certain, probable, or merely possible. In the immediate context, we know that we have reached the truth if we have sufficient evidence and that evidence entails the conclusion. I have already examined in sufficient detail the structure of this reflective grasp of the actually verified.

The remote criterion of truth refers to the broader context of human persons that are obliged to be intelligent and reasonable. Individual judgments usually depend on the context of presuppositions, principles, terms, and relations. The context can be very wide indeed. If the context is in itself skewed, then the individual judgment will not be reliable. How do we ensure that the context is correctly oriented, that it is not itself mistaken or deformed? We appeal to the general context of all knowing, where the dynamic that is operating is the pure, detached, unrestricted desire to know. It is the proper unfolding of that desire, which is the remote criterion of truth.

It is the implementation of that desire that is the only ultimate guarantee that the overall context of our individual judgments is sound. The desire to know is the source of the imperatives of being attentive, intelligent, and reasonable.

The remote criterion of truth might be described as an experience of closure. We come to a conclusion; we know we are right. We have faced all of the critical questions; we have filled all the gaps. We have refuted all counterarguments; our position is unassailable. The matter is closed; no further pertinent questions arise. We now move on to a new topic. In simple mathematical problems or crosswords, it is easy to recognize the correct solution. One can have that same experience while writing an article that interprets the hieroglyphics of an Egyptian pyramid; having exhaustively studied all the related material, the researcher knows that he or she is right. A mechanic faced with a funny noise from the engine considers many possibilities, tinkers with various parts, thinks again, and removes the carburetor. A washer is loose—a eureka moment confirmed by replacing and testing. In philosophical positions, it is more difficult to be sure about being right, to be sure about being totally honest, to have considered all counter arguments, to be totally open to the possibility of being wrong, to allow all pertinent or impertinent questions to arise, and to exclude all other alternatives. However, in principle, the only ultimate criterion of truth is the incessant stream of further critical questions, which consider all the possibilities, and finally, closes in on the one correct judgment.

A visiting professor to our campus recently explained how bored he was with propositional truth, and how he was really fired up with the idea of "giving meaning." Giving meaning in the field of art, mythology, literature, painting, poetry, symbolism, or comedy is fine. But in most areas of knowing, we are obliged to distinguish between true meaning and false meaning. I doubt if the same professor would teach his children to tell lies, or if he would applaud a doctor for a misdiagnosis. Would he be bored if he discovered that a scientific report was fraudulent, or that an article in the newspaper was patently untrue? Truth is not just a matter for speculative philosophy but for daily life, for relationships, for community, and for progress and development.

7

Understanding and Knowing Values

BEETHOVEN THE REVOLUTIONARY

Beethoven's remarks about this Symphony (fifth) are vague and elusive rather than concrete. The compositional problems he set for himself were abstract, musico-emotional ones that were little affected by external experiences, and not accessible to translation into mere words. . . .

In one of his few comments about the Symphony, he noted that, after the creation of the theme, "begins in my head the working-out in breadth, height and depth. Since I am aware of what I want, the fundamental idea never leaves me. It mounts, it grows. I see before my mind the picture in its whole extent, as if in a single grasp." By picture Beethoven meant not a visible painting, but rather an overview of the total structure of the Symphony, from its tiniest fragmentary component to the grand sweep of its total structure. . . .

So completely did composition occupy Beethoven's thoughts that he sometimes ignored the necessities of daily life. Concern with his appearance, eating habits, cleanliness, even his conversation, all gave way before his composing. There are many reports of his trooping the streets and woods of Vienna humming, singing, bellowing, penning a scrap of melody, and being, in general, oblivious to the people or places around him.[1]

Judging Moral Values

Beethoven's example reveals how the pivoting between images and ideas also occurs in musical composition. Beethoven has a fundamental idea

1. Pittsburgh Symphony Orchestra, *BeethovenFest*.

for the ninth symphony: he has a grasp of its total structure, the whole in a single picture. Then, he goes humming through the woods, imagining harmonies, appropriate instruments, human voices, themes, and variations that would embody these ideas. All of these are aimed at the beauty of a completed symphony; and surely, beauty is a value.

The method I have been using until now can be described in four simple points. First, human knowing arises spontaneously. No formal education is needed for children to ask questions, understand answers, and distinguish fact from fiction. Persons of common sense also ask intelligent questions, understand, and ask critical questions in order to distinguish between a real and a virtual world. They do so spontaneously, and in most cases effectively; one does not have to take a course in logic to distinguish between real life and science fiction. Scientists have to be more formal and careful in their procedures, measurements, definitions, experiments, and conclusions; they are in a theoretical mode. The experiments must be repeatable and the measurements precise in order to justify the conclusion. These procedures emerged spontaneously; Galileo was not following a manual on the logic of induction; he was following his gut instinct. Second, this spontaneous stream of activities can be described in detail; when you put all the parts together you get human knowing. This is what I have been doing in the previous chapters using examples from history, biography, autobiography, and additionally, from research of psychologists and from our own experience.

Third, there are certain norms that are immanent and operative in the process of knowing. Spontaneously we know that if you want to attain true knowledge we must ask all the relevant questions, consider all the pertinent data, and allow useful and opposing ideas to arise. We must ask critical questions, be willing to admit mistakes, be open and honest, and examine the arguments that link the data to the conclusion. Finally, when we reach closure, we move on to other topics.

Fourth, by comparison, there is an opposite track where we are cursory and careless in attending to the data, which is poorly understood. In this approach, we do not think the question through to the end; we cater to wishful thinking, bias, prejudice, and ambition; and we brush aside contrary positions. I will deal with the normative aspect of the process later when I discuss mistakes and misunderstanding.

The question now arises as to whether this method can be extended to the area of moral values. I have described the activities leading to a judgment of truth. Why should we not follow the same procedure and describe the activities involved in leading to a judgment of moral value? Instead of asking whether a judgment is true or false, we can ask whether it is a true or false value. The question of value arises, first, by attending to the evidence for a prospective judgment of value. Then, we identify the process of evaluation; describe its emergence, components, and causes; distinguish evaluating in various spheres; identify the steps in the process; and note how the process ends in a judgment of value. We instinctively discriminate between good evaluating and bad evaluating. This is what I plan to carefully elaborate on in this chapter. I identify the three activities involved in value judgments, namely, (1) asking value questions, (2) deliberating about value alternatives, and (3) passing final judgments of value.

We talk a lot about values. We talk about democratic values, economic values, American values, family values, personal values, aesthetic values, cultural values, and the like. Talking of values is part of our political discourse, our moral discourse, and our philosophical conversation. We consider our values to be a central aspect of who we are and what we stand for. We talk about value-free environments, about academic freedom, about appreciating a diversity of values, and about respect and tolerance for the values of other persons and cultures.

Yet in contrast to all of this talking about values, there remains very little discussion on what values are, where they come from, how we distinguish between true and false values, what the difference is between values and feelings, and how we ought to teach values. Why do we talk about moral values rather than moral laws or virtues and vices? The philosophical and theological traditions have discussed morality at length based on the natural law tradition, or based on the virtue ethics tradition. However, the language of values has now crept into our discourse. Marx started talking about values in his value theory of labor. Nietzsche undermined traditional moral values, but he also wrote about a transvaluation of values in a rather original way.[2] In the first half of the twentieth century the phenomenologists Max Scheler, Nicholai Hartmann, Dietrich von Hildebrand,[3] and others devoted some efforts to defining values, but the tradition has not been continued.

It is not surprising then that there is considerable confusion as to what a value is and whether we can know the difference between true and false values. Can we know the difference between good and evil? Alasdair MacIntyre asserts that the most prevalent view on values in our present culture is emotivism, namely, "that all evaluative judgments and more specifically all moral judgments are nothing but expressions of preference, expressions of attitude or feeling, insofar as they are moral or evaluative in character."[4]

2. Nietzsche, *Beyond Good and Evil*, index on values.

3. See, for example, Scheler, *On Feeling, Knowing, and Valuing*, chap. 10; Hartmann, *Moral Values*; Hildebrand, *Ethics*.

4. MacIntyre, *After Virtue*, 12.

He goes on to say that such expressions of feeling are neither true nor false, as the category of true or false does not apply to feelings. This attitude is very common. It is common to think of values as personal preferences, as arbitrary, irrational, relativistic, incommensurable, socially constructed, or beyond the scope of rational argument. It is common to dismiss a person's position with the casual remark, "But that is a value judgment!" In other words, once we enter into the realm of values, it seems that rationality goes out the window and it is a matter of personal preference and choice.

But this would seem to fly in the face of the fact that we are evaluating things all of the time and seem to be fairly successful at it. From morning to night, we evaluate the weather, the food we eat, and other people and their behavior. Professors evaluate their students, and students evaluate their professors. We are making moral value judgments all of the time, so it is hard to think of a full human life without such a stream of moral affirmations about the goodness or evil of people, institutions, governments, behaviors, and so on. We can and must make some attempt to defend the soundness of value judgments that underpin our priorities, our decisions, and our actions.

Whenever we use expressions such as good, better, best, or bad, worse, worst, we are engaged in the process of evaluating. We can evaluate well or badly, carefully or rashly, explicitly or implicitly. We seem to have an innate ability to evaluate and deliberate. The smallest child is quick to express likes and dislikes, what they want and do not want, what they value and do not value. The process seems to start with a question. Is it worthwhile? Is this good or bad? We consider the alternatives, the arguments, the pros and cons, the consequences, the feelings involved, the dangers, and the fears. The process seems to come to a conclusion in a judgment of value—this is the best thing to do, and there should normally follow the implementation of that value judgment into a course of action.

Our treatment of values builds on our earlier work on judgments of truth.[5] In the previous four chapters I elaborated on a cognitional structure of three levels of activities: experiencing, understanding, and judging truth. It is a detailed description of how we actually come to know. Truth is what we find when we have examined all the evidence, grasped the connection between the evidence and the conclusion, have no further relevant questions, and posit a judgment.

But there is a further level of activity involved in knowing good and evil. We usually do not stop when we have discovered a truth, a new idea, a scientific breakthrough, or a pure theory. A new discovery or insight almost

5. Please refer to the table of levels of consciousness (chap. 8) to note the parallel between judgments of truth and judgments of value. *p. 189*

inevitably leads to further questions. What should be done in light of this breakthrough? What are its implications? What is its worth? How can science be applied in technology? Science does not end in pure truth but in the implications, the applications, and the improvements in human living that can be introduced. Questions for truth are usually followed by questions of value. There are practical implications from most discoveries in medicine, economics, communications, science, and philosophy; thus, cognitional structure needs to be completed with an elaboration of the question of value, the deliberative insight, and the judgment of value.

What is this process of evaluating? Perhaps a simple, concrete example of this process might help to keep everything in perspective. Consider the mental activities we engage in when we set out to buy a new cell phone. The activities of questioning, deliberating, and concluding are always present. *Intelligence* is obviously involved. We ask a myriad of questions: where can I buy one? Why do I need one? What functions does it perform? How much does it cost? What is it worth? Where can I get the best bargain? *Feelings* are also involved. We see our friends using attractive, new cell phones, and we want one like that. We desire, we want, we need, we aspire to be connected at all times. We like one color and not another, we admire some functions and detest other annoyances. We are comfortable with our choice or uneasy. We can perform these activities well and get a good phone that satisfies our needs at a good price and we are happy. Or, we perform the activities badly, do not match our needs to functions, and end up returning the phone within a week. Identifying the activities in the process of buying a cell phone is helpful, because the same process and activities are involved in the more difficult judgments of moral value. In both instances, knowing and feeling are involved. In both cases, there is a process of deliberating, beginning with a question, followed by evaluation, and ending in a judgment of value. And in both instances, there is a good way of performing these activities and a bad way.

Both cognitive and affective elements are involved in buying a cell phone. Most obvious is the cognitive element: we ask questions, we seek information, we compare prices, we learn about apps and functions, and we seek advice from others. But the affective element also informs the process: we want, desire, and wish for a new and better phone. We are, perhaps, envious of our friends or ashamed of our old-fashioned clunky machine; we are frustrated with the complications of functionality, the price, and variety that is available.

There is also an element of choice, which is operative from the beginning in our questioning, in each step forward that we make, and to the final decision of paying for the purchase. We can decide to stop, to reverse, or to change direction at any stage of the process. Sadly, we can know what is the best thing to do in a particular situation and still do the opposite. Such is one aspect of human freedom.

The Question of Value Arises

The origin of values and value judgments is the question of value. Questioning is the first activity of understanding (see chapter 3). If values arise from questions, then, it is worthwhile to examine the characteristics of this question and the immediate implications of this position. In the following, I will try to pin down some of the characteristics of this process of questioning values by way of self-appropriation.

Children do not need to be taught to ask questions of value. A parent can teach the content of what is to be evaluated, provide the criteria to be used in evaluation, and give specific answers to specific questions. However, the question of value emerges from within the child; one might say it is *a priori* or innate in that sense, but I prefer to say that evaluating emerges spontaneously.

A baby operates in terms of likes and dislikes, what is agreeable or disagreeable, what is satisfying or not satisfying. This is a purely sensitive criterion of being attracted by what gives pleasure and repulsed by what gives pain. But gradually this criterion is transformed by the emergence of intelligence, the emergence of questions of fact and value. Once questions emerge, then intelligence and reason are operating. If intelligence is operating then a new criterion of truth and value emerges. Likes and dislikes give way to the more potent questions: Is this good for me? Can I have this now or later? Is parental approval more important than physical satisfaction? The child moves from the immediacy of the world of sensitive pleasure and pain, to the world mediated by ideas of value and judgments of value.

The most basic and pervasive form of the question of value is, "What is the right thing for me to do here and now in this situation?" We want to be reasonable and responsible; thus, implicitly at least, we form a value judgment that this is the best alternative, and then we do it. Normally, our choices are preceded by value judgments. In any one situation there may be many values in harmony or in conflict; there is some evaluating to be done. It is good advice to think before acting. Judge what is the best thing to do, decide to do it, then do it.

Is it possible to exclude choices and values from life? Is it possible to deny that values are operating? It seems to me to be impossible. To choose not to choose is already a choice. To decide not to decide is already a decision. To eliminate values from life is to judge that this is a valuable thing to attempt to do. Even the nihilist says that his or her philosophy of values is better than mine! No matter how we twist and turn, we are faced with the process of questioning values and deciding what to do about it.

We can, of course, eliminate some values from part of our lives: we can simply ignore, denigrate, disparage, and eliminate certain moral values. We can eliminate values from some of our relationships and be guided only by sensitive likes and dislikes. We can pretend that values are not operative: we can foster a pretense that an institution is value-free. We can affirm certain values in theory but deny them in practice. We can embrace certain disvalues instead of values.

One way of dealing with values is to try to eliminate or bracket them either completely or from a certain defined arena. The notion of a value-free sociology was propounded by scholars such as Max Weber; he had the laudable intention of making sociology an acceptable academic discipline and of distinguishing it from the value-laden ideologies of communism, socialism, and free-market capitalism. The idea was that sociology could have an objective method, rules of procedure, and clearly defined concepts. The private values of the researcher, interviewer, or theorist could be systematically excluded. This drew a picture of the neutral sociologist, like the neutral scientist, trusting in his or her methodologies to arrive at objective results. Values were viewed as irrational, arbitrary, private, and ideological. Values were viewed as irrational because they somehow go beyond knowing truth and do not seem to be amenable to reason and logic. They were viewed as arbitrary, because there seemed to be no way of measuring, controlling, reasoning about, or agreeing on values. They were viewed as private, because they characterize the person and the person's choices; that was considered their proper place. They were viewed as ideological, because they were intertwined with political systems, which were fighting for the minds and hearts of people during the industrial revolution of the nineteenth century. Because values are so hard to deal with, they tend to be pushed under the table. But they do not disappear! Lonergan remarks that a value-free theory of values resembles a theory of knowledge that prescinds from the knower![6]

There is no such thing as a value-free position. We are human beings who seek vital, social, cultural, moral, and religious values. Values are implicit in all of our choices. They may not be explicit but they are operative. One might argue that economic theory and research does not involve an explicit value system, but when economic policies are put into practice we can see the values emerging.

A neutral educational system claims to leave religious and moral values to the parents, to the private life of the person or family. It aspires to

---

6. Lonergan, *Philosophical and Theological Papers*, 403.

concentrate on science or intellectual development and claims not to discriminate or teach a particular value system. But in practice, it does imply a value stance: it is saying that religion and morals are a matter of private, arbitrary choice and that the academy cannot make any contribution to such choices. In sex education the facts of biology are explained in great detail with charts and diagrams, along with the accompanying claim that this approach is value-free; the biological facts are taught and the rest is up to personal choice. But the implicit value stance being propagated here is that the biological facts are important, but friendship, discipline, love, relationships, trust, intimacy, and fidelity have nothing to do with sex!

I have described in a rather compact, descriptive way how, when, and where the question of values arises. Because these questions arise in many contexts, it might be that there are different kinds of values, or it might be that they relate in terms of a scale of values. That is the hypothesis I will now consider.

Scale of Values

There are many different kinds of value questions. In the previous section, I detailed an example of evaluating and buying a cell phone. I identified a sequence of mental activities of evaluating from various viewpoints; the values at stake were economic, utility, and personal convenience. Moral evaluations require much the same process of activities, feelings, and judgments but add the criterion of moral values. Are all of these values of equal worth? Are values all the same? Is there a chaos of values? One can slice values in various ways, but the most fundamental is to follow the five levels of conscious activity that are constitutive of the human person. I have already examined three of these levels: experiencing, understanding, and judging truth. At present I am identifying the fourth level—the question of value, the deliberative insight into value and the value judgment. The fifth level is the level of religious involvement, which I do not examine in detail in this text. In this framework, we can distinguish vital, social, cultural, moral, and religious values in a hierarchical, structural scale of values.[7]

How can the levels of consciousness ground the distinction between five kinds of value? We do so by asking questions. What is the good proper to each level of consciousness? What is the value to be affirmed that is specific to each level? How is the good of each level to be realized? In practice, we

---

7. I include religious values here to flesh out a complete account of values. The table of four levels of consciousness can be expanded to a five-level structure to include a religious dimension of charity, faith, worship, grace, and salvation.

operate at many levels at the same time; the levels are distinct but not separate. We specialize at one level in the context of influences and dependencies on other levels. But if we apply this principle of the value proper to each level of operation, we get at least a preliminary scale of values that has solid foundations. Assuming the framework of five levels of consciousness, one way of dividing values is according to the level at which they are intended. Thus, I will elaborate on vital values at the level of experience, social values at the level of understanding, cultural values at the level of judgment, personal values at the level of moral deliberation, and religious values at a fifth level.

Vital values are characteristic of the human person as living, as sensing, as embodied, and as satisfying the needs of sensitive living. Vital values loosely correlate with the level of experiencing. Health, vitality, energy, food, clothing, housing, propagation, growth, sleep, and the like are examples of vital values. Certain foods are good for our health. Getting a good night's sleep is critical for our livelihood. It is nearly impossible to pick up any magazine without being given free advice on what to eat, how to exercise, or what is good for our health. We are all familiar with the adage, "A healthy mind in a healthy body."

Social values are characteristic of the good of order of a society. We are not just individuals seeking our own good, but social animals seeking the good of the community. There are various ways in which we structure social relations in a society of specialized roles, cooperation, law and order, principles of equality, and the like. Efficiency, order, differentiation, regularity, cooperation, and proficient use of resources are examples of social values. They presuppose vital values but in principle are at a higher order as they loosely correlate with the level of understanding. We satisfy individual needs only in the context of a well-functioning polis or society. Specialization and cooperation demand an organized society where the good of individuals will be balanced with the good of all.

Cultural values are the beliefs and values inherent in a given way of life. These values are embodied in the constitution, inculcated in an educational system, and underpin the judicial system. We value truth, education, science, and technology. We respect the values of tolerance and freedom and equality. The truth of our history is embodied in the myths, the institutions, traditions, stories, and songs of the group. Different cultures have various configurations or ways of expressing these cultural values. A democratic society will have a set of core values concerning ownership, voting, rule of law, and a balance of powers between different branches of government. A communist or dictatorial society will have a very different set of cultural values.

Moral values are the values implicit in our relations to one another as free and responsible human persons. Above and beyond the question of truth, there arises the question of moral value. What is the best way to live as a person in society? How do we develop as free and responsible persons who know, decide upon, and implement an integral scale of values? This is the good of the individual who realizes his or her freedom as a responsible person. Honesty, tolerance, justice, responsibility, freedom, equality, and respect are examples of moral values. It is not so easy to specify moral values, so I will do this in a later section.

Religious values are not my primary concern here, but for many people there are also religious values. What is the form of the question intending religious values? To be fully human is to be open to the divine. We can recognize this openness by the unlimited nature of our questioning, by our experience of the holy, by our longing of mind and heart for the possibility of God's intervention in our lives. Hence worship, prayer, grace, unconditional love, meditation, asceticism, self-sacrifice, service, love of neighbor, and so on are examples of religious values, which go beyond moral values.

The scale of values helps us to see that there are different levels of value, and that they are dependent on one another; the higher presupposes the lower, while at the same time, they go beyond the lower and introduce something new and more valuable. Just as understanding presupposes and goes beyond experiencing, so social values presuppose but go beyond vital values. Just as reflective understanding presupposes and goes beyond both understanding and experiencing, so cultural values presuppose and go beyond social and vital values. Just as deliberative insights presuppose and go beyond reflective and direct insights and experiencing, so moral values presuppose and go beyond cultural, social, and vital values. Similarly, religious values presuppose and go beyond moral, cultural, social and vital values. Not all values are at the same level; values are not all equal. The good is an analogous notion. The division into levels is not arbitrary but based on our complex nature as sensitive, intellectual, rational, moral, and religious beings. The image of levels should not be taken too literally; I am not trying to compartmentalize human valuing but to have a conceptual scheme for relating different kinds of values to one another.

Values are everywhere. They are embedded in every activity, every institution, and every policy. We find values in education, politics, laws, courts, governments, banks, hamburger joints, and so on. A value-free context is an illusion, and is usually a mask for a secular, relativistic, politically correct agenda. We have the innate potential not only to know the truth but also to know particular goods, namely, values. Values are not arbitrary preferences as maintained by emotivists; rather, they really give us objective knowledge of good and evil, value as true or false. That is not to say that we are always right or that we never make mistakes. But significantly, we can recognize our mistakes, learn from them, and avoid similar goofs in the future. Nor does it mean that we know all the answers. But at the very least, we have a method of asking the right responsible questions, considering the possibilities and evidence, and often reaching a conclusion in a true judgment of value.

Structure of Deliberative Insight

I now come to the crux of the matter. I have elucidated a precise idea of the question for evaluation and an anticipatory notion of the judgment of value; the focus now is on what happens in between. What is this process of evaluation, which in moral philosophy is traditionally called deliberation? How does it begin, how does it proceed, and how does it end? Does it have many different forms or is there one single, universal form? I am proposing that such an important process will have a single, basic form, even though there may be many specific variations. Using the various analogies available in the diagram of cognitional activities (see chapter 8), I am proposing that deliberation is a single insight into the sufficiency of the evidence entailing the conclusion in a judgment of value. I intend to call this a "deliberative insight," to be understood on the analogy of reflective insight. It is a cognitive activity by which we grasp the sufficiency of the evidence for the positing of a judgment of value. It is similar in structure to the reflective insight; it differs from the reflective insight in that it intends value and not truth. In the following, I explore the implications of such a hypothesis and check if it coheres with our own experience of where judgments of value come from. This is an attempt to give a systematic, comprehensive overview of the structure of deliberative insight.[8]

Deliberative insight will be an insight, an act of understanding, that embodies in some way the five characteristics of all acts of understanding:[9] First, it will come as a release of the tension of inquiry (in this case, the question, "Is it worthwhile?") as a result of consistently and deeply driving toward a solution. Second, it requires that we do the work—assemble case studies, study all aspects of the situation, and do some serious thinking. Third, it will come suddenly and unexpectedly: we cannot force such insights to come. We can provide optimal conditions of concentration, attention to relevant data, manipulating images, data, and examples—then, suddenly it comes. The emergence of the insight depends on inner conditions more than outward

---

8. Lonergan never used the phrase "deliberative insight," although he does speak of deliberation and evaluation. I give a detailed interpretation and analysis of deliberative insight in Cronin, *Value Ethics*, chap. 4.

9. Lonergan, *Insight*. 28–31.

circumstances. The inner conditions are the questions, the habits, the feelings, the intentions, the ambitions, the desires, and so on, which move toward evaluation, decision, and action. Outer circumstances, such as wealth, gender, time and place, or culture and language may be quite irrelevant.

Fourth, a deliberative insight pivots between the abstract and the concrete: universal moral laws have to be applied in a concrete situation. Which laws apply in this situation? Is this a situation of killing, murder, manslaughter, accidental killing, or what? Is this concrete situation an exception to the general definition? Fifth and finally, the deliberative insight will pass into the habitual texture of the mind: by means of individual judgments of value, we establish habitual value stances and priorities. If we realize that we did the right thing in one situation, we are likely to do it again in a similar situation.

Deliberative insight, then, will not be intuitive, that is, a simple, single, direct vision of value; it will be discursive, worked out painfully and slowly, and open to interference of various kinds. It will involve sensing, remembering, and understanding; it includes a context of facts, a context of ideas, and a context of previous reflective and deliberative insights. It will involve active focusing, researching, questioning, thinking, writing, and talking. It will also involve a passive component of waiting, listening, hoping, and receiving. Many existential elements will tend to intrude, for better or worse—fear of consequences, mixed motivations, selfishness struggling with altruism, or willingness in tension with unwillingness. Deliberative insight ushers us into the world mediated by meaning and value, not the world of immediacy of sensing. Deliberative insight will grasp a unity, a connection, a whole, a value, a relation, a form immanent in a multiplicity of images, situations, experiences, and events.

But a deliberative insight will be modeled on reflective insight because it is preparing to issue a judgment, in this case a judgment of value. If the structure of judgment of value is the same as the structure of the judgment of fact, then surely the form of deliberative insight will be similar to the form of reflective insight. Hence the unity we are looking for in deliberative insights is the connection between evidence and conclusion: is it sufficient, relevant, convincing, possible, probable, impossible, or improbable? The descriptive way of expressing this is weighing the evidence for or against the conclusion.

All good or value is conditioned or contingent (except for God, the formally unconditioned good). There is no absolutely necessary good, so all judgments of value will be of contingent values, values that will be real values, if certain conditions are fulfilled. The judgment of value will start with the conditioned and proceed to establish a link between the conditioned and its fulfilling conditions. It will determine if the conditions are in fact fulfilled; it will then proceed to enunciate the actually unconditioned value of this person, act, policy, or thing. The deliberative insight is the grasp of the sufficiency of the evidence in the premises for the conclusion. It is a single insight that unites a vast multiplicity of data, insights, facts, previous evaluations, and so forth. Hence deliberative insight follows the form of the hypothetical syllogism of reflective insight, that is: If A, then B. But A. Therefore B.

This analysis of the fundamental underlying structure of deliberative insight is important because it reveals the structure of the human mind as it grasps the good and knows value. We are not born knowing what is right, but we are born with the capacity to work it out for ourselves. Listen to any argument about abortion, capital punishment, just war, homosexuality, gender discrimination, and the like, and underlying all of the contributions, whether they are valid or not, is the following four-fold structure: (1) beginning with a question of value to be answered; (2) making arguments, connections, inferences, links, or relevance; (3) appealing to evidence, experience, facts, examples, memories, or previous experience; (4) ending with an appropriate conclusion, by which we affirm or deny the value. In all cultures, at all times, this is the fundamental underlying universal structure of evaluating. This is how all human mind works. This is the fundamental form of inference of value that I am in the process of identifying and objectifying.

We can formalize this procedure in more detailed, explicit ways so as to be clear how they apply to particular cases. We have the formal structure of deductive, syllogistic logic; we have the rules of inference and the fallacies that occur when the rules are broken. We have inductive logic and principles of scientific method; we have many forms of modern symbolic logic. Many disciplines develop their own particular forms of methodologies, procedures, and rules; all of these guide the process of inference from evidence to conclusions. All of these may be relevant to procedures of moral reasoning. The structure of moral evaluating is similar to the structure of scientific or philosophical reasoning. It is the *content and criteria* that makes the difference between reflective and deliberative insight. Reflective insights intend truth; deliberative insights intend value. The distinct notion of value motivates the intentionality of asking value questions until a satisfactory resolution is found. The notion of value recognizes value when it is found and provides the criterion of true value in the happy conscience of the good person. This is transcendental in the sense that it is beyond categories, applying to all human persons making judgments of value, of any kind, in any time or place. This is a very high level of generality. Allow me to try to be more specific and clear about what I am saying.

The criterion of truth operating in questions for reflection is relatively univocal: it has one meaning, one intention, which guides the activities to a successful conclusion. The criterion of value is much more analogous: value takes on different meanings depending on the context of the question that is asked. "What is the value of this food?" is a value question that considers vital values. "What is the value of this person?" is a value question that intends moral values. Persons, things, and policies can be evaluated from many different points of view. How do we know which point of view is operative? Fortunately, it is the question that usually sets the criterion that is operative and must be satisfied. The criterion is goodness from one perspective or another. It is only when we are clear about the criterion that is operating that we can assess the relevance of evidence for the truth or falsity of the judgment. We are constantly evaluating things in a loose sense as either good or bad. We apply these judgments to cars, to dogs, to schools, to books, to paintings, to tools, to institutions, and to just about anything in the universe. I will examine how and why we do this with a few typical examples.

How do we evaluate a book, and describe it as good or useless? Clearly we start with a criterion of what we hope to get from reading the book—recreational reading, escapism, help for an exam, a solution to a particular problem, general enlightenment, inspiration, and so on, all of which are legitimate values. We judge the book on whether it satisfies these criteria, how well it does so, with or without reservations or deficiencies or qualifications. We set the conditions to be satisfied by reading the book; if the conditions are fulfilled, we judge it as good. If they are not fulfilled, we judge it as a failure, a waste of time, a useless book. If we are buying a book, we clearly establish what we are looking for. We line up possibilities in order to judge prices, presentation, material, and so on, and finally pick out what we evaluate as the best option and buy it.

We can evaluate schools while operating according to different criteria. One might be looking for something affordable, some place within a reasonable distance from home, or some place that offers a major in a specific field of study. Other criteria that may be considered are whether the school is well administered, has good professors, has high academic standards, is committed to small classroom numbers, has a well-reputed athletics program, and so forth. While visiting the school and talking to teachers and pupils, one evaluates the information as to whether it satisfies these criteria of not. There will be a constant stream of tentative value judgments being made, leading to the final, definitive judgment of whether it is a good school overall.

The value of things will vary as to the criteria operating in the situation. A good book for holiday reading is not the same as a good book for passing exams. Gold is very valuable but not much use if one is stranded in a desert with nothing to eat or drink. When King Richard was surrounded by his enemies, he willingly would have given his kingdom for a horse to escape with his life. This does not mean that all values are subjective. What is valuable is a very flexible notion, depending on particular criteria operating in concrete situations with individual persons who are doing the evaluating. But there is a single, transcendental structure underlying each of the examples—a conditioned value, a link between the conditioned and its fulfilling conditions, the fulfilment of the conditions and hence the judgment of value—the actually unconditioned of value. Even though the notion of good and value is analogous, there is one series of activities producing knowledge of goodness, and one underlying heuristic structure by which we move from questioning to knowing value. This can be seen in either of the above examples.

Evidence should be relevant to the conclusion; we usually use the terms "inferring," "implying," "entailing," and "requiring" to express this relation. There may be a long process of reasoning to show the connection between the evidence and the conclusion; the connection might be direct or circumstantial. Forms of inference can be implicit or they can be formalized in moral arguments. Listen to a moral debate and evaluate the arguments. There can be all sorts of red herrings thrown into the procedure, items that deliberately distract from the issue at stake. Insults do not qualify as a good argument but are present in many debates. The person who shouts the loudest should not necessarily win, neither should the one who keeps talking to the end when everybody else capitulates out of sheer exhaustion. It is not a question of scoring points by cleverness or humor, or belittling the opponents. Understanding of good procedures of inference should be flanked by an understanding of fallacies, evasions, distortions, bias, blindness, the twisting of data, and the ignoring of data. Hence, we can see the necessity of a clear criterion of relevance, the need for a coherent structure of thinking, a philosophy which determines what is relevant, a correct grasp of argumentation and how it should proceed, and a grasp of fallacies and how they intrude and interfere.

Who decides what is sufficient? Are there any rules that will determine in all cases what is sufficient? The final criterion is simply reason itself in its practical application. In the case of judgments of truth, it is reflective understanding; in the question of judgments of value it is deliberative understanding.

We rely on juries to reach a verdict on the basis of "guilty beyond a reasonable doubt." To apply rules to a concrete situation supposes understanding the situation, as well as understanding the rules that might apply, and also the priority of some rules over others. In reality, the jury is continually making judgments of value about witnesses, about evidence, about arguments, about motives, and about responsibility. We trust a jury to determine if there is sufficient evidence and if the evidence is sufficient for a verdict. They do not need to study moral philosophy to evaluate impartially—though it might help.

Deliberation on a moral dilemma is purposive; it is aiming in the direction of a judgment. At first we may be totally puzzled by a new situation or question. We ask about it, do research, discuss it with friends, gain a personal acquaintance with the issue, and ask how we feel about it. Gradually, we find that we are moving in the direction of approving, that the evidence is pointing in one direction, that counterarguments are invalid or can be refuted. A point is reached when the mind is satisfied, when we have considered all the angles, when no further pertinent questions arise, and we know we are right. At that point, the deliberative insight issues in a judgment.

Very often we cannot be certain of our judgments of value. Consequences in the future are by their very nature difficult to foresee. Information on possible courses of action may be incomplete, unreliable, partial, and mistaken. We do not have time to collect all the relevant information; we have to trust in the advice of our friends, or believe what is written in the brochure. Values may be conflicting: there may be conflict between a vital value and a moral value. We want to use the money for a new computer, but we promised to use it to pay back a loan. There may be a conflict between different moral values, such as loyalty to the group and one's duty to report wrongdoing. Many of our moral decisions will be a question of probability, high or low as the case may be. The degree of probability will be determined by the weight of the evidence and the link between the evidence and the conclusion. There are many cases where we cannot fully understand the matter in hand, where full information is not available, where many values impinge on the situation, or where complicated moral inferences are involved; but we have to act, now!.

It is the function of understanding to unify and organize data of sense and data of consciousness. Similarly, the deliberative insight is a single insight, which unifies and organizes a vast amount of data in view of a judgment of value. The evidence is usually wider, more subtle, and more prone to bias and distortion than in the case of judgments of truth. Much of the data may already be previous judgments of fact and preliminary or tentative judgments of value. But all of this preparatory work coalesces in a single deliberative insight, a single grasp of the sufficiency of the evidence for the positing of a value judgment. The judgment simply affirms or denies. It is right or it is wrong; it is good or bad.

Deliberative Insights into Moral Values

Value judgments occur in all areas of life. I have used examples from the lived experience of evaluating books, schools, and cell phones to show how they operate and how the question leads to the process of deliberation and to the final judgment of value. Now I wish to apply that familiarity with the process to the more difficult and complex area of moral value judgments. The structure and the process of the judgment of value are the same, but the content, the criteria, and the intentionality are different. Moral judgments of value presuppose and presume vital values, social values, and cultural values, but they go on to recognize the value of the human person as free and responsible, having personal and social obligations.

It seems that an approach to moral philosophy by way of values and where they come from would be superior to theoretical approaches. There is no shortage of theories of moral philosophy. Natural law was initiated by Aristotle, elaborated by Aquinas, and is still appealed to by the Catholic tradition, the United Nations, and judicial systems. Virtue ethics, also initiated by Aristotle and expanded by Aquinas, enjoys a wider popularity today. A deontological ethics of obligation was initiated by Kant, which claims a source of normativity in the individual person's rational capacity to arrive at universal ethical maxims (e.g., the categorical imperative). There are also utilitarianism, social contract theory, consequentialism, situation ethics, divine command theory, personalism, care ethics, moral sentimentalism, and perhaps others. Introductory textbooks on ethics regularly explain these theories, but they often leave it to the students as to which one to follow or not to follow.

The first difficulty about theories is that we have to choose between them. We have to make a value judgment about which is the best theory! Theories, no matter how sophisticated or correct as theory, still require the individual subject to make a value judgment on the theory itself. The second difficulty about theories is that theories are general and each situation is unique and particular. To mediate between the theory and the situation, we need a further insight and a further judgment of value into which law or theory applies in this situation and in what order of priority. The third difficulty is that normative ethics often tries to provide yes or no answers to each and every particular situation that is ever likely to arise; to approve or disapprove of every specific action, practice, behavior, or life style; and to formulate rules as to what is the right thing to do in each situation. But there is never a simple fit between the rule and the unique situation. No matter how detailed we make the rules, in business ethics, healthcare ethics, medical ethics, environmental ethics, sexual ethics, and like specializations, the unique situation remains unique. Value judgments are still required.

My approach is to identify the process of making correct value judgments, which will be relevant to all situations and help subjects to recognize what is required for a responsible judgment of value in every case.

I have not been formulating theories and then applying them to practice; rather, I have observed the activities of understanding and knowing as they actually occur in concrete examples. The activities can be done intelligently and reasonably to produce true judgments, or they can be done carelessly to produce mistakes and confusions. The same approach can be used for value judgments in moral philosophy. We can describe how people make value judgments concerning the person, themselves, or others as free and responsible. We can describe how it can be done responsibly and produces good persons and good societies. We can further describe how it is done irresponsibly and produces evil persons and corrupt societies. My focus will be on identifying and appropriating this process of making good judgments of moral value. Perhaps the way to help people to make better value judgments is to identify and objectivize the cognitive and affective factors involved not only in making good moral judgments but also in carrying them out.

The Specific Meaning of Moral Values

Allow me first try to identify precisely what is meant by a moral value. It was relatively easy to identify the spheres of vital values, social values, and cultural values, which correlate to the levels of experiencing, understanding, and judging. It is not so easy to specify the sphere of the moral or personal values, which correlate with the level of value questions and judgments. One clue is that we often interchange "moral" value with "personal" value. Some initial observations:

1. There are moral values and they cannot be reduced to skills, economic values, or intellectual values. They are the highest in the hierarchy of the scale of values, in the sense that they presuppose the others but go beyond them to something new and different.

2. The moral sphere is where the value of the person as human, as free and responsible, is at stake.

3. In the moral sphere, the goodness of the whole person as an integrated unity of mind, heart, will, and spirit is involved. We often refer to a person as a good football player, as a very good teacher, or as a good economist. These are skills, parts of the person, aspects of the totality. Moral values, however, involve, not the goodness of the parts, but the goodness of the whole with an emphasis on freedom and responsibility.

4. The moral sphere implies that we are social beings; we have received everything we have from our families, our societies, our cultures and traditions. The good of the individual has to be balanced with the good of the society. We have duties to family as well as civic duties to schools and local communities. A person who makes no contribution to family, to community, and to other people can hardly be regarded as living by a high moral standard.

5. The moral sphere implies a general obligation to assert all values. However, not all values can be realized at the same time by the same person. If one donates money to one charitable cause, it is not available for other worthy causes. If one volunteers to help in an overseas disaster, the volunteer may have to neglect his or her family. Each choice excludes many alternatives; but these alternatives are still valuable choices.

6. Western culture generally emphasizes rights and brackets duties. My approach is to recognize duties and obligations first. I have identified the obligation to ask questions, to understand possibilities, to affirm the truth, and to seek and implement values for oneself and others. These fundamental obligations are rooted in being human persons. We do not have to invoke a putative social contract theory to justify such obligations.

7. If one seeks to live a good life and searches for and implements values, that person changes him or herself into a benevolent and beneficent person. Such a person is an originating value; the individual makes him or herself to be a good person. In contrast, the good that is achieved by building a school, writing a book, or rearing children is a terminal value. These are reciprocal: one becomes a good person by doing good for society; a good society is constituted by good people.

8. Freedom and responsibility are two sides of the same coin. We are responsible for our actions because we are free not to do them. Freedom can be understood and misunderstood in many and various ways.[10]

9. The moral sphere has to include the planet, the environment, and the integrity of creation. We have emerged from the universe, we are an integral part of the environment, we depend on the ecology of the area, we do not own the planet, and thus, we have an obligation of sustainability to hand it on to future generations.

10. Cronin, *Value Ethics,* chap. 7.

The Scope of Judging Human Actions

The moral philosopher makes judgments of value about method, principles, criteria, human nature, human action, human purposes, and the consequences of human action. We can usually distinguish moral philosophies by what they value most in human life, whether it be virtue as an end in itself (Stoicism), pleasure (Epicureanism, hedonism), or utility (utilitarianism, consequentialism). Sometimes power is elevated to the status of a final end or criterion as in the philosophies of Schopenhauer, Nietzsche, and what is called "real politik." Moral philosophy must make value judgments at the theoretical or methodological level, but also give guidance, criteria, or applications to the concrete details of everyday evaluations, choices, and actions. Many moral philosophies err by way of simplification. They may concentrate exclusively on one value to the exclusion of other values. They may emphasize the consequences of an action while excluding the motivations. They may extol the rational, universal, and moral imperative at the expense of human feelings, aspirations, and affects. Moral philosophy is fraught with multiple possibilities of going wrong.

Consider some of the areas in which deliberative insights operate in order to work toward a comprehensive grasp of human moral good:

1. *Moral Persons.* Deliberative judgments need to be made toward the real sphere of the moral as distinct from all other values. They will be concerned with the free and responsible development of human persons as good valuers, choosers, and doers. Deliberative judgments pertain to persons in their relations with other persons and to the goodness of activities of the fourth level of human consciousness. This is not a matter of skill, intelligence, strength, beauty, talent, personality, or temperament; it is a matter of what a person has done, is doing with his or her life as a whole in relation to responsible choices (e.g., promoting the good, doing the right thing, being virtuous, being a human person), and of flourishing in the fullest sense of that ambiguous term. Moral philosophy will depend on how we value the life of a human person, including the human person's development, purpose, and proper self-realization.

We normally distinguish between moral goodness and other kinds of goodness, and I have done my best to articulate this difference. We constantly judge people as good or evil, and these are either true or false judgments. We judge their ability as bankers, footballers, conversationalists, and teachers, but we also judge them as moral persons—"Underneath it all, he is a good person. He may not be very intelligent but he is a good person." We judge the integrity of a person's motivation—we live with them over a period of time and see how they react in various situations. We check for consistency between what they say and what they do.

2. *Judging Moral Actions.* We deliberate about specific human actions and classify them into kinds and categories. We distinguish between actions that are serious from the moral point of view—killing, stealing large sums of money, rape, and the like—from those we consider trivial such as white lies, bad language, and being impolite.

An extreme situation ethics claims that there are only an infinite number of particular concrete human actions and therefore we cannot apply general rules.[11] Yet we know that human actions, although unique in their concreteness, can be understood, classified, defined, and evaluated; thus, general categories can be reached and moral judgments affirmed in general. We can categorize human actions into typical action situations such as adultery, abortion, murder, genocide, corruption, lying, perjury, and fornication.

Judging human actions must include judging motivations, intentions, freedom, consequences, circumstances, and much more. We distinguish human actions that are free and responsible, from acts of the human being that are reflexes, instinctual, or biologically or psychologically beyond the control of will and responsibility. We judge when actions are due to ignorance or misunderstanding, and we decide whether it is culpable or inculpable ignorance. We judge the quality of the freedom: is the act premeditated, planned, chosen deliberately; or is freedom lessened by compulsions, instinct, passion, addiction, and so on?

3. *Moral Consequences.* We evaluate human actions partly in terms of their consequences. But consequences can be multiple and of different kinds. We can distinguish between direct consequences and indirect, remote, or unintended consequences. Consequences can be important or irrelevant or trivial; they can be short-term or long-term effects. In different ways, all of these will influence whether we view the action to be moral.

4. *Moral Intentions.* We also evaluate moral actions in terms of intention. What was the person intending to achieve? Moral idealism, in the sense of having high ideals, but little or no competence, will probably do more harm than good. Almsgiving can sometimes cause dependency, encourage addiction, and demean persons. Planting trees at random can do more harm than good. Good intentions by themselves are not enough.

5. *Motivation.* We also evaluate in terms of motive. What was the motive of the crime? What was the person trying to achieve by doing this? What was a person's motivation in choosing a career or embarking on a course of action?

11. See Fletcher, *Situation Ethics.*

6. *Means and Ends.* Aristotle claimed that we do not dispute about the end, because we all agree that it is happiness; however, we do argue about the means because there are various means to the end of happiness. It is probably correct that everybody seeks happiness as their ultimate end but that is at a very high level of generality. In reality, we do argue about ends and means. There are intermediate ends: we seek wealth, success, or pleasure in order to be happy. There are many means, good and bad, to get rich and famous. In this context we deliberate about both ends and means and the relation between them. The end does not justify the means, generally speaking, but that is also a judgment of value, and other factors must be taken into account.

7. *Moral Reasoning.* How then does a person answer the question: what is the right thing for me to do in this situation? A person thinking in terms of natural law theory will ask, "What kind of an action is this? Which moral laws apply here? Which law has priority?" The solution will be a deliberative insight into the application of moral laws to concrete situations. A person thinking in terms of virtue ethics might ask, "Which virtue is called for here? Which virtue has priority? If I want to become a good person, what do I do here? What would my role model do in this situation?" The solution will be a judgment of value in terms of grasping the virtuous course of action. A person thinking in terms of Kant's deontological ethics will apply the categorical imperative, judge that this action is not universifiable, and in duty, refrain from doing it because it is wrong. A person thinking in terms of moral values will understand the values of an action, the possibilities and alternatives, and the consequences in terms of moral and other values. The individual will deliberate, judge, decide, and act attentively, intelligently, reasonably, and responsibly. The person will be guided by conscience and ultimately answerable to a good conscience.

In the end, we judge that one course of action is the best and carry it out. All of the preliminary partial judgments of value coalesce into a judgment about the whole. It may seem rather complicated, but after some consideration, even the decision to apply to a certain university involves most of the aforementioned points. To be unqualifiedly good human persons, our actions must be wholly good, the intentions benevolent, the motives wholesome, and the consequences good for all. But that entire combination is a rarity in human affairs. Yet we must establish this as the standard of human moral judgment, and if anything is lacking the action must be judged to be somehow defective. Goodness belongs to the whole, evil results from some kind of defect, as Aristotle and Aquinas noted. Evil lies in some kind of absence of what should be there, whether it is in the action, the amount, the time, the intention, or the consequences. Many moral judgments of value will be comparative rather than absolute: this is better than that, rather than this is wholly good and that is wholly bad.

In each case the value to be ascertained is a conditioned value. In each case it will be a real value, if those conditions are fulfilled. We assemble examples, distinctions, evidence, and previous evaluations and line them up as the fulfilment of the conditions. The deliberative insight grasps the sufficiency or insufficiency of the evidence for the positing of the judgment of value.

The Affective Component of the Judgment of Value

I have given a detailed account of the role of intelligence in producing judgments of value. Does this mean that I have adopted a rationalist position? By no means. What then is the role of feelings in the process of evaluations, particularly of moral judgments? Again we can attend to questions of fact and to our own experience of moral evaluations. University students are familiar with nuances in the area of feeling and are able to name more than a hundred feelings within half an hour. Chief among them are desires, fears, love, hate, remorse, guilt, disgust, anger, responsibility, unease, being tense, being stressed, excitement, being perturbed, confusion, hesitance, confidence, and so on. Do these feelings enter into the process of moral deliberation? Of course they do. Our feelings motivate, direct, channel, and sometimes control our actions. We are feeling-oriented animals. We are very articulate in naming and distinguishing various feelings. But how and where and to what extent do they enter into moral deliberation?

We tend to think in terms of feelings that are good and feelings that are bad. We tend to judge anger, passion, and hate as bad. We tend to judge love, peace, and compassion as good. But it is not quite as simple as that. One can love evil and come to hate the good. There are situations of injustice where we should be angry. Compassion shown to a murderer might be misplaced. It does not seem to be the feeling itself that is good or bad but what the feeling is intending. The distinction we seem to need here is between (1) feelings that normally lead to good moral actions, and which normally result in self-transcendence, on the one hand, and (2) feelings that are morally neutral, ambivalent, or ambiguous, on the other.[12] Allow me to try to identify these two distinct vectors of affectivity. This is an application and

12. "In general, response to value both carries us towards self-transcendence and selects an object for the sake of whom or of which we transcend ourselves. In contrast, response to the agreeable or disagreeable is ambiguous. What is agreeable may very well be what also is a true good. But is also happens that what is a true good may be disagreeable" (Lonergan, *Method in Theology*, 31).

expansion on our previous distinction (chap 3) between intellectual feelings and sensitive feelings, now being applied to judgments of value.

First, there are feelings that tend toward moral self-transcendence. I have spoken about the importance of the pure, detached, unrestricted desire to know truth and value. This desire is the dynamic of the activities, the intentionality implicit in the activities, and the drive of knowing. It is also the criterion by which we know we have reached the correct answer. We feel it in our curiosity, our wonder, our questioning, our searching, and our joy in success or frustration at failure. Is the desire to know a feeling? I do not see any alternative to clearly and explicitly calling the desire to know a feeling.[13] If a desire to know is not a feeling what is it? We feel them, they move us in a certain direction, and they drive human living. The desire to know is one identifiable feeling that normally leads us in the direction of self-transcendence. It is deep, long lasting, provides direction to our search, and leads us to inquire relentlessly for truth and value.

What is the role of this desire? Is it extrinsic to the process of knowing or is it constitutive of the process? Try to imagine a knowing that does not start in a desire to know that is expressed in questioning. Could such knowing without desire provide the drive for research and deliberation, force one to make a judgment when sufficient evidence is grasped, and be content when the truth has been attained? It seems that without the desire to know, we do not ask questions, and thus, do not understand anything. Understanding is a dynamic activity and the dynamic is provided by the desire to know. The desire to know as a feeling is a constitutive element of human knowing of truth and value. The scope of the term "desire to know" might sound a bit narrow, but it can be articulated in the terminology of transcendental precepts such as be attentive, be intelligent, be reasonable, be responsible, or be in love. These are broader in scope but help to identify the feelings of obligation that lead to intellectual and moral development. The desire to know is not just a desire to know truth and value, but also a desire to be, to become, to live in conformity with truth and value, to seek the highest good.

Second, there are feelings, which in themselves are neutral, ambivalent, or ambiguous. These are sensitive feelings, feelings that involve chemical or biological changes; they are bodily based. They are morally ambiguous in the sense that in themselves they are neither good nor bad: it is only in the context of a free, developing moral person who is knowing, deciding, and acting that such feelings enter into the moral domain. Anger is an example

---

13. "It depends, however, on exactly what you mean by affectivity. If you include what I call the pure desire to know along with affectivity, then it is a matter of selecting one affectivity and favoring it against others" (Lonergan, *Understanding and Being*, 265).

of such a feeling. On the one hand, one can be filled with righteous anger over injustice, corruption, discrimination, child abuse, and the like. One should feel angry at such evils. On the other hand, one may exhibit the more selfish anger of road rage, anger at a crying baby on a plane, or anger at a policeman who rightly hands out a ticket for speeding.

Understanding our feelings is a legitimate process. In discerning our feeling orientation, we should be able to distinguish the deeply rooted sense of obligation to be attentive, intelligent, reasonable, and responsible from the more superficial, sensitive, transient, ambiguous feelings of appetite, attraction, or satisfaction.

I have considered the cognitive and affective components operative in our understanding and knowing of values. My focus is on the cognitive, as this study is centered on human understanding. I have devoted some attention to the affective dimension, as that is crucial and constitutive in the process of knowing. However, there are two other components operative in making moral judgments and deciding to implement them. I call them (1) the volitional and (2) the developmental.

The volitional component simply attends to the fact that if we do not want to do something and have set ourselves against it, then no amount of reasoning or feeling will likely change that. The proper unfolding of all the activities and affectivities of moral reasoning presuppose a good will, a willingness to accept the consequences, and an openness to the consequences of a correct judgment of value. How we decide in freedom would require a phenomenological study all on its own. This is beyond our remit in this text, but it is a crucial aspect of affirming correct judgments of value, deciding for them, and implementing them in action.

The developmental aspect simply attends to the subject as developing. Chapter 6 examined the process of developing understanding. There, I identified a process of formulation, of generalization, of moving from description to explanation, of moving from lower to higher viewpoints, and of the necessity of facing the reality of inverse insights into a lack of expected intelligibility. All of these processes also impinge on the moral subject as understanding, judging, and implementing values. We develop as existential subjects; value judgments pass into the habitual texture of our minds. We consider originating values that seek terminal values. We become the good, wise person who is the criterion and standard of goodness as Aristotle put it. We develop or we decline. In decline we make self-interest or sensible satisfaction our criterion of goodness and enter into a spiral of decline where cognition, affectivity, and freedom reinforce one another in distortion and destruction.

In the end, a comprehensive treatment of the judgments of value of a moral person would have to include four dimensions: (1) A cognitive dimension of reasoning, logic, intelligence, understandings, and judgment (mind); (2) an affective dimension of desiring, persevering, inquiring, and feeling (heart); (3) a volitional dimension that recognizes that all thinking, judging, and acting presuppose a good will, a willingness to do the right thing, good decision-making, and a free commitment (will); and (4) a developmental dimension, which recognizes the moral agent as developing, as moving from one way of thinking, evaluating, and acting to another (spirit). In this text, I have focused on the first two dimensions.

Judgments of Value

Finally, I consider the characteristics of the judgment of value. Our questions of value intend judgments of value; our questions intend an appropriate, proportionate answer. The answer is expressed in a judgment of value. Who is the best professor? What is the best cell phone? What is the best way to study? How do I deal with this person who is harassing me? All of these questions intend judgments of value, and later, decisions and actions. It is perfectly normal, reasonable, and responsible; we do it all the time. We are constantly evaluating and passing many judgments of value. Are they justified, reasonable, and responsible; or are they self-interested, private, and arbitrary preferences?

Judgments of value are structurally similar to judgments of truth and share the same four characteristics of a judgment of truth. I have discussed these characteristics of judgment of truth (see chapter 6) and am now briefly applying them to judgments of value.

First, I already distinguished questions for intelligence and questions for reflection: the question for intelligence asks for further information and understanding; the question for reflection is the critical question of asking whether it is true or false. The question that intends a true judgment of value is of the critical kind. It is a deliberative question: is this good or bad? The appropriate answer must be simply yes or no, or something in between. The deliberation over evidence and arguments has been exhausted; it is time for a conclusion. The conclusion is a simple affirmation or denial: yes, this is good, or no, this is bad.

Second, no further content is added to the hypothesis except the affirmation or denial. When a jury declares a person guilty, they are not adding to the evidence; they are bringing all of the procedures, the witnesses, and the arguments to a closure in a yes or no answer. The judgment of value is of fundamental importance for what we are as seekers of value.

Third, we are personally responsible for our judgments of value just as for our judgments of truth. Our values define what we are and what we stand for at a deeper level than our judgments of truth. In affirming particular values, we constitute ourselves as morally good or evil persons. We have no excuses as we affirm values or their opposites freely, responsibly, and deliberately. We could have refrained from the judgment.

Fourth, in the judgment of value, knowledge comes to term. We judge that in this particular circumstance, this is the best professor, this is the best book, this is the best course of action in dealing with a relationship, and so on. Our knowledge and wisdom is built up of a multitude of such particular judgments of value. They bring the present deliberation about the current affair to a conclusion, but of course, further situations will arise and may have to be dealt with differently.

Conscience as Criterion

Two criteria of truth operate with reference to judgments of truth, a proximate and a remote criterion (see chapter 6). The proximate criterion is the actually unconditioned, the factually verified. If there is sufficient evidence, and if the evidence entails the conclusion, then the conclusion must be true. The remote criterion is broader. It depends on the proper unfolding of the pure, detached, unrestricted desire to know. The specific judgment presupposes a context of openness, genuineness, a willingness to face consequences, a freedom from bias and prejudice, and a readiness to ask all relevant questions and face the answers. Both of these criteria are also operative for deliberative insights and judgments of value. The proximate criterion of a moral value judgment is the sufficiency of the evidence for a specific judgment of value. Moral conscience is the remote criterion of value that operates at the level of deliberation.

Conscience is not just a little voice or a feeling of guilt. It is an awareness of the feeling of moral obligation and our fidelity or infidelity to that imperative in our deliberation, judgment, decision, and action. Conscience encompasses the whole process from beginning to end. I gave an account of the activities of questioning, deliberating, judging the value, deciding, and implementing in action. I analyzed the four components of the process, which are cognitive, affective, volitional and developmental. Conscience is both a feeling and an intellectual process, unfolding in responsible freedom. To be human is to be moral. We are aware of our good deeds as well as our twists and turns away from the good. Conscience is supreme in the sense that in the end, we are responsible for what we value and make of ourselves. We decide for ourselves what we are to make of ourselves.

Conclusion and Summary

Allow me just to summarize the argument so far. This text has been trying to identify the activity of human understanding and the different kinds of acts of understanding. I examined in detail acts of direct understanding by which the mind grasps an idea that emerges from the data and formulates it in a concept or theory or hypothesis. I moved on to the act of reflective understanding where we ask a critical question, assemble data, and line it up in terms of arguments that lead to a judgment of truth. In this chapter, I noted that a further question usually arises that involves a moral implication: what should I do about this judgment? Is this good or bad? Thus, I have analyzed the process from the question of value, to the deliberative insight, to the judgment of value in the various fields of social, political, economic, and moral life. I also analyzed the affective side of the desire to know, moral obligation, and the imperatives at work.

The method I have been using is that of self-appropriation. The data I have largely been talking about is the data of consciousness, namely, what is going on in the head of the person who is asking questions, trying to understand, and trying to do the right thing. I have been describing the mental dynamics of feelings, understanding, knowing, deciding, and acting as it actually occurs in human subjects. If we want to know about human knowing, surely the one place we should go to is the subject who is engaged in the dynamics of thinking, reflecting, and concluding. Knowing what is good and evil is part of the dynamic of knowing; it is simply asking and answering the question of value in various fields.

What is the fundamental dynamic pushing these activities forward? In earlier chapters, I spoke of the desire to know as that which initiates, motivates, directs, produces, and recognizes a correct answer. In this chapter I spoke of the desire to know value and the affectivity of being attentive, intelligent, reasonable, and responsible, which is how the desire to know manifests itself in the unfolding process of mental dynamics. In the moral field, obligation is a part of being human, not a conclusion of a syllogism; moral reasoning does not produce feelings of moral obligation out of nothing. A human person with no sense of moral obligation is classified as a psychopath and will probably end up institutionalized. It is as normal to feel a sense of moral obligation as it is to be curious about the truth or falsity of a proposition. One cannot prove that we are morally obliged by argument or reasoning; if it is not already there, it cannot be produced out of nothing. However, we do use moral arguments to discern what particular actions, policies, institutions, and values are good or bad.

Being sure about the foundations of value judgments does not mean that we can answer every question in moral philosophy. Judgments on specific moral questions demand a familiarity with the field. If we are passing moral judgments on financial policies, then we need to know economics. If we are passing judgment on medical matters, then we need to know medicine. If we are passing moral judgments on a person, we must be sure to know that person well. Value judgments presuppose the necessary and important judgments of fact on which they are based. Hence we need a bioethics, business ethics, medical ethics, justice and peace ethics, and an ethics that specializes in each area of human life.

This chapter has sketched a position on judgments of value that obviously is in need of greater elaboration, which I have done elsewhere.[14] I have mainly been concerned to show that values are not irrational, arbitrary, and a matter of personal choice, but can be understood, thought about, identified, argued about, defined, affirmed, and classified. There is both a cognitive and an affective element involved. These two elements are not necessarily opposed to one another. There is also an element of choice and the context of the developing person to be considered. It is important that a consideration of the scope and limits of human knowing should include our knowledge of good and evil.

14. Cronin, *Value Ethics.*

8

Cognitional Structure

A Chess Champion Blunders

On November 15th, 2014, Magnus Carlsen of Norway was playing the sixth game in the World Chess Championship against Vishy Anand of India. The series was tied at one win apiece. Carsen is White and the game develops into a Sicilian, where the Queens are exchanged but Carlsen has the advantage of having two Bishops and is pressing hard but does not yet have a clear win. To the amazement of analysts, on move 25 he blunders. He places his King on a square where it is vulnerable to a check, and Anand could take two pawns, get his Knight into a safe position, and swap Rooks. Carlsen knows immediately he has blundered, but he keeps his cool; the analysts and the audience hold their collective breadth. After five agonizing minutes, Anand plays a harmless rook pawn move—he did not see the blunder! After Carlsen's, next move the opportunity is no longer there. Carlsen goes on to win the game and in the end to win the series.

Anand was asked afterward why he did not see the opportunity for taking the pawn and checking the King. "I was focused on moving the rook pawn forward and did not see it. It was a positional game, and I did not expect tactics to play a part in this game. I did not see it!" Why did the analysts see it, and Carlsen saw it, but Anand not see it?

What does it mean to say, "I did not see it!"? Clearly Anand could see it; he was not blind. The board was visible in front of him; he could see the pieces clearly. He was not referring to physical seeing but to something more, namely, attending to and understanding. He did not attend to all of the possibilities: he was not looking at the whole board, he did not imagine checking the King, he forgot about the pawn in the center of the board, and he did not grasp the sequence of four moves that could have saved the game. He was focused on one possibility to the exclusion of others. He was thinking of position, not of tactics. One blunder by Carlsen was followed by a blunder by Anand![1]

How many times do we hear the admission: "I did not see it," "I did not think of that," or "My attention was elsewhere"? How many times do we blunder in our judgments because we do not pay attention, we do not see? But is seeing the same as understanding?

A Synthesis and Summary Thus Far

Descartes recommends a method of analysis and synthesis.[2] If one has a complicated problem, break it down into smaller parts and solve all the problems concerning the simpler parts; then, put them together again into a correct, clear, synthesis of the whole. I have examined the parts of the process of knowing in great detail; now it is time to put them together into a whole, coherent, correct, cognitional structure. This chapter will summarize what I have done so far, serving as a kind of synthesis and a reprise of all cognitional activities. There is a basic unity within the whole process of knowing. It is not the unity of a single activity, but the unity of a multiplicity of activities bound together in the dynamism of a single structure of knowing. I will show how all the pieces I have examined so far fit together into this dynamic unity.

These conclusions are based on the method of introspection or self-appropriation. This is not based on the authority of Aristotle or Aquinas or Kant or Lonergan. It is based on attention to how, in fact, questioning, studying, understanding, defining, criticizing, evaluating, and judging truth and value fit together into a coherent whole. There is actually nothing startling or original about this sequence of activities, as it is hard to imagine that any reader is unfamiliar with them. If we are to propose a theory of human knowing, surely it is appropriate to pay some attention to how knowing occurs! We tend to think that knowing is something different and higher and more magical than the mundane activities of questioning, studying, thinking, defining, and so on. We readily look to more exotic theories.

1. Details of the 2014 World Chess Championship, Game 6, can be found at the Internet Chess Club Archive. Accessed https://www.chessclub.com/.

2. Descartes, *Discourse on Method,* rules 2 and 3.

The Sequence of Activities that Constitutes One Knowing

Below I present a chronology of what I believe to be an inevitable, invariant sequence of activities, which together, constitute knowing truth and values. I cannot see what can be left out or what structural elements need to be added. I maintain that it is the only way to human knowing of truth and value:

1. *Questioning.* Intellectual human knowing starts with a question. Asking a question supposes that one is looking for an answer. The source of the question itself is the desire to know, which expresses itself in particular, specific questions. All men by nature desire understanding, as Aristotle said. All human knowing begins in wonder. If you do not ask the right question, you will not get the right answer.

2. *Experiencing.* We ask questions about what we have seen and heard, what we have experienced, what we have noticed, or what has aroused our curiosity. At a primal level, children point to something they see, ask what it is. As knowledge accumulates, we continue to ask questions about unfamiliar objects of sense, about ideas that we do not fully understand, and about the application of principles to concrete situations. At a certain point, we can ask questions about ideas, principles, and laws, but they all originated in experience. To verify the most extravagant of ideas, we are obliged to return to experience. Questions about the ultimate cause of the universe are a special group of questions, which are still rooted in an experience of the universe but seek ultimate rather than proximate causes. All knowing begins in the senses but does not end there.

3. *Information-gathering.* What do we have to do in order to answer our questions? Fairly clearly, we must do some research, gather information, observe, experiment, or do whatever is appropriate in that particular line of work. It may involve hours in the library, or in the laboratory, or on the Internet. It will involve thinking about the matter, organizing notes, highlighting important portions of a text, consulting others, group discussions, and more.

4. *Understanding.* We struggle to produce this act of understanding, line up images, memories, and possibilities, but in the end we wait for it to come, suddenly and unexpectedly. It may be appropriate to take a break, sleep on it, focus on something else, and allow new ideas to emerge. When the matter is properly disposed the insight emerges. The more appropriate the image, the closer we get to the idea.

5. *Formulation.* When we have understood, we struggle to put the idea into words, to find the best and most accurate expression of our discovery. We formulate a definition, a concept, an explanation, or a theory. We want to tell people about it or write an article or a book. We want others to also understand.

6. *Critical Question.* Unfortunately, a bright idea or concept is not knowledge. A clear and distinct idea is not necessarily true or correct or useful. An explanation is not necessarily the only explanation and might be incorrect. A further critical question needs to be asked. Is it right? Is it correct? Can it be verified? We shift gears into a critical mode.

7. *Reflection.* We assemble the evidence, line up our points, and face counterevidence. A historian will assemble texts, documents, letters, and files as evidence for his or her conclusions. A scientist will show the results of experiments or research, but the evidence must also be relevant to the conclusion, entail the judgment, and be adequate to the proposed affirmation.

8. *Reflective Insight.* We have a single reflective insight that unites all of the data, information, and evidence and links it to the conclusion. We grasp in one insight the necessity of affirming or denying.

9. *Judgment of Truth.* We pass a judgment, we posit a conclusion, we take a stand, we affirm or deny, and hopefully we reach a truth. The conclusion depends on the evidence, the arguments, and the data. The conditions for the truth of the conclusion are independent of the knower. The knower does not make it to be true by his or her knowing.

10. *Implications and Value.* What are we going to do about the finding? Is it useful or useless? Can it be applied to medicine, technology, or education? What is its value or worth? Can it be patented? Various questions of value emerge spontaneously.

11. *Evaluation of Value.* Answers do not come immediately. Again we need to do research, get the background information, check on the facts, seek competent advice, and review previous conclusions. We evaluate various possibilities: who will it benefit, does it represent progress or decline, will I profit, or will others profit from this? How do we balance financial gain with justice, equality, and freedom? We line up our evidence and arguments with counterarguments and alternative strategies.

12. *Deliberative Insight.* Then, the deliberative insight comes. We see that one alternative is by far the best. In one insight we see the connection between a vast amount of evidence for one of the alternatives. We know what is the best thing to do.

13. *Judgment of Truth.* Finally, we conclude with a judgment of value, a final affirmation of what is the best thing to do—who is the best person to vote for, what is the best book to read, what is the best thing to do for a troubled teenager, what to do with your newly discovered value, and so on.

The only major exception to be added to this list might be belief, namely, accepting something as true on the basis of trust in an authority. But even in belief we are being intelligent, reasonable, and responsible. In immanently generated knowledge, we rely on evidence and arguments. In belief, we rely on the trustworthiness of the source and the credibility of the belief.

Epistemologists often simplify their account of knowing. Some claim that all knowing is sensing, and then most of the above activities are interpreted as sense perceptions. While sensing is part of knowing, the part is never the whole. Others opine that knowing is understanding and only understanding, and that clear and distinct ideas are the criterion of truth. If that were correct, then activities 6–13 would be redundant. But we are performing such activities all the time. Knowing correctly is a rather protracted affair. A theory of human knowing has to include all of these activities in sequence.

It is a sequence in which the later stages emerge from the earlier and are dependent on them. Questioning precedes understanding, and understanding precedes formulation. It is hard to imagine formulating something that you have not understood, or understanding without a question that provokes the answer. Similarly, the question of truth precedes the reflective insight, which precedes the judgment of truth. It is hard to imagine making a judgment of truth without understanding the evidence in favor of it and the connection between the evidence and the conclusion. It is hard to imagine a judgment of value that is not preceded by a value question, a deliberation on the issue, a process of evaluation, and a deliberative insight into the sufficiency of the evidence for the conclusion.

The final product sweeps all of the preceding activities into a single knowing. The formulation puts together all that is of value in the questioning of the data and the relevant understanding. The judgment of truth puts everything together from sensing, to the activities of understanding, to reflective understanding in order to reach a single knowing of one truth. The judgment of value further gathers together all the activities of sensing, understanding and judging of truth in order to express a single specific judgment of value.

Cognitional Structure—Explaining the Table

Below, I chart how the different activities can be related to one another in one, instructive table that suggests fruitful relations and parallels. The table represents a summary of all that I have said about the activities of human knowing. The sequence of activities is presented on four levels: experiencing, understanding, judging truth, and judging values. The levels are distinguished by the kind of question that is being asked. They are different kinds of questions, so the activities required to find the solution vary. The insights differ, and thus, the products of the insight will differ. There is a unity in that the question is answered appropriately in the final judgment.

The four levels are parallel and proportionate to one another. We can fruitfully explore the similarities and differences between the three questions, the three kinds of activities in seeking an answer, the three acts of understanding that come suddenly and unexpectedly, and the three products of understanding in definitions, judgments of truth, and judgments of value. It does not seem that any activity or level can be entirely left out.

The notion of "levels" is an image or metaphor. It is presumably taken from the image of a house or a building. It captures the notion of successive degrees of dependence and of ascending from sensing, to understanding, to knowing truth, and to knowing value. However, it is not to be taken too literally; it is only a pedagogical image. The mind can hop from one idea, to another image, and to a judgment of value in an instant or be working at different levels at the same time. The mind is more flexible and dynamic than the image of levels in a building might suggest.

The table helps us to see the relationship between the activities. A theory is an explanation. Explanation relates things to one another. This table allows us to further understand each activity by seeing each of them in relation to the others and seeing the function of each part in relation to the whole unfolding of human knowing. We can see parallels and patterns suggested by the table. It is a bit like the periodic table of elements in chemistry where, even if one box is empty, we can still predict some of the properties the element will have, even if it has not yet been found.

Imperatives	Levels	Questions	Activities	Receptions	Expressions
Be Responsible	4. Level of Valuing	Questions of Value	Evaluating Goodness, Worth, Actions, etc.	Deliberative Understanding	Judgments Of Value
Be Reasonable	3. Level of Judgment	Questions for Reflection	Criticizing, Checking, Reviewing Data	Reflective Understanding	Judgments of Truth
Be Intelligent	2. Level of Understanding	Questions for Intelligence	Research, Observe, Study, Think, Draw	Direct, Inverse Understanding, Higher Viewpoints	Formulations, Definitions, Expressions
Be Attentive	1. Level of Experiencing	Desiring, Sensing, Instinct	Remembering, Imagining, Responding	Free Images	Utterances, Gestures, Groans

Table 1: Phenomenology of Human Understanding: Parts that Make up the Whole

curiosity   cf. p 165

Each row includes the questions, activities, receptions, and expressions of each level. Levels 2–4 all start with a question. The question inspires certain activities of researching, observing, thinking, criticizing or evaluating. But we cannot force an insight to come, and there might be a period of waiting and then a reception. Finally, we express the insight into a definition or a judgment. Again, note the parallel between the three questions, the activities, the reception, and the expression at the various levels.

The only level that does not fit this pattern is the level of sensing, where no questions arise and hence no intellectual activity ensues. There are sensitive desires, hunger, lust, fear, and the like. On this level, there are certainly activities of sensing, processing, and coordinating input from various senses. There is an interplay between memory, imagination, and instinct, and there is also an output, a response, an action, or an utterance. There is sense learning by remembering, by association, by imitation, by imagining, or by chance.

The table has a column for "activities" and a column for "receptions." I identified an active element in the process of knowing as well as a passive element. As active, we take the initiative in searching for a solution: we may do research, search databases, do experiments, or consult more knowledgeable colleagues. We do the thinking, the defining, and the clarifying. We line up the evidence and the counterevidence. We check, review, evaluate, and reevaluate. We use our memory, our imagination, and our intelligence. We criticize, question again, and move forward. We have to do the work and put in the hours.

But we cannot force insights to come: there is a passive element, a reception. We need to take a break, have cup of coffee, allow insights to emerge, and receive the gift of understanding. There are no rules for making groundbreaking discoveries.

In the first column of the table, are the imperatives appropriate to each level, which are immanent and operative in the activities at that level. These will be explained in detail below. The dynamic of the desire to know is manifested in these transcendental precepts. As with most things, there is a good way to perform these activities of knowing and a bad way. These norms are not learned from logic; they are learned from living and understanding. Jumping to conclusions without sufficient evidence usually results in having an uneasy feeling, a sense of guilt or of uncertainty, and may reveal that the conclusions are wrong.

All of these activities are conscious, and thus, it is the activity that determines the level of consciousness on which we are operating. We can distinguish an empirical level of consciousness where only activities of sensing are operating. We can distinguish an intellectual level of consciousness where we are asking questions for intelligence and seeking insights and

definitions. We can distinguish a rational level of consciousness characterized by the question for reflection, which leads to a judgment of truth. We
can also distinguish a level of moral consciousness where we are faced with
a moral dilemma, ask the question of value, reach judgments of moral value,
and follow our conscience. The levels of consciousness are distinguished
according to the intentionalities of the question, the activities that follow,
and the product that results.

This is a table of cognitional activities; thus, I have put aside decisions
and actions that are not an integral part of the cognitional process. They are
obviously of enormous importance, but I am concerned with knowing and
not about free, responsible deciding or the implementation of decisions. It is
true that if one does not make good decisions and carry them out that this
will have a deleterious effect on our knowing, and a process of distortion
and rationalization might occur. Conversely, good judgments of truth and
value pass into the habitual texture of the mind and one becomes a good
knower of truth and value.

Knowing has a structure. A structure is a whole made out of function-
ally interrelated parts.[3] Our clearest image of a structure is a house with a
foundation, three stories, and a roof. The parts have their own integrity but
are also subsumed into the unity of the whole. The whole is dependent on
the parts; the parts can only exist within the whole. Of course, like most images, the image of a building limps when it comes to details. Particularly, the
image of a building does not reflect the dynamic aspect of knowing. In the
case of cognitional structure each of the parts is dynamic, alive, and active.
The whole is also dynamic, always in action, always moving, always desiring
further understanding.

The table is an idealized version of what should happen and when it
should happen in the unfolding of knowing. We all know that in the topsy-
turvy of scientific or academic life, it is not always so neat and systematic. We
do not always follow the order or sequence; we work forward and backward.
We jump from one image or idea to another. We get distracted. Particularly
in a confused state—when we are not sure what we want to say, are not clear
about how to say it, or do not know whom we are addressing—our minds
may be all over the place. We do not know the wood from the trees. We do
not know the beginning from the end. It is the stage of frustration, which
pervades one's whole project. However, usually things slowly begin to fall
into place, an outline of topics begins to form, a picture of the whole comes
together, and consequently, a better grasp of the parts comes into view.

3. Lonergan, *Collection*, 205–21. See also Danaher, *Insight in Chemistry*, 47–55;
Gregson, *Lonergan*, 23–58.

Conversely, when it comes to simpler matters, many of the activities have either become habitual or are compacted into what seems to be a single activity. An experienced chess player does not need to perform each of these activities separately, or sequentially, in order to make a move. Most of the principles of good play have passed into the habitual texture of the mind. He or she is familiar with the position and has thought it out before. The player remembers the alternatives and the consequences; all coalesce into a few seconds of thought before a move is made. Much of our own thinking in our own area of expertise has also become habitual; we perform the activities in seconds. It is only when something new arises that we have to stop and think. Our pedagogical principle is to differentiate in order to integrate. We move from the stumbling efforts of the novice to the polished performance of the professional.

Immanent and Operative Norms

The naturalistic fallacy claims that one cannot argue from a premise of "what is" to a conclusion of "what ought to be," that one cannot deduce value from fact. This is logically correct. We cannot have something in the conclusion of an argument that is not there in some way in the premises. We cannot prove that there is an obligation by using a syllogism unless the obligation is already in the premises. However, my approach is not derived from a syllogism. I am showing that *there is* an obligation and an imperative already operative in asking questions and seeking answers. It is simply a fact that these obligations operate; observation and attention to the process of knowing reveal these norms in action. Any student knows that there is a good way to write an essay and a bad way. The best way is to prepare notes in advance, make an outline, think clearly about the argument, present the points in order, get advice, check alternatives, review the paper, and present it to the professor. Such a paper results in an A grade. Alternatively, a student can leave the task until the last day, cut and paste from various sources, fill up the pages with some kind of relevant information, yet draw no conclusions. Such a paper results in C grade, or worse. The same is true with doing laboratory experiments, observing human behavior in the human sciences, thinking out a philosophical position, or in any area of human knowing: there is a good way to go about it and a bad way. Norms, obligations, standards, and sanctions are operative, and we can experience and observe these imperatives at work in any unfolding research projects.

The dynamic is the desire to know, which pervades all of the activities and is satisfied only when knowing is reached. The stages of knowing have their own immanent and operative norms: be attentive, be intelligent, be reasonable, and be responsible. These norms are immanent, because they are part of the very structure of knowing; they come from the inside rather than from the outside and are operative in any human knowing. All learning presupposes the operation of these obligations. Guided by what I have already elucidated about the complete process of knowing, I further explain these immanent and operative norms:

1. *Be Attentive.* In general, this means to be alert, to notice data that *be curious* might prove significant, to be sensitive, to use all of the senses and to exploit their potential to the full, and to extend the range of the senses by using instruments. Our knowing begins in sense experience and continues to depend on the senses for verification. All scientific conclusions must have some sensible consequences. Conclusions are verified by pointing to some data through observation, experiment, or research.

This is an imperative to be attentive to all the data and not to exclude on a priori grounds any data. Most scientists attend to the data of the external senses; they rule out of court appeals to mental activities as unverifiable. However, the data of consciousness are equally part of what is given in experience. Just as we can attend to dissecting a frog, so we can attend to dissecting the act of understanding. It is obscurantism to brush aside data just because it does not fit within our already-established categories. In our example from the chess game Anand was attending to certain possibilities but not to others: he missed his chance.

Significance is grasped by intelligence. Animals have senses and are attentive but only to what is relevant to their survival and the satisfaction of their needs in the biological pattern of experience. Our senses are under the guidance of the desire to know, in the context of the intellectual pattern of experience. Seeing is guided by a question, which directs us to what is relevant, significant, and of possible importance. Searching is guided by the expectations of theory. For example, theories formulated in the 1960s suggested where and how to find the Higgs boson. It was consequently found in July 2012 using the Large Hadron Collider. I reject entirely the principle of the empty head, which presumes that theory will interfere with the objectivity of seeing. Empiricists seem to adopt this position because they think verification is in the seeing, and not in understanding the significance of what is seen. But the work of intelligence is not interference, but rather, is necessary guidance toward understanding the intelligible in the sensible.

All the data must be explained. It may not be explicable in terms of classical laws, but then we have recourse to the statistical method. There are degrees of intelligibility attainable in different areas, from description to explanation, to different kinds of causality. We do not expect the same precision in ethics as in mathematics. The sensible simply as such is significant in that it is that about which we ask questions and from which we abstract answers.

2. *Be Intelligent.* Our ideas must be coherent; they must fit together with the data, facts, and definitions of our own discipline and area of study. Logic is useful to determine the coherence of definitions, divisions, arguments, and conclusions within a given system. Mathematics usually plays the same role in the empirical sciences. One of the normal developments in thinking is to move from confusion to clarity. We discover many inconsistencies by simple clear, straight thinking about a problem. Here, I am drawing attention to the imperative to be clear, precise, sophisticated, differentiated, and coherent in moving toward a correct formulation.

Being intelligent means being open to possibilities, looking at a problem from every angle, and making connections. It involves thinking outside the box. Often our imagination and memory confine us to limited perspectives; they act as blinders excluding other possibilities. Intelligence is an infinite openness to make or to become all things.

3. *Be Reasonable.* We can assert as true only that for which there is sufficient reason or justification. The critical question arises spontaneously; possibilities have to be evaluated based on whether they are correct and true. Judgment is the criterion of what is true and real, not imagination, not our sense of the real, not feeling, not tradition, not prejudice, not profit. These and many other extraneous influences tend to skew the process from evidence to conclusions.

Affirmation adds only the yes or no of judgment; it does not include an image that goes along with the judgment. Affirming the suitability of an image is often a separate affair. To affirm that a person has a soul is a judgment; to imagine the soul as a ghost in a machine is quite another.

4. *Be Responsible.* Questions arise as to what is the best thing to do in a certain situation, for the good of the person and for the good of the family or society. They are questions of value and above all of the moral value of the person as free and responsible. We are conscious of an obligation to do the right thing. If we do it, we are at peace; if we don't do it, we feel guilty, uneasy, or remorseful. These feelings emerge spontaneously in the child and are formed by a process of moral education as to what is right and wrong. Aristotle claimed that the whole of moral education consisted in teaching persons to feel good in doing good deeds, and to feel guilty in right measure for evil deeds.[4] Only a psychopath does not experience the feeling of moral obligation. No amount of reasoning will produce such feelings if they are not there already. Arguments,

---

4. "Hence the importance (as Plato says) of having been trained in some way from infancy to feel joy and grief at the right things: true education is precisely this" (Aristotle, *Nicomachean Ethics* 1104b15).

principles, and definitions such as found in Kant might help in the judgment of what is the right thing to do. They may direct feelings of moral obligation, but they do not produce them. Feelings are not very responsive to syllogistic arguments.[5] Value questions enter our lives in many ways. Being responsible in our value judgments permeates our daily activities.

These four norms are operative at every stage of knowing and in every discipline or subdivision of knowing. They operate at the level of common sense: an argument in a pub in its own confused way applies these norms. Someone caught in a contradiction has lost. Another person points out data that has not been considered, counterexamples are produced, or demands a better definition of the terms. The norms operate in a more refined way in science, in the human sciences, and in philosophy. They operate in all cultures, in every nation, for all peoples, and at all stages in the development of humanity.

These immanent and operative norms are also sanctions; those who violate the norms are punished. There is a self-correcting process at work in the unfolding of any area of human knowing. I opened this chapter with a chess blunder; it was only a blunder because it was a world championship match. An average player would not even have noticed. There is a punishment for making mistakes. We learn to play chess by getting beaten and resolving to learn from our mistakes. The same dynamic is operative in all fields of scholarship. The professor who gets a bad review on a book likely deserves it; the professor tries to learn from the experience in order to improve his or her argument.

There is something fundamentally wrong with being inattentive, unintelligent, unreasonable, or irresponsible. It is not the wrongness of breaking a law but of a subject being incoherent and self-contradictory. We are not really free to choose between being attentive or inattentive, intelligent or stupid, reasonable or unreasonable, responsible or irresponsible. Any argument presupposes that we are trying to be attentive, intelligent, reasonable, and responsible. There are very few authors or writers who explicitly espouse a position of being stupid or unreasonable!

A Verifiable Cognitional Theory

It may sound ambitious to talk of a verifiable cognitional theory, but that is the point I am advocating by reviewing the evidence, understanding the implications, and affirming the conclusions. We usually use the term "verifiable" with reference to scientific theories, but if we accept the data of

---

5. "In general, feeling seems to yield not to argument but only to force" (Aristotle, *Nicomachean Ethics*, 1179b29).

Archimedes .

consciousness as data, then we can talk of evidence for or against cognitional theories. In what sense can we speak of a verifiable cognitional theory?

History has offered various theories about how the mind works and the processes by which we come to know. We can distinguish and state the theory of Plato, Aristotle, Aquinas, Descartes, Hume, Kant, phenomenology, materialism, and postmodernism. All of these are different, and many of them are contradictory to one another. But how do we choose between these theories? Is it just a question of liking one and not liking the other? If a scientist is faced with five different theories as to why a plane crashed, he knows that it is not a matter of indifference as to which is true. It is a matter of safety—the cause must be identified and the correct theory or explanation faced with all of its implications.

Similarly, it is not a matter of choice, or a matter of indifference, as to which cognitional theory is true. Truth has consequences. In chapters 10 and 11 I will build an epistemology on the basis of my cognitional theory. From there, one can build a metaphysics and an ethics. All in all, I am aiming at a philosophy of life, a wisdom, a worldview, with sound ethical principles. Cognitional theory makes a difference for education, for method, and for living in the real world. We have to do what the scientist does and look for the relevant evidence, in this case by paying attention to how the human mind actually works and how sequences are involved that begin in questioning and lead to correct answers. Is knowing understanding correctly? Or is it remembering, sensing, imposing ideas on reality, an intuition, or a mystery? Each answer leads into a different direction and to a different philosophy of life.

True knowledge is attained only in a correct judgment. The question now is whether this statement is verifiable, and if so, how? As with any judgment, we can suppose it as a hypothesis and see what is necessary to turn it into a verified conclusion. In brief, my argument has been to appeal to evidence that is available to anyone of sufficiently cultured consciousness, that is, anyone who is conscious of his or her own thinking processes. The evidence is right there in our mental activities. We can identify the critical question and ask all relevant questions. Having done all of that, I am justified in saying that there is sufficient evidence that entails the conclusion that knowledge is only attained in a true judgment.

Scientific conclusions are often hypothetical and probable: I would like to show that our conclusions about the process of knowing based on the data of consciousness are more certain and permanent than those of any of the empirical sciences. In the context of our contemporary culture, the empirical sciences are highly respected. They are considered to be successful, methodical, objective, and the most trustworthy kind of knowledge. All one has to do to bolster his or her argument is to call in a scientific expert to prove the point or get a computer printout. By contrast, the assertions of philosophers are often considered to be unverifiable, personal speculation, unreliable opinions, and thus, the polar opposite of the precise, verifiable formulas of science. In light of the position I have now reached, allow me to contrast the procedures of the empirical scientist with the procedures I have recommended for the philosopher and evaluate how they match up on specific points of method. Which is the most reliable, the most certain, and the most foundational?

1. *Effects of New Data.* In the empirical sciences there is always the possibility of new data requiring adjustments or extensions of a theory. Much of the history of science consists in these constant adjustments as new data emerges. New data can totally overthrow an existing theory, as the use of the telescope showed that Aristotle's theory of the perfection of the heavenly bodies was simply mistaken. New data can require extensions, adjustments, qualifications, or exceptions to be made to an existing theory. Thus, a scientific theory is always open to revision because of the possibility of further contrary data becoming available.

Does this apply to cognitional theory? Can our account of human knowing be overthrown by further data becoming available? The data on which I have grounded this account of human knowing are the data of consciousness. I have been concerned with identifying activities rather than contents. The contents could embrace an infinity, but there is a basic simplicity and unity about the activities. There is one activity of physical seeing, but there is an infinity of shapes, colors, and forms to be seen. There is one activity of human understanding, but there is a quasi infinity of relations, causes, connections, substances, and the like to be understood. There is one form of reflective understanding leading to a judgment, but the content of the judgment includes all that has been known, is known, or could be known. It is not necessary to explore all the contents of the act of understanding to grasp its basic nature. It is necessary, as we have seen, to examine some examples very carefully; we need to identify, appropriate, discriminate, and relate these activities. However, after attaining a facility in self-appropriation, there comes a point of diminishing marginal returns where examining further examples adds little or nothing to our understanding. Hence, new data has a very limited effect on the conclusions of cognitional theory. We have exhaustively examined the relevant data, allowed further questions to arise, and found that every example of human knowing must conform to this basic pattern of operations. No conceivable new datum of consciousness can arise to require a radical revision of our cognitional structure.

2. *Not Open to Basic Revision.* Empirical sciences are open to basic revision of their principles and axioms, whereas cognitional theory is not. For scientific theory to be explanatory, it must rest on certain basic axioms,

definitions, and assumptions. Euclid clearly defined these for himself before setting up his system of theorems and corollaries. But where did these principles and postulates come from? What if we revise them? If we start from other principles, we get different systems of geometry. Today there are many such systems. Newton assumed a certain basic understanding of time and space; Einstein changed this basic understanding and produced a new physics. Quantum physics has added a further twist to the tale. Science is always open to basic revision, because the principles on which it is founded can be reexamined and redefined. Paradigm shifts are to be expected in the development of the empirical sciences. Such shifts do not prove the irrationality of scientific method; on the contrary, at times, a total shift in presuppositions, concepts, axioms, and definitions is necessary for the progress of science.

By contrast, my account of cognitional structure is not open to such basic revision because any attempt at revision invokes the basic structure it is trying to revise. By not being open to basic revision, I mean that the structure of terms and relations that are implicitly defined in the table is not open to fundamental change. One can neither conceive of another level being interposed, nor of a level being left out, nor of the sequence of activities being changed or reversed. In its basic structure, this account of human knowing cannot be fundamentally wrong.

I am not saying that this account of cognitional structure cannot be improved. Hopefully, it will become easier and more common to become aware of activities of knowing, to improve the terminology available, and to compare and contrast various accounts. There may be many subtleties that could be included. As people become more familiar with self-appropriation, there ought to be a great improvement in the methods of teaching, in the choice of examples, and in the depth of awareness of what is going on within us when we know. Perhaps, cognitive psychology and neuroscience will break free of materialist presuppositions and become a very fruitful source for the study of the subtleties of intelligence in act. But whatever improvements might arise, there can be no change that will subvert, replace, or fundamentally alter the structure in its basic outline. In case this sounds like an arrogant claim, I can show that any attempt at basic revision will only serve to reinforce the structure.

Imagine a hypothetical reviser who seeks a new theory about the structure of human knowing. The reviser will have to explain this new theory in order to communicate it to others. This will require defining terms and relations and putting them together in a coherent way. The reviser will have to appeal to data to show that the new theory is verifiable and better than the old one. And he or she will have to show that the new theory is true and can be justified and verified in the data.

Thus any hypothetical reviser will not be able to challenge this account of cognitional structure without invoking (1) the experience of data, (2) the intelligent formulation of theory, and (3) the verification of theory by recourse to data. There is something that is very basic and unavoidable about the three levels of experiencing, understanding, and judging. Even a hypothetical reviser must be attentive, intelligent, reasonable, and responsible. This account of human knowing is coherent with the activities which constitute human knowing; it is not open to basic revision.

3. *Description and Explanation.* In chapter 5, I noted that all of the sciences proceed from description, to explanation in the technical sense, and then return to description. In other words, the empirical sciences start by relating things to our senses, move to relating things to one another, and finally return to relating things to our senses for verification or application. In the normal unfolding of empirical science there is a divergence between description and explanation, between common sense and theory. Explanation introduces a hypothetical element, a supposition, or a theory, which is then verified by reference back to the data of sense. But the hypothetical element introduced is never totally eliminated by the verification. Galileo repeated his experiments many times, but he did not perform the experiment for every distance, for every time period, or for every possible material. He did it for a sufficient number of times to reach a reasonable conclusion.

What is important for us here is to note the significant difference between the procedure of the empirical sciences and the procedure of cognitional theory. I noted that the empirical sciences start with description, move to explanation, and then return to description. But cognitional theory is an area where description and explanation coincide rather than diverge. I have defined description, as relating things to ourselves and explanation as relating things to one another. Hence, description in the case of the data of consciousness is explanatory at the same time as being descriptive. If relating things to myself is description, and we admit that I am also a thing, then relating things to myself is a particular case of relating things to one another. Hence, the movement away from description to explanation does not happen in cognitional theory, because these two procedures of knowing converge rather than diverge. Examining cognitional structure is explanatory in the sense of relating things to one another, but it is also descriptive in that one of these things is oneself.

Because of this convergence in cognitional theory between description and explanation, no hypothetical element is introduced. Each and every instance of knowing is a verification of the explanation that I have given of cognitional structure. As Lonergan puts it, "Explanation on the basis of consciousness can escape entirely the merely supposed, the merely postulated, the merely inferred."[6]

4. *Antecedent/Consequent*. In empirical science the logical form of the demonstration is often in the form of positing the consequent. Strictly speaking, the logic of this procedure is invalid. In the hypothetical syllogism one can posit the antecedent and the consequent follows; but one cannot on logical grounds alone, posit the consequent and claim that the antecedent follows. The form of positing the consequent is:

> If A, then B. (If he is an Irishman, then he eats porridge.)
>
> But B. (He eats porridge.)
>
> Therefore A. (Therefore he is an Irishman.)

It is easy to see that there might be other people who eat porridge who are not Irishmen. Similarly, Einstein on the basis of his theory of general relativity predicted that light rays passing through the gravitational field of the sun would be bent. Eddington took his photographs in 1919 and showed that light from the stars was, indeed, bent. Everyone considered Einstein to be vindicated. Strictly speaking, this is not valid. It is an example of positing the consequent. There could have been another explanation for the bending of light. The only reason that it seems valid is that it is very difficult to visualize any other law that would explain these measurements. Much of classical scientific thinking is under the shadow of positing the consequent.

The basic logical form of my argument is always in the form of positing the antecedent. From the antecedent the consequent follows of necessity. If A, then B. But A. Therefore B. My position on knowing is on a more solid basis than Einstein's general theory of relativity!

5. *Intelligible/Intelligent*. We can attain a valid knowledge of substances, causes, laws, essences, and the like. Our universe is contingent, not necessary; whatever knowledge we attain happens to be the case, but it could have been different. The intelligibility we grasp is extrinsic, passive, and secondary. Often the scientist attains correlations and not causes—that x follows y but not why x follows y. Even Aquinas acknowledged the difficulty we have in knowing material substances even though they are the proper object of the human intellect. We know them from the outside.

By contrast, our knowledge of our own process of knowing is a grasp of intelligence in act, that is, of our being intelligent. The laws of the mind are not imposed from outside, not passive or extrinsic, but an intelligent and rational process in itself. We learn of intelligence not from the outside but from the inside as active intelligent beings. We too are contingent and

6. Lonergan, *Insight*, 358.

could have been different. But we are intelligent! We can grasp the passive, extrinsic intelligibility of our universe and the active, intrinsic processes of intelligent and rational acts.

6. *Belief.* In empirical science, surprisingly, we are usually dependent on belief. No scientist can ever repeat all of the experiments of his predecessors. Nor can he check all the research of his colleagues. Nor can he check the reliability of his tables, instruments, and equipment. Science is a collaboration of specialists. Much has to be taken on trust; it is a matter of belief rather than immanently generated knowledge. Hence it is open to mistakes, prejudice, fraud, and the self-interest of others.

But in cognitional structure, we are relying on our own immanent experience, understanding, and judging; we do not have to rely on what any scientist, philosopher, or author says about knowing. We can reach a personal foundation, which cannot be skewed by others.

The above comparisons have shown that scientific theory is always open to basic revision because of the potential revision of principles or paradigms; it is always open to adjustments and revision because of the possibility of new data. Scientific theory attains probabilities rather than certainties, because of using the method of positing the consequent, because of the hypothetical element that cannot be eliminated, because understanding any concrete event involves a combination of classical and statistical methods, because science often attains correlations rather than real causes, and because science is a collaborative effort and one can never personally verify everything for oneself.

In contrast, explanation based on the data of consciousness escapes many of these limitations. In self-appropriation we grasp directly intelligence in act; it is a personal experience and in no way dependent on belief. Theory based on the data of sense suffers the limitations outlined above. Theory based on the data of consciousness is special; it is on a firmer basis and is not open to fundamental revision.

All of these points show that, paradoxically, we can be surer of our conclusions about the structure of knowing than we can be about the conclusions of the empirical sciences. In a culture where science is so highly respected and where theories about knowing are so diverse, this is a surprise. Yet it highlights the fruits of the method of self-appropriation; we can establish for ourselves the foundations of our knowing and keep in perspective the frequent upheavals in other areas of the physical and human sciences.

Performance and Content

The pillar of our approach to the theory of knowledge has been self-appropriation. The foundation of self-appropriation has been to start with the actual activities of human knowing—to describe them, define them, relate them together, and formulate an explanatory account, where at each stage and for each term there will be a validating reference to the data of consciousness. The key, then, to this approach has been coherence between the activities and the theory: the activities verify the theory; the theory explains, relates, and objectivizes the activities.

There is only one basic set of interrelated activities that produce true human knowing. It is one human knowing, whether it is common sense, empirical science, or philosophy. It is the same human knowing whether it is Aristotle or Sartre, Ireland or America, the first century or the twenty-first. If there is only one set of essentially unrevisable activities, there is also only one explanatory theory that adequately relates, defines, and objectivizes these activities. Hence, there can be only one theory of knowledge that is coherent with the actual activities involved in human knowing. I am not talking about differences in terminology or detail, but about the fundamental stance on the structure of knowing.

It follows, as night follows day, that in all other theories of knowledge, which differ fundamentally from the above, there will arise an incoherence between what the philosopher is actually doing and the theory he or she uses to explain these activities. There will be a fundamental incoherence between performance and content.

The performance of the activities of knowing are a constant. These are the activities of attending to data (doing research, making observations, performing experiments), of being intelligent (grasping the relevant and leaving aside the irrelevant information, defining terms clearly, thinking things through to the end, moving from images to ideas, and from ideas to concepts and theories), being reasonable (checking results, evaluating, asserting, denying, proposing as true, publishing and proclaiming), and being responsible (asking about values, deliberating about worth or goodness, passing responsible judgments of value). These are the activities Descartes actually performed as he sat down to write his *Meditations*, or when he instructed the Queen of Sweden about his new philosophy. These are the activities performed by Hume as he worked on his *Enquiry Concerning Human Understanding*. He was not satisfied with what Locke had written; he thought he could do better. He wanted to show that his understanding was indeed better, clearer, truer, more to the point, and more radical. These are the activities performed by Kant in his study at Königsberg and in his daily walks through the town.

In his theoretical account of knowing, Descartes thought that clear and distinct ideas were the criterion of truth. However, if he had attended to his own knowing, he would have found many clear and distinct ideas which were not true, and many confused and vague ideas which were true. He taught a distinction between matter and thought, but was this based on understanding correctly or on the imperatives of the imagination? He taught that science could be deduced from principles of philosophy, but is that the way scientists actually work?

Hume taught that all mental activities could be reduced to sensation. But were his books produced by sensation or by thinking, criticizing, reflecting, and judging? Are images and ideas really the same? What about the creativity of his own work, the evaluations, the concepts, the judgments, the progress, the truth or error? His theory of knowledge did not seem to allow him the possibility of writing about a theory of knowledge.

Descartes and Hume did not use a method of self-appropriation; they did not check their conclusions—except partially perhaps—against the data of their own consciousness. We cannot really expect them to have done so in their age of theoretical thinking. Nevertheless, we do have to point out the fundamental incoherence in these philosophers between the activities they performed and the content of their theories of knowledge. Because they did not perform self-appropriation, they could not articulate the dialectic unfolding in their own minds, between sense and intelligence, looking and knowing, the animal sense of the real and the real as the correctly affirmed, and the world of immediacy and the world mediated by meaning. Being unaware of this dialectic, they were unable to resolve it. And so their theories reflect this unresolved dialectic, containing elements that are truly and correctly affirmed that are mixed in with other elements of imagination and the animal criterion of the real.

The same critique can be aimed at postmodernists who claim that our world is fragmented and incoherent; that we cannot have metanarratives; and that philosophy can only provide one little idea about one area, and even still remains contextual, temporary, suspect, subjective, and relative. They claim that there can be no overarching vision of the universe and human life that is true and permanent.

But what are they doing? Where did this vision come from? Surely, they are asking about previous philosophies, criticizing their optimistic assertions and rejecting them as wrong. Surely, they are thinking about a philosophy that should replace such naïve optimism and they articulate a position of skepticism, of pessimism about general truths, of the fragility of human knowing, and of the possibility of being wrong. They believe this postmodern position to be better than what preceded it. They hold that postmodernism represents progress in the development of human thought and culture. They hold that it is true and that what preceded it is false and to be rejected. In rejecting the old optimism and in accepting a new pessimism, they are actually asking questions about what they have experienced in order to understand and express it into words. They have been asking what is right and wrong, what is true and false, what is best and worst. They have come to a clear conclusion and argue for the truth of that conclusion on the basis of reflecting on the merits and demerits of different positions. They have inevitably performed the activities of questioning, experiencing, understanding, and judging truth and value; they have spontaneously used the structure of the human mind in the search for truth. But they have sadly arrived at a theory of human knowing that is in stark contradiction to how they actually arrived at these conclusions. According to their theories, metanarratives are indefensible illusions; yet, they are actually foisting on the innocent public the most outrageous metanarrative of all, namely, that there can be no metanarratives.

9

Understanding Misunderstanding

IMAGINING THE REAL—AUGUSTINE

"I came to the point where I conceived of You as existing in the physical reality of space. I still preferred to believe that you were incorruptible, invulnerable, and unchangeable, as opposed to being corruptible, vulnerable, and variable. I considered whether Your being was infused into the world, or diffused infinitely through the universe. The problem was that I could not imagine a being that transcended material reality might be real. If You were outside of everything, I reasoned that You were altogether nothing. If a body could be taken out of a void, so that the void was truly empty of material, earth, water, air, or star matter, would not such a place be no more than a spacious nothing?

These mental wanderings were thick-headed and not clear even to myself. Whatever did not have measurable bulk, whatever could not be diffused, whatever could not contract or expand to some sort of dimensions—such things, I thought, must be altogether nothing. My faith was no larger than what my eyes could see. It never occurred to me that the very mental processes I used to reason such things were real enough to do wondrous things and form marvelous images, yet it did not have a form of the sort I was demanding that my God fit.

That was my guess, since I was unable to consider an alternative. But my idea was false."[1]

---

1. Augustine, *Confessions*, 117–18.

Conflict and Disagreement

Given my account of human knowing up to this point, one might expect that if philosophers followed these injunctions, then philosophy would advance systematically, cumulatively, and progressively and we would become more wise and good with every passing generation. But it does not seem that philosophy is progressing in such a manner and may well be moving in the opposite direction. Every generation seems to be seeking a new and different system of philosophy than previous ones. Even great philosophers of the same generation with the same language and culture have disagreed deeply and irrevocably with one another—think of Plato and Aristotle, Aquinas and Bonaventure, or Hume and Kant. The history of philosophy is very much a history of misunderstanding, of disagreement, and of contradictions and confusions. Surely it is not because of the lack of intelligence of philosophers, nor their lack of seriousness or dedication to the cause. They are supposed to be the wisest of human beings, were sincere in their convictions, and were conscientious and methodical. They were not indifferent, stupid, careless, or slipshod in their work. So why so much misunderstanding?

In contemporary times the same divisions are evident. We have schools of philosophers who cannot even talk to one another, as they differ on basic starting points upon which one might initiate a dialogue. They have no foundations, no common ground or principles; some even rejoice in having no foundations. We have no shortage of contradictions, disputes, misunderstandings, and controversies. We have ever new and varied perspectives—hermeneutical, existential, empirical, idealistic, skeptical, therapeutic, and pragmatic to mention a few—but nothing seems to bring philosophers together. There is little they seem to be able to agree on. Surely if philosophers are all aspiring to be wise, they should be able to talk to one another, understand one another and work out differences, and agree on a common position. But it does not seem to be that way. The war between the giants and the gods that Plato spoke about continues apace. So why are there still such disagreements, divisions, and contradictions?

My account of understanding "understanding" must provide some explanation for such misunderstanding, and thus, can strengthen my account by showing that it can also understand "misunderstanding." Can we identify the source of such deeply intractable disagreements, controversies, and confusions? Obviously many things can go wrong. I will divide them into minor sources of misunderstanding, and the major source, which involves a dialectic between sensing and understanding. The minor sources are many, various, and familiar. The major source is more difficult, much deeper, and more fundamental and pervasive.

Minor Sources of Misunderstanding

The minor sources of disagreement are relatively easily identifiable. Usually, it is clear where and what went wrong, and it is relatively easy to admit error, to correct it, and to reach an agreement. We all make mistakes and learning from mistakes is as much a part of philosophy as it is of life itself. I am not going to go into great detail of these various aberrations; rather, I will just give some examples so that I can clear away the clutter and concentrate exclusively on the major source of disagreement.

Mistakes can take place at the level of collecting the data, doing the research, making observations, or getting questionnaires filled out and correlated. The data can be incomplete; it can be biased; and it can be skewed by expectations, wish fulfillment, denial, repression, or prejudice. The data can be inadequate as a basis for the conclusions drawn; it can be fraudulent, one-sided, or a pack of lies. The wrong questions might be asked, contrary data might not be taken into account, relevant data might be excluded, or the classification process might be inappropriate.

At the stage of understanding and formulating, one might be jumping to conclusions, oversimplifying, accepting wrong interpretations, making mistakes in the calculations, or using undefined terms or simplistic definitions. There might be confusion between prose, poetry, play, art, religion, and morals. Aristotle expounded on how to make correct definitions and divisions but do we follow his advice? Data can be forced to justify preexisting positions rather than to seek correct understanding.

Mistakes can be made when we are critically reflecting with a view to affirming a judgment. Arguments, inferences, and implications can be misconceived, and thus, reach wrong conclusions. Fallacies may enter into the arguments. Here there is a role for clear logical principles, for proper deductions and inductions. We may be influenced by tradition and not by the evidence. We can be subject to group think. We must think the matter through to the end, until no further relevant questions arise.

When it is a matter of value judgments other factors may intrude. One might be inclined to favor economic values over moral values. One might be starting with a skewed idea of human happiness. Likes and dislikes, pleasure and pain, true and false, and values and disvalues may operate on our judgments in an undifferentiated confusion. One's priorities in life might already be distorted, thus, leading to further distortions; one may be seeking selfish value and not that of the family, the community, or the common good. One might be overcome by the influence of political correctness and go along with conventional wisdom without making a personal evaluation. Mistakes can be induced not just from within the internal process of understanding and knowing but because of the social and psychological context in which the intellect operates. Feelings are a powerful influence in life and might distort the pure, detached, unrestricted desire to know. Resentment, power, bias, hidden agendas, and the like might twist our motivation and conclusions. Personal ambition, careerism, pride, hatred, and revenge all amazingly interfere with objective scholarship.

Roger Bacon (1212–1292), in his *Opus Majus,* enumerates four principal causes of human ignorance and failure to attain truth: subjection to unworthy authority, the influence of habit, popular prejudice, and making a show of apparent wisdom to cover one's own ignorance. Francis Bacon (1561–1626) outlined the mistakes that captivate the human mind and need to be purified:

1. The Idols of the market place, where words or language become an obstacle to new understanding;

2. The Idols of the Cave, when we can only see things from our own narrow point of view;

3. The Idols of the Tribe, when the will, affections, or wishful thinking interfere with the thinking process;

4. The Idols of the Theatre, which refer to false philosophical systems that we have to discard if we are to think straight.[2]

It is not easy to get everything right. But the above sources of misunderstanding can be identified, named, and overcome. These mistakes can be made but usually can be rectified. Most people can recognize these kinds of disagreement. We can recognize these in others even if we find it hard to eliminate them from our own thinking. And yet these sources of misunderstanding do not seem to adequately explain the confusion and disagreement between philosophers in the modern and contemporary period.

Dialectic at the Heart of Human Knowing

The quotation from Saint Augustine provides an entry into what I think is the major source of disagreement and misunderstanding. Augustine had accepted the materialism of the Manichees in the early stages of his intellectual quest. Now he is thinking his way out of it, but it is a deep, spiritual struggle. Can something be real if it is not material? If God is real, then he must be material in some sort of a way. How could something beyond material reality be real? Beyond material reality there is simply "a spacious nothing," a void, a vacuum. He states, "My faith was no larger than my eyes could see."

2. Bacon, *The New Organon* 1.33–101.

Note how he puts it, "I could not *imagine* a being that transcended material reality might be real" (italics mine). With help from neo-Platonist writings, Augustine was able to liberate himself from the grip of the imagination. He comes to realize that imagination is not the criterion of what is real, but rather, intelligence and judgment: we know not by imagining but by understanding. Thus, he was enabled to overcome this instinctive imperative that for something to be real it had to be material. He was set free to do his psychological introspection on the mind itself, to write on memory, on truth, on evil, on the Trinity, on free will, and on many other topics.

This struggle between imagination and judgment is one that every human person must negotiate. Like Augustine we all start as children in the world of sensation and imagination: something is real if we can chew it, throw it, touch it, or see it. We are all born as materialists! But soon we start naming, understanding, and making judgments about what is true and false. Then, we have a struggle as we encounter tensions between the criterion of sense and the criterion of judgment. It is a struggle to enter into the intellectual pattern of experience and to be at home there; we struggle to balance the expectations of imagination with the imperatives of intelligence. It is very difficult to identify and communicate this struggle, because it is not a direct insight we are seeking but an inverse insight—an insight into misunderstanding. We are looking for something that is not there, but it should be there.

Aquinas, in his efforts to explain human knowing, often contrasted it to animal knowing on the one side, and divine or angelic knowing on the other. Angelic knowing is purely spiritual knowledge of ideas or universals. It involves no sensation, no imagination, no processing from what is potentially intelligible to what is actually intelligible, no active and passive intellect, no discursive struggle to understand, and no formulation in language. It is pure understanding, pure intellect. In contrast, animal knowing is sensing, imagining, remembering; it is knowledge of the individual, sensible object. It can involve learning by imagination and memory; it is successful in its own sphere, but never rises to the level of questioning or understanding. In the middle of these two extremes lies the human knower who shares characteristics of angelic and animal knowing in a unique, new integration. We inherit all the characteristics of animal knowing, but we are also able to ask questions, to discover ideas, to formulate definitions, and to affirm propositions about truth and value. But this is not a syncretistic mixture, but a new integration, a new reality, with its own unique and complicated process of human knowing. Although it is one process of human knowing, the tension remains between the exigencies of sense and the criteria of intelligence.

It is this dialectical tension between sense and intelligence that is the major source of misunderstanding and division. This is an area that philosophers cannot name, identify, define, or talk about. This is the dialectic that divides the materialists, the idealists, the dualists, the analysts, the behaviorists, the continental philosophers, and the critical realists. It introduces a real incommensurability between different positions. It centers on the nature of human knowing and the dialectic between sense and intelligence, imagination and understanding, two different criteria of what is real. This dialectic is very subtle, pervasive, hard to identify, and very difficult to overcome. It is operative even as we are unaware of its massive implications. My task here is to unmask these unstated assumptions, to uncover the unquestioned imaginative assumptions that mix and blend with the criterion of intelligence and so produce incoherent and confused conclusions.

By dialectic, I simply mean two linked but opposed principles of change. Within the unfolding of one human knowing, through the developments of understanding from adolescence to senescence, there lies a struggle at the heart of human knowing between two principles. They are linked, because it is one human process of knowing; yet they are opposed, because they pull in opposite directions. They are principles of change, because knowing is dynamic and is always either developing or declining. The crux of the matter is to identify these two linked but opposed principles of change. For the moment, we can identify them as the principle of sense and the principle of intellect.

The principle of intellect should not pose any problem. I have spent eight chapters outlining the activities of experiencing and understanding, followed by judgments of truth and value. I have described the activities and also the immanent and operative norms that drive these activities, namely, be attentive, intelligent, reasonable, and responsible. These are readily identifiable and understandable through a direct insight. They are not just intelligible, they are intelligence in act.

I have already assigned a positive role to sensing in the unfolding of human knowing. We usually initiate the process by asking questions about what we have experienced through the senses. We rifle out memories and imaginations to assemble and organize data, images, ideas, examples, and experiences with a view to understanding. Judgment usually returns to data of sense or data of consciousness in order to verify its conclusions. The conclusions are usually applied to the concrete in technology, medicine, or some practical field.

But there is a negative aspect of sensation, which tends to distort the whole process of intellectual knowing. We can only grasp this negative aspect by an inverse insight: it should be there, but it is in fact not there. I can only communicate this through images and examples and not by a positive definition. Consider again the mindset of Augustine as he struggled between imagination and intelligence with reference to the question of what is real.

The thesis is that the dynamics of sense knowing, and particularly the imagination, tend to impose unquestioned imaginative assumptions on our attempts to understand the process of knowing. The imagination suggests that knowing is a contact between who we are "in here" and a reality that is "out there." The whole question of knowing, then, becomes a question of how we cross the bridge from in here to out there. This is a deep, operative assumption that often dominates our attempts to understand the process. It is unquestioned: imagination does not ask questions; it is intelligence that asks questions. We think we know what knowing is before we even start asking questions about it. Because it is unquestioned, we are unaware of its influence, unaware of its massive implications, and unconscious that it is skewing the whole direction of our inquiry. It is subversive and undermines the whole epistemological project. If knowing is posed in terms of contact between in here and out there, then knowing will be something like sensing. Physical seeing seems to suggest a simple model of knowing as a contact between the seer in here and the seen out there. Therefore, we automatically assume that intellectual human knowing must be the same kind of activity, namely, simple direct vision, or intuition, or perception, or contact between the knower in here and the known out there. Hence, the simpler and the more direct the contact is, the more successful and true is the human knowing that ensues.

This results in the tendency to reject any representations that mediate between in here and out there. They can only be obstacles to uninterrupted human contact between the mind and reality. Once we have an intermediary, how do we know that we have knowledge of the reality that is mediated by that intermediary? Thus, there is no place for impressions, images, ideas, or activities that might interfere with direct contact between the knower and the known. There can be no mediation, no mediating factors, because they are obstacles to human knowing. Human knowing in this context is an act of intuition, vision, contact, seeing, looking, and the like.

If an epistemologist poses the question of human knowing in terms of contact between in here and out there, then the whole enterprise is skewed by a false problem. The question sets the criteria that are to be satisfied in a correct solution; but if we ask the wrong question, we are heading in the wrong direction and can only save ourselves by realizing that the question is skewed. My question about human knowing was simply to ask what it is, to seek a correct and detailed description of the activities involved in real examples of successful human knowing, and to note the imperatives that are immanent in the process. I depicted it as a sequence of mental activities, which are integrated together in a cognitional structure. The description was factual and verifiable;

the conclusion was that knowing is a sequence of activities culminating in a judgment. At no point in the previous chapters did I invoke the image of knowing as a contact between in here and out there.

The question of in here and out there is a legitimate question when it is posed more formally in terms of objectivity and subjectivity. But it is better to separate out this question and deal with it when we have already worked out what activities are involved in knowing. Once we have a handle on human knowing, then we can distinguish and relate subjectivity and objectivity in an adequate and objective fashion. Nothing but confusion ensues when we fuse and confuse two basic philosophical questions, namely, what is human knowing and the question of objectivity.

Why does this dialectic make a difference? Why is it important? Almost all of the theories of knowledge proposed since the time of Descartes labor, to a greater or lesser extent, under the shadow of this false, unquestioned assumption about human knowing. If we try to philosophize within the framework of a false or skewed epistemology, then we cannot possibly avoid skewing our conclusions about metaphysics, ethics, politics, theodicy, and philosophy of science. My claim is that this dialectic is the source of the deepest kinds of misunderstandings and disagreements that have occurred in philosophy, especially in the modern period.

Uncovering this dialectic should not be seen as an effort to discredit this series of great philosophers. Each and every philosopher or scientist who has been explicit about the process of human knowing has made some contribution to that uncovering. This is both a hermeneutic of suspicion and a hermeneutic of recovery. If we recognize the dialectic operating in the tension, misunderstandings, contradictions and false assumptions, and images and ideas of the philosophers, we are, thus, in a position to stand on the shoulders of giants and to distinguish the two poles of the dialectic that are operating in these philosophers. We can line up all of these contributions as contradictory contributions to the clarification of a single goal. We can identify the dialectic of progress and decline in the unfolding of the history of modern philosophy. We can appreciate the contribution that each philosopher and each school of philosophy has made to the unmasking of this subversive dialectic.

It is critical that we differentiate between the imperatives of intelligence and the unquestioned assumptions of imagination and sensing. The examples of this dialectic in other philosophers and scientists might help to identify these processes in one's own mental experience. Now, it is time to recognize the mistaken assumptions, the subversive power of the imagination, the tendency to ask the wrong questions, and the temptation to fit the complex activities of understanding within the model of simple, direct sensing of what is there to be sensed.

I proceed by applying a kind of hermeneutic of suspicion with a view of unmasking the two poles of the dialectic. I approach this from three points of view, with three different terminologies and images, but with all of them aimed at provoking the same understanding of misunderstanding. First, there is the dialectic between imagination and intelligence. Second, there is the struggle to answer the question of what is really real. And third, I consider the illusion that knowing is like looking, and hence, that insight is the same as an intuition. There is a certain overlapping in these sections as I am talking about one reality while using three different terminologies and metaphors.

Imagination and Intelligence

We can distinguish between the proper and the improper role of imagination in the process of human knowing. As I noted in chapter 4, the act of understanding begins when we ask questions about something that is experienced. Intelligence orders, manipulates, and plays with the data and images in order to facilitate the insight. In the act of understanding, an idea emerges from images. Ideas are always from intelligence; they are abstract, universal relations, causes, or explanations in some way. They are answers to questions for understanding. Images are sensible and particular. We may have an insight into present data of sense through remembered sense experiences; through imagining situations which never occurred; or through the creation of diagrams, connections, or symbols. Understanding cannot occur without images; we cannot think without images. Thinking and knowing take place through an intricate pivoting between images and ideas. The more appropriate the image, the nearer we are to understanding. The less relevant the image, the more difficult it is to reach understanding.

The improper role of imagination occurs when we allow the imagination to dominate the process. The imagination tends to impose its own imperatives and criterion on the activities of knowing. As well as being intelligible, the solution must also be imaginable; it must satisfy the demands of imagination. There must be a picture, a sound, an image, or something that can be touched or felt. It is hard to imagine the meaning of "insight into phantasm"; it is easy to imagine a subject being in contact with an object. It is easy to imagine knowing as sensing and only sensing; it is difficult to imagine understanding as a series of related activities that culminate in an intentional identity between the knower and the known. It is easy to imagine two things as distinct and separate; it is not so easy to imagine two things as distinct but not separate. As a result, imagination tends to take control and to overshadow the more recondite criterion of understanding and judgment. To elaborate on this ambivalent role of the imagination, I examine animal knowing and then human knowing as it is slowly transformed by intelligence and ideas.

Animals live in the biological pattern of experience. Generally speaking, they have five external senses, and they do have a limited ability to remember, to imagine and to coordinate responses to different stimuli. Their particular interests are very limited and specialized; what is outside those interests does not get their attention. The whole orientation of their sensing is for successful survival, the satisfaction of basic needs, protection, propagation, and the preservation of life. However, animal senses can be sharper, more sensitive, and more specialized than our own human sensing.

We can talk about "animal knowing" in the restricted sense of a knowing limited to sense or to experience. But it is a knowing that is pre-intellectual and pre-conceptual; it is knowing of the particular as particular and not as a particular instance of a universal species. Animals do not ask questions, they do not have insights, and they do not make judgments. We may speak of some animals as being intelligent and others as being dumb, but this is a very loose use of the word "intelligence"; few would put animals in the same category as humans when it comes to intelligence. There is a limit to learning in animals, which is largely based on principles of stimulus and response, on reward and punishment, on association, and on imitation. All knowing by nonhuman animals can be satisfactorily explained in terms of the biological pattern of experience of sensitive living. Dogs recognize their masters, cats recognize mice, a kitten will recognize a saucer of milk, and a male weaverbird will recognize a female weaverbird. But again, what we mean by "recognize" here is simply at the level of biological seeing with a minimal reference to memory, to imagination, and to instinct. It is purely sense knowing, and it is massively oriented to the outside; it is animal extroversion.

We can characterize this elementary knowing as the already, the immediate. An animal finds the world *already* constituted; there is no transition from potentially intelligible to actually intelligible. The animal does not grasp intelligible relations, causes, and species: it sees what is there to be seen. It automatically opens its eyes and sees on the level of sensation. There is no activity of questioning, no understanding, no hypotheses, and no judgments. Animals do not have identity crises or epistemological problems, and do not reflect on their destiny or lot. What is real for the animal is an object of sense, and it is real if it comes within the range of the interests of survival. It is *there now* in the sense that animals have to situate objects in time and place, but they live predominantly in the present. They do not have an abstract notion of space and time.

Animals do have a criterion of the real. They can distinguish between a saucer of milk and a picture of a saucer of milk. They can often distinguish between a man and a scarecrow; they can sense traps, fear guns, suspect an unfamiliar smell, and so on. Their elementary knowledge is often highly successful and ensures that they preserve their niche in the ecological system. What is real is what can be sensed and what is important in the biological pattern of experience. Animal sensing is dominated by the external senses and the predominant orientation of their sensing toward the already, the immediate.

We can apply this analysis to the development of human knowing. The infant starts in this animal world of immediacy.[3] What is real is the sum total of what is seen, heard, touched, tasted, smelled, and felt. The infant is a center of sensations, emotions and experiences. What is real is what can be grasped physically, what can be felt by the hands, and usually put in the mouth. The infant lives in the present, is dominated by its needs and the satisfaction of those needs. There is little to distinguish the development of the infant from that of the animal at this stage. An infant's sensorimotor development is very slow compared to other animals and the period of dependence on the parent is longer than for other animals. This is the world of immediacy, the world of what is immediately present to the senses. The criterion of what is real in this world is what the infant can see, grasp, and put in the mouth. The pre-intellectual child shares all of the characteristics and expectations of animal knowing. That is what is in place already before the emergence of intelligence.

But the infant slowly and exultantly moves into a world mediated by meaning. Perhaps, the first clear expression of intelligence is by way of naming; the parents are named and hence identified, recognized, and distinguished from other objects and persons. Other basic objects and needs are named as the process of moving into the world of meaning advances. All sorts of other developments take place. In identifying shapes, distinguishing noises and colors, and knowing the cause and the meaning of objects, associations are built up and general categories and conclusions are reached. The world of immediacy gives way to the expanded world that is mediated by meaning. Eventually the child's world is not simply the present but also a past that is remembered, promises that were made and have to be fulfilled, a rule that was laid down that must be kept, a routine that has to be fulfilled. There is also the future, the possibility of postponing gratification, plans laid down for future activities, and looking forward to future events. The world

3. Lonergan, *Method in Theology*, 238.

is not only what is physically present but what is absent for the moment; places can be named and visited. People who are absent are still part of the child's consciousness and concern. What is learned by understanding passes into the habitual texture of the mind.

In children beliefs about God, fairies, monsters, and Santa Claus mingle in a confused bundle of fiction, fantasy, and fact. Each culture teaches the child its own language; its own myths and stories; its own way of behaving; and its customs, clothes, music, prayers, and duties. Being so dependent on adults, the child accepts most of what it is told on the authority of the parents. The child will move into that world of values, beliefs, causes, and mores which is usually a mixture of fact and fantasy. The child is usually very anxious to know about these things and incessantly asks, "Why?" But some answers do not satisfy; a period of silence might ensue while the child digests the answer and then replies, "But . . . ," thus, raising an objection to the proposed answer. It is reason that is immanent and operative, which now begins to distinguish between what makes sense and what does not make sense, between what there is evidence for and what contradicts the evidence. At a certain point, the story of Santa Claus no longer stands up to criticism, the evidence is against it, and suspicions are aroused. A test is made: the presents are found hidden in a closet, a myth has been exploded, and the child moves into the hard reality of fact.

A new criterion of meaning and truth is becoming operative: it is verification, in a basic, rudimentary way. This is the world of meanings conferred on objects, values that guide behavior, truths about how things work. This is the world of mathematics that determines what can be purchased with so much money, how things are to be shared, and how things are made. Natural properties are recognized: gravity in sliding down an incline, fire that burns, water in which one can float and swim, paper airplanes that fly through the air. This is the world of meaning that is constructed by insights and generalizations, and is gradually checked against the available evidence. This world mediated by meaning will expand enormously through education; it can develop in many different directions depending on the culture, the educational possibilities available, and the choices of the person. The person can move into the world of nuclear physics, scriptural exegesis, historical scholarship, computer programming, literary studies, or theology or mysticism. These are worlds not given in the direct data of sense but mediated by insights and judgments, and embodied in technology and systems of theories.

However, in the background, the criterion of sense is probably still operative. Our senses constantly orient us toward the outside world. We live in the world of what we see, what we hear, what we touch, and what is present now as real in our lives. Our senses direct our attention outward; they are extroverted. We work, we eat, we play, we converse, we get things done. Rarely do we close our eyes, even rarer do we reflect on what we are doing; seldom indeed do we gather our thoughts and reflect on our mental activities. It is not surprising that our imagination suggests a schema of knowing as contact between in here and out there.

Two different criteria of what is real are operative, and we typically oscillate from one to the other. For the infant in the world of immediacy, it is the senses that prove what is real by touching, seeing, and tasting. But in the world mediated by meaning, it is the more intangible criteria of verification, sufficient evidence, and the correctness of a judgment that determine what is real. The criterion of verification emerges spontaneously in the context of the prior criterion of sense. The two criteria coexist in a state of tension and perhaps create conflict and confusion. Most people of common sense never realize that these two criteria are there. The survival of unquestioned assumptions, expectations, and presuppositions of elementary knowing in what is supposed to be fully human knowing is the source of endless confusion. This does not do much damage in ordinary, everyday life, but it can be disastrous if it is introduced to science and philosophy. The move into theory, epistemology, and philosophy require explicitly distinguishing between these two criteria.

Consider the mindset of an empiricist philosopher of the classical type, for instance, David Hume. He has no problem with sense knowing. Objects of sensation are real because they can be sensed; this knowledge is mediated by impressions, or images. This knowledge is verifiable and sound, because it satisfies the criteria of sensing and imagining. But there is a problem with the reality of causes, relations, universals, natures, essences, genus and species, laws of physics, and other nonmaterial entities. The problem is that they are not objects of sense, and thus, cannot be seen. We can see a succession of positions as a football player kicks a ball, but we cannot see the footballer cause the ball to move. Therefore, on this account, causes are not real; they are not out there in the world in the same way the football is. But how come most people hold that the kicker is responsible for causing the ball to move? Hume appeals to the laws of association of imagination and ingrained habits of the mind. We accustom our minds to organize sequences of actions and to imagine them as a succession of causes and effects. We put things that look alike in the same category for convenience's sake. Ideas such as cause or laws of motion are simply faint images in the mind that are governed by imagination rather than intelligence.

Empiricism is an epistemology and a philosophy arising out of the unconscious and unresolved conflict between the criteria of sensing and the criteria of understanding and judging. Clearly, on this account, sensing and imagination have won a total victory, and the activities of understanding and judging are reinterpreted as activities of imagining. Empiricism is motivated by a critical spirit to make philosophy verifiable, to remove unnecessary entities, and to make philosophy simple and clear. But sensation has triumphed in the content of the epistemology and becomes the criterion of what is real. However, intelligence, understanding, and judging have not gone away. After all, Hume is trying to understand; he is assembling data and facts in favor of his stance. He is making the judgment that this philosophy is truer and better than any previous philosophy. There is an incoherent mixture of two kinds of knowing, which are not acknowledged, not brought to consciousness, and not integrated. It is an attempt to eliminate one pole of the tension in the dialectic of human knowing. Examples abound where the unacknowledged operation of the dialectic leads to strange conclusions; let us examine some of them as illustrations.

Renaissance scientists were confronted with the problem that some aspects of the world could be subsumed under their scientific mathematical laws, whereas some aspects remained dependent on the perceiver and seemed to be stubbornly subjective and could not be measured. It was thought that some aspects of reality resemble the ideas that we have of them, and therefore the qualities we perceive belong to the object in reality. For other aspects of reality, there was thought to be no resemblance between what is in reality and what is in the perceiver; the real thing only has the power to produce these sensations in us. John Locke formulated this distinction explicitly in terms of primary and secondary qualities.[4]

Primary qualities are those qualities of a body that really belong to the body out there and cause our ideas of that body; the ideas in our mind really resemble the ideas in the body out there. There are five primary qualities: extension (size), figure (shape), motion (or rest), number, and solidity. These qualities are inseparable from the matter and are found in every part of it. Subdivide a quantity of gold, and the primary qualities will still belong to each and every one of the smallest parts. Significantly, the primary qualities can easily be measured, and thus, it was claimed that they were objective and were part of science. It can also be noted that primary qualities are usually perceived by more than one sense.

Secondary qualities are perceived qualities like color, taste, smell, sound, heat, and the like. They are causes of our perception of them, but the ideas in our mind do not resemble the qualities of the bodies out there in reality. Secondary qualities are not true qualities of matter, but merely powers in the

---

4. Hirst, "Primary and Secondary Qualities," 455–57. See also Locke, *An Essay concerning Human Understanding.*

objects to produce sensory effects in us. Secondary qualities can be influenced by the conditions of the sense organs, the health or sickness of the perceiver, the conditions of lighting, and the like. It is difficult to measure secondary qualities, as they are often the object of one sense only. Hence, Locke concluded, these secondary qualities are not really real, do not belong to bodies, are basically illusions, and are to be excluded from science.

There are difficulties to this distinction that Locke did not face. The main problem lies not so much in the definitions but in how he asked the question in the first place. He is comparing our ideas in our minds with what is out there in reality to see if they correspond. For primary qualities, there was a verifiable contact. For secondary qualities, there was no assurance of direct contact and hence these had to be excluded from scientific knowledge. The unquestioned assumption that knowledge was contact between in here and out there is the wrong question and results in an incorrect answer.

Newton's distinction between relative and absolute space, time, and motion is a further example of the unwarranted intrusion of imagination on the verifiable criteria of science. He insisted on the basic principle of science: that everything must be verifiable and verified in sense experience. He implemented this principle rigorously until he came to the question of space, time and motion. Certain relations of space and time that could be verified he called relative space and time, because there was always some measurable relation by which space and time was defined and verified. But he was unable to accept this as the whole story; his imagination and expectation was so strong that he postulated an absolute space and time that was not relative. He defined this absolute space as, "in its own nature, without regard to anything external, remains always similar and immovable."[5] Absolute motion is the translation of a body from one absolute place into another, whereas, relative motion is the translation from one relative place into another. He claimed to verify this postulation by means of the bucket experiment[6] and also invoked theological notions. We can understand this position as satisfying the exigencies of the imagination, but they are totally unverifiable and unjustifiable in terms of science or theology. If all space, time, and motion is relative, it seems to present a very unstable world. It needs to be bolstered with something permanent and enduring. And so he created this notion of absolute space, which gives

5. Newton, *The Principia*. 408.

6. Lonergan, *Insight*, 176. A bucket of water suspended from a twisted rope is allowed to spin. Slowly the surface of the water forms a hollow because of the centrifugal force of the spinning water. Stop the spinning and the hollow will persist for a time. Newton argued that as the hollow occurs both when the bucket is spinning and when it is stationary, therefore the spinning must be in relation to an absolute space. This is quite specious.

stability to the universe and satisfies the imagination, but is totally unverifiable. Newton's expectation that to be real something must be touchable, seeable, and imaginable was so strong that he could not believe that the reality of space and time was fully encapsulated in his laws and relations of relative space, time and motion. His absolute space is akin to the invisible, intangible, empty receptacle, which Plato imagined to have preexisted the work of the Demiurge in the formation of the world.

This position remained in the scientific community up to the beginning of the twentieth century, when Eddington presented his dilemma of the two tables.[7] By that time science had shown that atoms were mostly empty space and that the particles were constantly moving. The table of the scientist is mostly empty space, with a few particles whizzing around at enormous speeds and has no color. But the table of common sense is very solid, is certainly not moving, and is very clearly brown. Which one is the real table? How do we resolve the apparent contradiction? Following the tradition inherited from Locke and others, Eddington had to hold that the scientific table was real and that the table of common sense was merely an illusion. We are not so sure.

In contemporary times, most practicing scientists seem to be materialists or physicalists, as they prefer to be called. This seems to be the default position of most scientists. The position is not usually elaborated with any kind of sophistication. Moreover, it is taken for granted as obvious to everyone. Merriam-Webster's defines materialism as: "a theory that physical matter is the only fundamental reality and that all being and processes and phenomena can be explained as manifestations or results of matter." It is easy to hold that apples, dogs, and stones are really out there in the real world. It is not so easy to imagine that essences, causes, relations, or laws of physics and chemistry are also out there in the real world. Where are they, after all? Materialism is a nice, simple philosophy which satisfies the imagination and political correctness, but it leaves serious unanswered questions of intelligence. The real question about the above definition is the word "only." What scientific or philosophical justification can a scientist have for asserting that only matter exists, which is a metaphysical position?

Many scientists also espouse a position of reductionism. What are things made out of? Reductionism holds that everything can be explained satisfactorily and exclusively in terms of its smallest parts. But is this a response to imagination or intelligence? What is an animal made out of? The reductionist biologist will probably reply that it is made out of water, carbon, sulfur, and nitrogen in such and such percentages. These are the smallest parts that make

---

7. Eddington, *The Nature of the Physical World*, xi–xv.

up the animal. In this kind of thinking, an animal is simply a very complicated machine, no more than the sum of its parts. An atom is nothing more than it subatomic particles. A chemical compound is nothing more than a combination of atoms. A living cell is a very complicated chemical compound. An animal is simply the sum of its cells, tissues, bones, and the like which are ultimately atoms and subatomic particles. This satisfied the criterion of imagination as it offers a readily imaginable picture of a flat universe totally explicable in terms of matter. But is the question, "What is it made out of?" the same as the question, "What is it?" Is the formal cause the same as the material cause? Again, the criterion of the imagination supervenes over the criterion of intelligence and provides an imaginable but unintelligible answer.

Closely related to this is the question of unverifiable images. In the field of descriptive relations, there are verifiable images, which, by definition relate things to our senses. But in the field of explanation there are no verifiable images, because by definition explanation relates things to one another. On the criterion of imaginative, out there real, this is unacceptable. If something is real it has to be imaginable; the image is the criterion of the real. Atoms are little marbles, particles constituted by a nucleus with electrons spinning around in various orbits like the planetary system. Electrons, protons, and neutrons are smaller marbles, which are also real because they can be imagined. If there are smaller particles out of which these are constituted then those quarks are still smaller particles. If one points out that nobody has ever seen an atom, people operating out of this criterion of the real are not put out. They say that this is what atoms will look like when we do see one! If one insists that atoms are verified explanatory concepts, and not verifiable images, they will accuse you of idealism and still insist that atoms are real, and hence, imaginable.

The problem with this whole line of thinking is that the atom is a unit of explanatory knowledge. It is defined in terms of relations of things to one another; it is one of the terms defined by the relations of an explanatory system. There is no verifiable image. There is no out there, and thus, no real. There is no foothold for the imagination. For pedagogical reasons, we construct a model that embodies and symbolizes the relations of things to one another, but the reality is in the equations and not in the model. When the scientist, having verified his equations and laws, tries to tell us what the subatomic world really looks like, he or she is foisting on us unverifiable images. The scientist does this because he or she fails to distinguish between the real as what is out there from what is verified in instances. Such confusion is a perennial source of nonsense.

Consider one last illustration. Einstein made revolutionary discoveries about space, time, and gravity in his special theory of relativity and his general theory of relativity. Although they were revolutionary, the theories were still within the mind-frame of classical science. They fitted in with the deterministic worldview implied by Newton's mechanics that was more or less presumed by all scientists at the time. Then, along comes quantum mechanics with its principle of uncertainty, its indeterminacy, its probabilities, and its challenges to the classical, deterministic worldview. According to quantum mechanics, probability and indeterminacy are intrinsic to a correct understanding of the motion, position, and properties of subatomic particles. Einstein could never accept this and spent the rest of his life trying to reconcile the data on subatomic particles with his classicist, deterministic worldview. Does God play dice with the world? Einstein answered with a resounding "No!" I think it is now accepted that Einstein was wrong and the element of indeterminacy, uncertainty, and probability have been accepted as intrinsic to the world of physics. But why could Einstein not accept this? Why was he stuck in his world of determinism? Perhaps, this investigation into imagination and intelligence might help. To think of the universe as a clockwork machine is a powerful image and very satisfactory in showing how everything is interrelated and interdependent. Once a person has accepted this image, it is hard to let go. Sometimes imagination trumps intelligence. It is hard to imagine a universe based on probabilities.

To conclude, I am identifying the meaning of dialectic as linked but opposed principles of change. These opposed principles are the criteria of imagination and of intelligence. These examples identify the potential negative functions of the imagination in the process. This is one way to understand the source of deep misunderstanding throughout the history of philosophy and between contemporary schools of philosophy.

Naïve Realism or Critical Realism

In this section, I continue to focus on understanding misunderstanding, but I now approach this in terms of the question of what a particular philosophy explicitly considers to be real. Once again, I will utilize a few sample philosophers in order to penetrate their often unspoken assumptions about what is real. At the heart of every philosophy, there is the question of what that philosophical viewpoint considers to be real. Some philosophies do give an explicit answer to this question. In others, the answer is implicit in the criteria they use and the conclusions they reach. Sometimes it is very difficult for a philosopher to face up to this fundamental question and the answer may not always be clear. It is such a fundamental question that the position on the real sets the parameters for the rest of the philosophical position.

1. *Naïve Realism.* The naïve realist is blissfully unaware that there are two dialectically opposed criteria of what is real, namely, knowing as sensing and knowing as understanding correctly. I have already described the confused mind of the naïve realist and the unresolved tension between two kinds of knowing above, so no further discussion here is warranted.

2. *Plato.* I cannot pretend here to do justice to the wealth of Plato's thought on knowledge and his related metaphysics. There have been so many critical studies of Plato's thought that one is almost afraid to say that he held any particular position. This sketch intends only to illustrate his way of thinking and some of the apparent presuppositions behind that way of thinking. My route into the mind of Plato is through the expressions of the characters in his dialogues. I center on the question of what is real—not so much on the answers themselves, but on how Plato posed the question. What was the mindset behind the particular answers? We can only assemble some fragments hoping that it will be sufficient to make my point. Plato had not reached a full critical realist position and was still in the throes of the real as sensible and imaginative, out, there, now.

Plato—according to the common understanding—posited the existence of a world of Ideas, which was separate and apart, somewhere in the heavens. The Ideas were perfect, spiritual, unchanging. Now what led him to this position? Against the Sophists he had to hold that knowledge is infallible and of what is. If knowledge was stable, then it had to be of something stable. But the objects of sense knowing are always changing, so they cannot be the objects of infallible and stable knowing. What then is the really real? It cannot be the concrete, sensible things that are always changing. So the real must be of spiritual realities, which reside in the heavens ever perfect and ever the same. The really real is out there, up there, always permanent and stable. This is basically an imaginative schema, which satisfies imaginative exigencies, but does not satisfy critical reflective questions leading to judgments of truth.

The problem of negative or false statements was one area of great difficulty for Plato.[8] His difficulty stemmed from his expectation that for every concept or statement in the mind there was something outside the mind corresponding to it. For positive statements he thought of the world of Ideas as the corresponding reality. But what exists outside the mind that corresponds to negative or false statements? This expectation suggests the ultimate absurdity that there is a nonbeing that corresponds to these negative or false statements, namely, that nonbeing is real. Plato was not willing to accept this, so he had to leave the question unresolved. It did not strike him that he might question his unquestioned assumption that knowing was an imaginative correspondence between in here and out there.

8. Plato, *Theaetetus*, 187–90.

In the *Sophist* Plato explicitly faces the issue of reality and unreality.[9] He begins with a consideration of the history of the question. Some have said there are three real beings, some have said two, and the Eleatics say there is only one real thing. All of these fall to the same argument. If we take the Eleatics as an example, they say that the real is only one. But the one is not the same as the real, and the real is not the same as the one; thus, there are at least two things, the one and the real! Reading the passage and the rather labored arguments, it seems to be that Plato's real difficulty lay in the expectation that corresponding to every concept in the mind like real, one, being, hot, or justice there must be a corresponding Idea or Form outside the mind in a sort of one to one correlation with the concept.

Another of Plato's assumptions seems to have been that real knowledge must be "infallible and of what is."[10] When he then comes to distinguishing between different kinds of knowledge he divides it into sense knowledge and intellectual knowledge. Only the latter constitutes true knowledge because it is knowledge of what is and what does not change. Intellectual knowledge can be of what is because of the existence of the subsistent Ideas. The implication of this theory of knowledge is that outside the mind corresponding to sense knowledge is the material, visible, changing world; corresponding to, and, as it were validating, intellectual knowledge are the changeless, perfect subsistent Forms. The dominant, unspoken assumption of all of this discussion is the attempt to correlate what goes on in the mind to the corresponding realities outside the mind. But does this image of correspondence derive from imagination or understanding?

I tend to think that Plato had not negotiated the question of the real as Augustine had. Plato thought that to be real something had to exist and to exist is to be in a place. If ideas do not belong to the sensible world, then they must belong and exist in a separate world. This might satisfy the imagination but it entails all sorts of intellectual problems.

3. *Descartes.* Proceeding from his methodological doubt, to the cogito, to the existence of God, and to the reliability of our knowledge, Descartes then faces the question of what he considers to be real. Of central importance here is the notion of substance. Aristotle had a differentiated notion of substance. In the *Categories* he noted that substance is a concrete individual, a man, or a horse. Substances are not *said of* or *present in* a subject; substance underlies what changes. Substance is a *this*; it has no contrary, it

9. Plato, *Sophist*, 242–46.

10. Plato, *Theaetetus* 152c. The metaphor of the Divided Line is to be found in *Republic*, book 6, and the Allegory of the Cave at the beginning of book 7.

has no degrees.[11] In the *Metaphysics* he favored the notion of substance as essence.[12] The Scholastics accepted and elaborated on all of that. Clearly Descartes did not learn of this notion from the Jesuits of La Flèche, so he constructs his own definition of substance as "nothing other than a thing which exists in such a way that it needs no other thing in order to exist."[13] God obviously fulfills that definition but he extends it also analogously to Matter and Spirit. Thus, there are only two real substances. Matter is identical with extension and therefore there can be no vacuum, no void, and no space with nothing in it. Spirit is thought and does not occupy space.

Matter is extension. Thus extension in length, breadth, and depth constitutes the nature of corporeal substance. Matter is identical with extension. On this account, qualities such as extension, weight, and size really inhere in the thing, whereas qualities such as color and taste are not really there but are only the power to produce that impression in us. He accepted the distinction between primary qualities which really exist in the thing and secondary qualities which exist in the mind but not really in the thing. We can catch a glimpse of the unquestioned assumption that to be real is to be really out there, while to be unreal is to be a power that makes an impression in us. But does the model of in here and out there provide the criterion of the truth? He ends up with a metaphysical dualism which Burtt describes as:

> On the one hand there is the world of bodies, whose essence is extension; each body is a part of space, a limited spatial magnitude, different from other bodies only by different modes of extension—a geometrical world—knowable only and knowable fully in terms of pure mathematics. . . . On the other hand, there is the inner realm whose essence is thinking, whose modes are such subsidiary processes as perception, willing, feeling, imagining, etc., a realm which is not extended, and is in turn independent of the other, at least as regards our adequate knowledge of it.[14]

It follows that the human person is composed of two substances, matter and thought, which leads to a serious problem. How can the human person experience himself as one, and be one person, if the subject is constituted by two different kinds of substances? If there are two real things, matter and spirit, how are they related, particularly in the case of the human person, who is both body and mind? Descartes seems to have thought of spirit as invisible, intangible, and outside time and space, yet meaning something like a ghost,

11. Aristotle, *Categories* 2a12–4b19.

12. Aristotle, *Metaphysics* 1041a6–1041b30.

13. Descartes, *Principles of Philosophy*, 23.

14. Burtt, *The Metaphysical Foundations of Modern Science*, 118–19.

or an imaginable, ethereal entity. If matter is coterminous with extension, it is hard to see how it can be affected by spirit. How can mind, which is spiritual, affect body, which is material, when they belong to such distinct realms? Descartes solved this for himself by postulating one point of contact in the pineal gland. This may have satisfied his imagination, but his successors were more critical and had to invent more complicated theories of occasionalism and parallelism to account for contact between mind and body.[15]

Descartes started modern philosophy off on a false dichotomy between spirit and matter, mind and body, the ghost in a machine, from which it has not yet recovered. Once the question is posed in these imaginative notions of matter and thought, it is almost impossible to understand how they can interact. If we accept the two substances of matter and thought, we are forced into dualism. If we deny the reality of thinking substance, we are forced into materialism. If we reject material substance, we are forced into idealism. The only way out of this confusion is to start again and examine how to answer correctly the simple question, "What is real?" Ryle suggested the phrase "ghost in the machine" as best describing Descartes's view of the human person.[16] It is probably a correct characterization of Descartes's views, which are inadequate because of the imperatives of imagination in which the question is posed. Do we reject the ghost or the machine or both? It is better to start again using judgment as our criterion of the real.

4. *Immanuel Kant.* Although Kant attempts to break into a new critical philosophy and leave behind the rationalistic scholasticism of Leibniz and Wolff, his thinking continues to depend on some of the basic assumptions of these philosophies. One of these was the imaginative assumption of inner and outer, with knowing being inner and the known being outer.

According to Kant, "There can be no doubt that all our knowledge begins with experience."[17] He continues: "The capacity (receptivity) for receiving representations through the mode in which we are affected by objects, is entitled sensibility."[18] Phenomena can be known because we have an intuition of them; even though sensibility needs the a priori forms of space and time, it is clear that at the level of sensibility, we have knowledge of what is really out there by way of the senses. By sensible intuitions we have direct contact between the mind and phenomena.

15. Occasionalism claimed that the body moved on the occasion of the mind deciding; God is the real cause, the mind is the occasional cause. Parallelism, proposed by Malebranche, claimed that the two realms of psychic and physical were preordained from the beginning to run parallel and in harmony.

16. Ryle, *The Concept of Mind.*

17. Kant, *Critique of Pure Reason*, 41.

18. Ibid., 65.

But at the level of understanding there is a problem for Kant. If all our knowledge comes through the senses, how can the senses know causality, substantiality, unity, and the like? He writes, "But all thought must, directly or indirectly, by way of certain characters, relate ultimately to intuitions, and therefore, with us, to sensibility, because in no other way can an object be given to us."[19] The only channel between the knower and the known, the inner and the outer, is the sense intuition which, by definition, can only receive sensible representations. Therefore, we have no way of contacting substance or cause to know if they are really out there. In Kant's terminology, we have no way of knowing the thing-in-itself, the noumenon.

If the reality of substance, cause, and the like cannot be grounded in the out there, then Kant's Copernican Revolution proposes that we ground it in the mind itself. "Hitherto it has been assumed that all our knowledge must conform to objects. But all attempts to extend our knowledge of objects by establishing something in regard to them *a priori*, by means of concepts have, on this assumption, ended in failure. We must therefore make trial whether we may not have more success in the tasks of metaphysics, if we suppose that objects must conform to our knowledge."[20] We cannot have contact with the thing-in-itself out there, so let us suppose that the reality is in here in the mind and that we impose these categories on the outside real. Hence, he elaborates his twelve categories, among them the category of inherence and subsistence. He uses both the notion of permanence and the notion of substratum in proving this inner reality of substance: "In all changes of appearances, substance is permanent; its quantum in nature is neither increased nor decreased."[21] He continues: "But the substratum of all that is real, that is, of all that belongs to the existence of things, is substance; and all that belongs to existence can be thought only as a determination of substance."[22]

This thinking led Kant to the impossibility of pure reason knowing the thing-in-itself, the noumenon; nevertheless, he supposed that the noumenon lies out there behind appearances. His theory of knowledge denied him the possibility of knowing noumena, but his imagination demanded that we presume their existence. Thus, he was left with the strange position of grounding knowledge in the a priori categories, but still supposing that there are noumena out there that correspond to these concepts. As I interpret these passages I see the dominance of the imaginative assumption of knowledge as contact between in here and out there.

19. Ibid., 65.
20. Ibid., 22.
21. Ibid., 212.
22. Ibid., 213.

Plato, Descartes, and Kant in their own different ways were dominated by the imaginative assumption that knowing is a matter of crossing the bridge from thinking in here to reality out there. To understand this misunderstanding, we need to grasp how imaginative imperatives impose themselves on our thinking. They are unquestioned, imaginative assumptions that massively impose themselves on the details of our understanding and knowing. However, it is correct judgments that define what is real. It is not a question of imagination but of judgments. The question of subject and object, subjectivity and objectivity, will be addressed in chapter 11, but it will be done in terms of judgments and not in terms of unquestioned, imaginative expectations.

Intuition: From "Looking" to Knowing

A further such assumption is that intellectual knowing proceeds in the same way as sensing. On this account, it is assumed that the senses work simply, directly, and immediately; we open our eyes and see what is there to be seen. On a parallel track the intellect operates by way of an intellectual vision: a seeing that is direct and immediate; seeing becomes a predominant paradigm for intellectual knowing. Just as looking is one simple operation of direct sensation, for these philosophers intellectual knowing is a simple, direct perception, a vision, contact, or intuition. The sense of seeing is predominantly passive, that is, we open our eyes and we see what is there to be seen; in the same way, intellectual knowing is passive, that is, we see with our intellectual vision what is already there to be seen. Just as seeing is immediate—there is no obstacle or intermediary involved in the direct vision of objects—so intuition is a direct vision of essences, causes, being, or universals. In this section I will consider a few philosophers who have elaborated a theory of knowledge based on this assumption that intellectual knowing must be something like seeing, and thus, speak of knowledge as intuition. By "intuition," I mean the sort of knowing that is modeled on "looking." Merriam-Webster's defines intuition as "the power or faculty of attaining to direct knowledge without evident rational thought and inference."[23]

Intuition is quite different from insight. Insight is understanding of forms perceived in data under the influence of questioning; it can be direct or reflective. Knowing is not understanding alone but questioning, experiencing, understanding, and judging. Understanding is a sequence of activities; it is discursive. John Duns Scotus deviated from Aquinas in asserting an intuitive knowing of particulars as actually existing as well as an abstractive knowing of universals. He was followed in this by Jacques Maritain and Etienne

23. *Merriam-Webster's Collegiate Dictionary.*

Gilson who claimed to be Thomists but relied very much on the metaphor of intuition, which was certainly not to be found in Aquinas. Henri Bergson also appealed to intuition as the direct awareness of the actual movement of life. For Bergson analysis is the method of science but produces a lifeless, static system. Intuition is immediate consciousness of an object that is always in motion, the élan vital. However, I will concentrate on Immanuel Kant and Edmund Husserl as proponents of intuition as central to their account of understanding, and then some further contemporary proponents of intuitions.

I have interpreted the Kantian position as invoking a notion of the real as contact between in here and out there. Now I focus on the notion of intuition, which has a central role in Kant's system. According to Kant, we do have sensible intuitions of the phenomena, and thus, sense knowing is of the phenomena. But we do not have intellectual intuitions of things-in-themselves and so we cannot directly know the noumena; we know them only in the sense of the mind imposing a priori forms on reality. But what precisely did he mean by intuition, and what role did it play in his account of human knowing? Giovanni Sala explains:

> The Transcendental Aesthetic begins with a statement that in my opinion expresses the essence of knowledge according to Kant: "In whatever manner and by whatever means a mode of knowledge may relate to objects, intuition is that through which it is in immediate relation to them, and to which all thought as a means is directed" (A 19). In other words, intuition is in the last analysis the only way and the only means by which knowledge, *all* knowledge is related to its object. If we compress the principle articulated here into a concise formula, we can say that for Kant knowing is looking (intuiting).[24]

In his own words Kant affirms the centrality of intuition as an immediate relation to objects. I now outline the role of intuition in Husserl, and afterward, will examine the metaphor of intuition as part of human knowing.

Husserl is a very difficult thinker to deal with as he wrote extensively, his thinking was evolving throughout his life, he went into more and more detail as he continued to write, and he left many matters unclear. However, it is clear that he uses the notion of intuition as a crucial element in knowing truth. It is not so obvious what he means by intuition, the kinds of intuitions there are, and how intuition relates to understanding and judging. In this brief account I will rely mostly on *The Theory of Intuition in Husserl's Phenomenology* by Emmanuel Levinas, which I take to be authoritative and authentic.

---

24. Sala, *Lonergan and Kant*, 45–46.

Levinas asserts the importance of intuition for Husserl at the beginning of his treatment when he says: "The mode of consciousness or of representation through which we enter into contact with being has a determinate structure; it is, let us declare at once, intuition."[25] Husserl distinguishes between a signifying intention and an intuitive act. The signifying intention or act of meaning aims at, but does not reach, its object. The intuitive act, on the contrary, reaches its object; in intuition, we relate directly to the object. Perception, imagination, and memory are intuitive acts that possess and reach their objects. Meanings aim at their objects; intuition, and in particular perception, reaches them.

There are gradations of intuitive acts; there are degrees of extension, vividness, and reality to each intuition. Perception is a privileged, intuitive act, a primary intuition. Perception realizes an object as it is in-itself; perception gives us being.

There are sensible intuitions and categorial intuitions, but they are profoundly similar. Intuition seems to be more originary and primordial than sensibility or intellectual acts. Levinas writes, "Sensibility and understanding, inasmuch as they reveal truth, can be subsumed under the single concept of an intuitive act."[26] He continues: "Intuition, however, understood as direct vision of objects, seems to be independent of whether it takes place in a sensible or in an intellectual act."[27] Truth is conferred on understanding and judgments by this intuition, understood as an intentionality whose intrinsic meaning consists in reaching its object and facing it as existing.

Husserl criticizes the traditional definition of truth as *adequatio* of mind and reality, on the grounds that there is no standpoint outside the subject from which to judge the correspondence. This according to Husserl is the source of all problems in philosophy. His solution is to go back to the original phenomenon of truth in order to understand its very essence. Levinas writes, "This aspect is intuition, understood as an intentionality whose intrinsic meaning consists in reaching its object and facing it as existing."[28] In intuition, Husserl seems to be saying, the intuiting and that which is intuited, the mind and reality, are in direct contact.

Husserl is not devaluing discursive reasoning and judgment, but regards truth as a more primordial reality, which is realized in particular judgments. Levinas writes, "If a judgment may be true it is not *qua* judgment, *qua* asserting

---

25. Levinas, *The Theory of Intuition*, 65.

26. Ibid., 79.

27. Ibid., 83.

28. Ibid., 84.

something or other, but *qua* intuition, *qua* facing its correlate, a *Sachverhalt*, in the same way that perceived things are faced by sensible intuition."[29]

Levinas sums up Husserl's notion of intuition in this way: "Husserl was looking for the primary phenomenon of truth and reason, and he found it in intuition, here understood as an intentionality which reaches being. He found it in 'vision,' the ultimate source of all reasonable assertions. Vision has 'justification' as its function, because it gives its object in a direct manner; inasmuch as vision realizes its object, it is reason."[30] Now it is clear why intuition is central to Husserl's thought. It is the foundation of truth and underlies perception, memory, imagination, understanding, and judgment. There are both sensible intuitions and intellectual intuitions. Note the characteristic of intuition: that it reaches its object, is in contact with its object, faces its object, reveals its object, and sees its object, as opposed to merely signifying or intending. The image of vision is used to explain the intuition as simple, forceful, and effective in reaching its object. Reason and judgments are useful and important but only because they get their force from intuition.

I turn briefly to the contemporary philosophical context where perception, intuition, and vision are central to an account of human knowing. Richard Rorty interprets the traditional way of knowing as the mind mirroring reality.[31] He rejects what he calls representationalism where ideas and images mediate our knowledge of reality. If there is a representation in between the subject and the object, then we know the representation and not the real object. Descartes, Locke, and Kant are all charged with the same fallacy of putting intermediary ideas or images between the mind and the real object. So philosophy along with the search for truth in its traditional form has to be abandoned. He claims that Wittgenstein, Heidegger, and Dewey have liberated themselves from this disastrous representational approach to knowing in favor of direct contact with the real. In the place of traditional approaches to truth, he presents philosophy as therapeutic conversation leading essentially nowhere.

Charles Taylor recognizes that modern philosophy since Descartes has been dominated by the image of knowing as in here and the known as out there in much the same way as we have. However, his solution is quite different from ours. He seems to be in agreement with Rorty in dismissing what Taylor calls the "mediational metaphor" for knowing dominant since Descartes. He described such mediational knowing as, "In its original form, this emerged

---

29. Ibid., 89.

30. Ibid., 89–90.

31. Rorty, *Philosophy and the Mirror of Nature*. For a more detailed treatment see Snell, *Through a Glass Darkly*.

as the idea that we grasp external reality through internal representations."[32] He assigned four characteristics to this epistemology. First, that knowledge occurs "only through" some features of the mind/organism. Second, that the content is clearly and explicitly defined. Third, that we cannot go beyond or below these explicit formulated elements. Fourth, that this all presupposes the distinction between mental and physical. He criticizes the mediational metaphor from these four points of view. The linguistic turn, the materialist turn, and the critical turn in modern philosophy are all victims of relying on this same metaphor of mediation and hence are to be rejected. He prefers a contact metaphor as instantiated in Hegel, Wittgenstein, and Heidegger. "For contact-theories truth is self-authenticating. When you're there, you know you're there. But for the mediational variety, this can never be."[33] In contact theories there is no intermediary placing an obstacle in the way between the knower and the known. One has direct contact with the object. Although he does not seem to use the term "intuition," he seems to consider knowledge as a direct, simple, unmediated contact between subject and object.

John Searle, in his aptly named book, *Seeing Things as They Are,* proposes a similar argument as Taylor, namely, that representations are an obstacle to knowing rather than part of the process. He regrets the confusion caused by philosophers from Descartes to Kant in introducing ideas, impressions, and images as intermediaries in knowing. In his account of direct realism, he tends to use the term "perception," I think, with the meaning of intuition. He is not much in favor of self-appropriation: "Many truly appalling mistakes—from Descartes' Representative Theory of Perception all the way through to Kant's Transcendental Idealism and beyond—would have been avoided if everybody understood you cannot see or otherwise perceive anything in the subjective perceptual field."[34] Searle lays great stock on seeing; I am not sure that his perception adds much to seeing. On his account, one sees the world directly as it is out there, and there is not much room for questions, insights, formulation, criticism, and judgments.

I now critically examine whether the notion of intuition leads to understanding or misunderstanding of the process of knowing. I have shown how important a role intuition plays in Kant, Husserl and others, and how influential these thinkers have been in molding our views on knowing. Again, in a loose sense, in commonsense discourse, intuition is used in much the same way as insight, meaning a hunch, a guess, an illumination, a hypothesis. That is fine in the world of common sense, but if we move into

32. Taylor, "Retrieving Realism," 61.
33. Ibid., 74.
34. Searle, *Seeing Things as They Are,* 107.

the world of philosophy these terms must be strictly defined. For Kant and Husserl and many others, the notion of intuition is an integral part of the definition of the process of knowing. Intuition suggests that knowing is like looking, that knowing is a simple, single act of intellectual seeing. On this account, knowing is a confrontation or contact between the subject knowing and the object known; this simple intuition puts us in contact with being or the object or reality. This can be a very simple, attractive, and inspiring way to talk about knowing. However, I respond to the view of knowing as an intuition with a series of questions and comments.

First, do images and ideas play a part in the process of knowing? Most normal folks have no problem admitting that they have ideas and images, and they use them in the process of knowing. Most would accept a description of thinking as a stream of ideas and images, competing, jumping from point to point, pivoting from image to idea, rambling from one image to another, and perhaps, finally reaching a conclusion. Most teachers entering a classroom have a series of points (ideas) that they want to communicate, a series of examples and images to use to illustrate the points, start class with a revision of previous ideas, and conclude with homework assignments to hammer home the message. I have not yet met a professor in any discipline who prides himself that he has not taught his students a single idea, and has never used examples or images when teaching. Knowing is a discursive process, involving a series of activities, utilizing images and ideas, and often ending up with a conclusion. It seems to me that Searle and Taylor bypass this discursive process in their rejection of mediation or representation and embracing of a direct contact realism. Surely impressions, images, and ideas play some role in human knowing. Perhaps, the role they assign is different from the above, but it would be helpful if that was spelled out.

"Perception" is a word used with a variety of meanings, ranging from simple sensation to a full act of human knowing. I have avoided using the word for that reason. It is also used with the same meaning as intuition. I think of perception as sensation that is influenced by ideas and, thus, plays a part in full human knowing; but knowing is complete only with a judgment.

Second, is it possible that there are two kinds of knowing, the discursive knowing outlined in this text and an intuitive knowing that I have overlooked? A correct answer requires a clear distinction between discursive and intuitive knowing as provided above. After that it is a matter of cognitional fact. Do intuitions in the defined sense occur or do they not occur? All I can say is that I do not experience intuitions as direct, simple, contact with reality. None of my students have ever reported such experiences. Intuitions occur as hunches, guesses, or hypotheses but not as direct vision or contact with reality. I have experienced insights, acts of human understanding with five essential characteristics, ideas emerging from images, and usually leading on to critical reflection and judgments. That I consider to be knowledge of reality. It is possible that some misunderstanding occurs because the words intuition and insight are not clearly defined. But the distinction must be made and has vast implications for a theory of knowledge.

Third, do intuitions give knowledge of reality? Even if there were intuitions that give direct contact with reality, would they give true knowledge of reality? In my presentation I emphasized that direct insights produce ideas or hypotheses which may or may not be true; they are possibilities. The issue of true or false is settled by asking and answering the further critical question in a reflective insight and a judgment.

Intuitions if they are simple intellectual operations at best would give ideas, essences, causes, hypotheses. But these are only possibilities; there are always a number of possibilities; how do we know that this possibility is correct, true and real? Possibilities are not knowledge. The further question arises, are these intuitions true, real, and correct? To answer that question one would need some kind of evidence that would justify promoting the possibility into a judgment of truth. We reach knowledge of reality not in possible ideas but in judgments. Intuitions are not judgments. Intuitions if they exist are simple and direct. Judgments arise from asking a critical question, having a reflective insight that produces a true judgment. One thing that neo-Scholasticism held on to was the principle that truth is found not in simple apprehension, that is direct insights, but in the judgment.

Similarly, for the notion of perception when it is used in the same sense as intuition. Presumably, an act of perceiving is a simple cognitional act which attains what is perceived. But how do we know that what is perceived is real, correct and true? Further questions surely arise as to which perceptions are true or false; that is the critical question for judgment which can only be answered by finding sufficient evidence to justify that the perception has attained what is real and true.

Fourth, true knowledge of reality is mediated in many ways by many factors. It is mediated by images, ideas, and concepts. It is mediated by language as knowledge is expressed and defined. It is mediated by a tradition of thinking, research, teachers, schools, and universities. It is mediated by books, computers, instruments, experience, and belief. Knowledge is more and more a collaboration of specialists in an ongoing process of discovery and innovation. It is the very nature of human knowing that it be mediated by images and ideas, that it be a series of activities and not one single activity, and that it be discursive and not intuitive in the above sense.

Fifth, ideas, concepts, and images can be considered to be obstacles to correct knowing in the following contexts:

In an explicit conceptualist system we have knowledge of concepts and not of reality. Later Scholasticism is an example of such a system where philosophy consisted largely of definition and division of concepts and not reality. But the implications of that position are rather drastic, as we can no longer have knowledge of the real world; hence, we cannot have a process of verification and no longer have a criterion of true and false. In this case, concepts are an obstacle rather than a means to knowing reality; but that is not my position on the role of ideas and concepts.

A representationalist interpretation of knowing imagines knowing as contact between the mind in here and reality out there. In this imaginative scheme, anything that comes in between mind and reality can be an obstacle to direct contact and hence to knowledge. But I do not develop a theory of knowledge on the basis of imagination but of intelligence; intelligence uses ideas and images in order to reach knowledge of reality.

The correspondence theory of truth can also be presented in an imaginative form of in and out; and in such a framework it is impossible for the mind to compare the ins and the outs to establish a correspondence. But this is a total misunderstanding of the notion of correspondence based on imagination and not on intelligence. Aristotle defines truth and falsity in the *Metaphysics* simply as follows. "This is clear if we first define what is truth and what is falsehood. A falsity is a statement of that which is that it is not, or of that which is not that it is; and a truth is a statement of that which is that it is, or of that which is not that it is not. Hence, he who states of anything that it is or that it is not, will either speak truly or speak falsely" (1011b). Truth is to be found in the judgment and only in the judgment. There is no need for imaginative correspondence between in here and out there. A judgment emerges from an act of intelligence not of imagination. In my terminology the critical question, Is it true? is answered through a reflective insight issuing in a judgment, as explained in chapter 6.

Sixth, Aristotle has a rather enigmatic principle, which states that sensing in act is identical with the sensible in act.[35] Is there anything in our cognitional experience that might help us to understand this principle? I suggest that Aristotle might be referring to knowledge as identity and not knowledge as confrontation. The knowledge referred to in the fourth point above is knowledge by identity and the knowledge in the fifth point above is knowledge by confrontation. Sense knowing by identity refers to the notion that the "seeing" is identical with, coterminous with, coincident with the "being seen." It denies the notion that at some stage the seeing stops and the being seen begins, which would be confrontational.

35. Aristotle, *De Anima* 426a15.

Seventh, Aristotle also had a principle that the intellect in act is identical with the intelligible in act.[36] The same point can be made that he is distinguishing a knowledge by identity from a knowledge by confrontation. In knowing by identity the activity of understanding is identical with, coterminous with, or coincident with that which is understood. There is no point at which the understanding stops and the understood begins. For Aristotle if we understand a frog, we understand the essence or form or idea of the frog; the idea in the mind corresponds or is identical with the idea in the individual frog. Kant, by way of contrast, claims that we can know the appearance of the frog but not the reality; we can know the phenomenon but not the noumenon. That is knowledge by confrontation. We can know the appearance, but the reality is behind the appearance; the appearance is where knowing stops. The appearance is a block to knowing what is behind the appearance. Which of these accounts of understanding can be validated in the actual experience of studying frogs? I do not know any biologist who finds it useful to distinguish between the phenomenon and noumenon of a frog. I do not know any biologist who does not distinguish between the genus and species of frog and the particular characteristics of this individual particular frog. If you want to know the essence of this particular frog ask the biologist. If you want to know how the human mind can reach a knowledge of essence in general consult a good epistemologist.

Startling Strangeness

This has been a long and difficult chapter using many terminologies and examples to identify the dialectic at the heart of human knowing. I hope that this material has made explicit the influence of these two principles in the process of knowing. The tension between imagination and intelligence, the sensible criterion of the real and the real as correct judgment, and the difference between physical seeing and the activities of understanding and judging can all be identified in one's own experience. It is worth the effort because of the enormous implications of the position that I have articulated. If I am right, then I have uncovered the key to the deep intractable disagreements between philosophers in the history of philosophy and in contemporary debates. If I have succeeded in understanding the deep source of misunderstanding, surely what I have suggested here provides the way to overcoming or removing the cause of such confusion and disagreements. If I am right, we can understand the history of philosophy as dialectical contributions to the clarification of a single, correct philosophical position. All

36. Ibid., 430a1–5.

philosophers are in practice aiming at correct understanding and reaching a correct view of the universe and our place therein. That is their performance. But the contents of their epistemologies deny precisely the notion that knowing is correct understanding and substitute some imaginative notion of knowing as contact between in here and out there.

Can the tension of the dialectic ever be resolved? Neither pole can be eliminated. Imagination and sensation have an essential role to play in human knowing from the beginning to the end; it is human knowing we are talking about and not pure intellect. Empiricism tries to reduce all human knowing to sensation; however, they utilize intelligence, reason, and judgments to argue that this philosophy is better than others. The dialectic can be left in a limbo land of the semiconscious to pull us in opposite directions without us even being aware of the interference.

The tension can be resolved by becoming aware of its presence and openly and deliberately affirming the only criterion of the real: "The real is the verified; it is what is to be known by the knowing constituted by experience and inquiry, insight and hypothesis, reflection and verification."[37] We have to move from an imaginative presentation of the real as sensed, to the real as what can be sensed, what can be understood, what can be judged to be true, and of true value. There is a startling strangeness in the realization that we know by correct understanding. We move into the world of asking good questions, searching for an idea, formulating it in words, reflecting and checking, and finally, reaching true knowledge and knowing we have arrived. It is amazing how many philosophers claim to attain reality in ways that can do without making judgments. But if you ask the question, is it real?, you can only answer it with a judgment based on some thinking and appeal to evidence that entails a conclusion.

If this dialectic is so central to progress in philosophy, why is it that the community of philosophers is so unaware of its devious influence? I suggest that it is because of the lack of attention to the actual, real activities involved in knowing. The dialectic is not a problem that can be solved in one book or one simple distinction. It cannot be solved by logic, by distinctions and divisions, but only by self-attention. The only way to an appreciation of true human knowing is self-appropriation. It is only by attending to our own personal insights and judgments and where they come from that we can move to a correct appreciation of the human mind and its real power to know. This calls for an enormous shift in how philosophy is studied and taught nowadays. Meanwhile we wait for the self-correcting process of human knowing to emerge—for questions to be asked, for insights to occur, for contradictions to be overcome, and for judgments to be reached.

37. Lonergan, *Insight*. 277.

10

Establishing Critical Realism

Psychology of Knowledge

What I have been doing over the past nine chapters could be called a psychology of knowledge. It could also be called cognitive psychology or cognitional theory; or it might be called a phenomenological description of knowledge understood as a simple, accurate, detailed, sequential description of the activities involved in knowing in common sense, science, or philosophy. It has been an empirical study in the simple sense of describing what actually happens in the process of understanding and the sequence in which it happens. One would imagine that such an important aspect of the human mind would be the province of psychology and that psychologists would be the experts to go to for expertise in answering this question. Unfortunately, behaviorism excluded the study of the human mind from psychology and it has not recovered since. Cognitive science seems to have fallen under the sway of neuroscience and does not deal in actual descriptions and analyses of human knowing. Those who do describe the actual process of knowing do not seem to have discerned the basic definition of the act of understanding, nor the sequence and structure of activities leading to full human knowing.

Psychology is recognized as an empirical science. Its purpose is to establish the facts of human personality, feelings, and motivation; surely it should also include human thinking, knowing, and evaluating as activities that all human beings perform. Its subject matter is human behavior and human personality, and thus, its methodology will be different from those of physics or chemistry. Behaviorism however tries to give a reductionist, materialist account of human knowing and so is not much interested in studying mental activities as such. But to exclude the mental from the study of human beings is like excluding atoms from the study of physics. Psychology must use the data of consciousness rather than the data of sense. Data of consciousness is not private and unverifiable. When I describe the characteristics of an insight to a class of students and give relevant examples, they seem to understand. When I ask them to describe their own acts of understanding, they can do so, and I can verify that they have understood. So the method I have used in this psychology of knowledge has been introspection and self-appropriation: actual descriptions by scientists, artists, students, and professors compared and corrected with reference to my own cognitional experience and checked again in communications with others.

It was necessary to journey through a psychology of knowing ourselves. I have been answering the question, "What are we doing when we are knowing?" I demonstrated that the data of consciousness is something about which we can ask and answer intelligent questions. I used a method of introspection or self-appropriation to describe these activities, noted the sequence in which they occurred, became familiar with them, and gradually took possession of the mind. Anyone has the capacity to turn his or her attention to the activities of the mind, name them, distinguish them, note the sequence in which they occur, note how they start and finish, and note the judgment that brings the process to an end.

It is true that the starting point is subjective; it is a study of the subject as struggling to know. But this is only the starting point and not the end point. The purpose of this chapter and the next is to move from authentic subjectivity to genuine objectivity. We do not do this in terms of moving from in here to out there. The main conclusion after nine chapters is that we know not by imagining but by judging. Hence, I will proceed to posit a set of strategic judgments, which will implicitly define subject and object and will allow us to be able to establish the objectivity of knowing.

The detailed, psychological description of the activities of knowing is just a starting point. It is the most effective starting point because we are at home with subjectivity, interiority, consciousness, introspection, and the phenomenological. Once we have established this starting point, we are free to build on a firm foundation.

So far, I have made no ontological claims. I have not even claimed that the activities of knowing actually gain objective knowledge of the real.. I have tried to introduce no philosophical presuppositions or conclusions. I have presented a detailed description of the process of what is commonly called "knowing." I have tried to explain the position of materialism, dualism, and idealism because of their attention or lack of attention to the process of knowing. I have prescinded from metaphysical statements about the world or the self. My hope is that the reader has performed these same activities of self-appropriation and thus, can confirm the process that I have described.

Transitioning to Philosophy

I have presented a phenomenological description of the process of human knowing, but now that knowing process needs to be implemented in an orderly sequence that will provide a foundation for a critical philosophy. We must establish that a subject can know objective reality, that the subject is real, the object is real, and that the knower knows the real object. In precritical times, one could take this for granted, but we are now living in critical times. We have to face the critique of Kant, the critique of skeptics, and the various philosophies using the senses as their model for knowing. We have to face the challenge of establishing foundations for philosophy, which do not involve presupposing what we are trying to prove. The only thing I will be presupposing is the correctness of the account of knowing that I have already established in great detail.

The question now is, "Why is it that by performing those activities we know? Does the subject, who performs the operations previously described, know objective reality and be sure that he or she has attained knowledge?" I am shifting gears from simply describing activities commonly referred to as knowing, to implementing that power of knowing; hence, we will be able to make true statements about the universe and about ourselves. By simply describing the activity of understanding, I have still been sitting on the fence in regards to the scope and objectivity of our knowing. Now it is time to move from empirical psychology to a philosophical understanding of the objectivity of knowing. How can we be sure that, by performing cognitional activities described in this text, we know the real world?

I am not sure that phenomenology takes this extra step beyond merely describing the process of knowing. The question still rages as to whether Husserl was a realist or an idealist. He does not seem to have been explicit and clear on the issue. In *The End of Phenomenology*, Tom Sparrow argues that Husserl was an idealist: essences can be known as real only in a circumscribed sense. In response, Sparrow outlines the position of a number of speculative realists in the phenomenological tradition who have developed a realist position.

My strategy to make this transition is to consider three fundamental judgments and explore the implications of this set of judgments. This is a way of transitioning from psychology to philosophy, from cognitional theory to epistemology, and from describing the activities of knowing to a strategic implementation of that power of knowing.

The previous ten chapters have argued that truth is found in the judgment and only in the judgment. Hence, if we are to attain truth it must be by way of judgments and not imagination, sense, hypothetical understanding, feeling, political correctness, authority of tradition, or anything else. It is not an imaginative correspondence between the in here and the out there. It is not to be found by eliminating subjectivity and espousing an objectivity that can do without human minds. It is not a direct, intuitive contact with reality. Truth is to be found in asking the critical question, assembling evidence for and against, connecting the evidence to a conclusion, and grasping the rational necessity of affirming or denying the conclusion. It is an impalpable, invisible, complicated, intellectual activity. It is a culmination of many preliminary preparatory acts of understanding. If we are to make a transition from the subjective activity of knowing to its objective counterpart in the known, we must do so in judgments and the cognitional activities required to make a correct judgment. Hence, the focus will be on a set of three interrelated judgments, which are of strategic importance for establishing this transition. Here I present an overview of these three judgments to be discussed in detail afterwards.

1. *Self-affirmation.* The first judgment is whether we can affirm the statement, "I am a knower" as true and undeniable. Most of this chapter will consider this point.

2. *Simple judgment of objects.* The second affirmation is a simple judgment, such as, "This is a computer." We can consider as many simple examples of judgments as we wish. The point is that if we are knowers, we can pass judgments, provided there is sufficient evidence and a link between the evidence and the conclusion. The last section of this chapter considers this point.

3. *Distinguishing between knower and known.* Can we then affirm that, "I am not this computer"? There are real distinctions in our universe between knowers and the known. Further, these distinctions are objective in the many correct meanings of this much abused word. The following chapter will address this point.

The strength of the argument is in the combination of the three judgments. Together, they implicitly define subject and object, knower and known. The argument depends on the truth of the three individual judgments, and not on a further judgment about objectivity. If the three judgments are true, then we have already established the principal notion of objectivity. The three judgments are relatively innocent and simple; combined they give a rational, rather than an imaginative, grounding for the notion of objective knowing of the real. I am actually establishing foundations for a philosophy that takes a stand on the fundamental issues of any philosophy, namely, knowing, being, and objectivity.

First Strategic Judgment: Self-Affirmation

Consider the first strategic judgment, the simple affirmation that "I am a knower." It is not as if we ever doubted this rather basic statement, but now we are in a position to affirm it as true. Whereas previously such a judgment was implicit in all of our knowing, now we posit this strategically, explicitly, critically, and foundationally. The previous chapters have defined the meaning of knowing; all the work thus far prepares the way for this judgment. Making this judgment will open the way for the possibility of further judgments.

We can put this in the form of positing the antecedent in the hypothetical syllogism, which makes the procedure explicit:

> *Hypothesis:* I am a knower.
> *Link between Conditions and Hypothesis*: If I am a conscious self who experiences, understands and judges, then, I am a knower.
> *Fulfillment of the Conditions*: But I am a conscious self who experiences, understands and judges.
> *The Verified Conclusion*: Therefore, I am a knower.

What do we mean by knower? A knower is a person who experiences, understands, judges, and evaluates—all terms I have explained in detail already. However, we need to examine the other terms in the proposition "I am a knower" carefully.

What do we mean by the self? Thus far, I have dwelt at length on the activities of imagining, thinking, reasoning, and judging in all their forms and details. We have become conscious of these mental activities by working on a puzzle or problem, and then reflecting back and identifying the activities by which we solved the problem. The next step is to become conscious of the subject, who is always there concomitantly with our awareness of objects or activities. How can we become aware of this subject, the I, the self?

It cannot be done directly. If we try to turn around and become directly aware of the self, we can to some extent succeed; however, what we become aware of by this direct reflex action is the subject as object and not the subject as subject. To the extent that it is possible to direct attention explicitly at the self, then the self becomes an object and not a subject. To become aware of the subject as subject we have to heighten the awareness of the self, which is concomitant with the awareness of activities or objects.

This awareness of the self is there in all conscious activities; that is the meaning of a conscious activity (see chapter 2).

This experience of the self is given; it is the one subject who performs all the cognitional activities at the different levels; this is what unifies the different activities so that they are activities of the same subject. The experience of the self continues over time—from emerging childhood memories, to maturity, and old age. It is the same self who wakes up in the morning, washes, dresses, eats, prays, studies, travels, works, relates to others, relaxes, plays, returns home, goes to bed, sleeps, perchance to dream. This experienced unity is given; without it, knowledge would be impossible. It starts as an experience but can become self-knowledge. The one subject is conscious empirically, intelligently, rationally, and responsibly.

Hume challenged the notion of the self as given in experience. His position was that the self is sensed and that all knowing is by sensation. Hence, senses provide a sequence of individual sensations, but not the idea of continuity, sameness, permanence, and substance. These latter ideas are habits of the mind, by which we conveniently associate sensations together. But they have no reality in themselves. This seems to have been the beginning of the modern attack on the self as a personal, enduring, and real subject. If all human knowing was sensing alone then Hume would have drawn a correct conclusion. But human knowing is not experiencing alone; it is questioning experience in order to understand, and reflecting on that understanding in order to utter a judgment.

Awareness of self turns into knowledge of the self by a simple process of reduplication. First, we are aware of ourselves as subjects perduring over time, and as subject of many operations of thinking, deciding, sensing, and the like. Second, we can understand this self and define it for what it is, from what it does. Third, we can affirm it to be true and real in a correct judgment. Consciousness of self turns into knowledge of the self. (Whether the self is material or spiritual is a further question best left for metaphysics.)

Now, what do we mean by being conscious? It is simply the difference between being unconscious and conscious (see chapter 2). To be conscious is to be aware, awake, alert, paying attention, aware of objects, and aware of the self concomitantly in one conscious act.

Are we then prepared to affirm the judgment, "I am a knower" in a personal way? There should be no difficulty making this judgment. The terms have been explained, not just as concepts, but as corresponding to identifiable activities and experiences. The evidence is there in the act of self-appropriation. The evidence is given in the data of consciousness. The evidence is in the fact that we ask questions, struggle to solve a puzzle, wrestle with truth, or wonder if our friend is lying to us. The evidence is in the intricate mental processes we go through to perform a simple task such as purchasing a cell phone. Making a judgment rests on evidence and the link between the evidence and the conclusion. It seems to be that there is ample evidence for the judgment of self-affirmation, if we advert to our own mental acts. It seems to me that the conditions are amply fulfilled.

Are alternative answers possible? A judgment can be a yes, a no, anything in between, or I don't know. In this case, which of these answers are coherent? Which answers are possible? Is it possible to say, "No, I am not a knower"? It is possible but deeply incoherent. In this case, the person understands a question, experiences the relevant data, understands what is referred to, and passes a judgment; yet the person claims not to be a knower! This is deeply self-contradictory: the content of the judgment is in fundamental conflict with the activity of affirming the judgment.

Is it possible to say, "Well, maybe I am a knower, but I am not sure"? There is a sense in which this is legitimate. If a person has not fully understood the terms of the question, or has not fully understood the preceding discussion on this topic, it would be reasonable to say, "Wait a little bit until I go over this again." That is a perfectly reasonable procedure. But having done the bit of review required, having understood the terms of reference, the data, the conditions, and the link between the hypothesis and the fulfilling conditions, can one still be reasonable and sit on the fence? Once one has grasped the implications of the syllogism, then it becomes incoherent to affirm definitively "I am not sure." Once one has sufficient evidence, it is no longer reasonable to refrain from judging.

Is it possible to say, "I do not know"? Again this is incoherent. It involves a profound contradiction between the content of what is being affirmed and the activity of affirming a judgment. A judgment is being passed, but the content of the judgment is saying that no judgment can be passed. This is not just a clever way of rebutting an adversary; it reveals an intrinsic contradiction between performance and content.

The answer, "Yes, I am a knower" is coherent. This is the only answer that makes sense. It is in harmony with the evidence. There is harmony between the activity of knowing and the content of the judgment. It builds on what we have been saying all along. It prepares the way for many other prospective judgments.

This lays the foundations for a multitude of other judgments. If I am a knower, then other judgments can be posited, if, of course, there is sufficient evidence. We can make judgments of common sense, accepting the limitations of descriptive knowing, while recognizing that it is still valid human knowing. We can make judgments of the classical scientific type, if we have moved into theory, which involves defining our terms explanatorily and experimentally showing the truth of our laws. We can make judgments of a statistical type, if we have established the ideal frequencies from which actual frequencies diverge nonsystematically. In this way we can build up a body of knowledge based on correct judgments. It is not that we first doubted or suspended our knowledge of common sense and science and can now reintroduce them. The starting point has been the subject as he or she tries to gradually sort out his or her confusion and disorientation. Now at least one pillar is in place: at least we can affirm that I am a knower, in the sense that has been defined throughout this book.

Contrast with Descartes

My approach to self-affirmation may be reminiscent of Descartes's *cogito, ergo sum*, so allow me to explain where I agree with and where I differ from Descartes. The method by which I arrive at this judgment of self-affirmation differs from Descartes's, but we agree that there is something basically right about the conclusion, *cogito, ergo sum*. Despite this agreement in the conclusion, I part ways with a number of Descartes's positions.

Descartes approached the *cogito* by way of the principle of methodological doubt; he systematically doubted everything until he found some principle that was indubitable. But if we start down that road, we find that what we consider indubitable becomes rather arbitrary. The criterion of indubitability is too demanding as a criterion for most human knowing. Some have managed to think of themselves as a brain in a vat and have no way of refuting such an absurdity. So the *cogito* is not indubitable to really skeptical souls. Descartes's preparation for the affirmation of the *cogito* was totally negative by way of doubting everything. On the contrary, I have prepared the way to the judgment of self-affirmation by way of a detailed, positive, and comprehensive account of human thinking and knowing.

Descartes's approach was to doubt everything that could be doubted. My approach has been to investigate how in fact we come to know, how questioning leads to understanding, which leads to judgment. I have investigated how we tend to make mistakes, but then, how we recognize mistakes, correct them, learn from them, and build up mastery in a field.

Further, Descartes made little attempt to define his terms, especially the term "knower." For him there was little difference between a thinker and a knower; he affirmed the existence of a thinking subject, not a knowing subject. This distinction has been the crucial task of this text. Everything I have been doing has been related to the self-appropriation of the knowing subject. Descartes, more or less, presumed a kind of rationalist approach to knowing.

Knowing was having clear and distinct ideas. Once he affirmed the self as a thinking subject, it was deductive logic that got him to God, to knowledge of the senses, and then to scientific knowledge of the concrete universe.

All in all, Descartes really did not say much about the I, the self, the subject. There is very little discussion of the self, the conscious subject, consciousness of self as concomitant with consciousness of objects, or the movement from subjectivity to objectivity. Descartes is credited with beginning the turn to the subject, but it is a very incomplete turn.

Yet there is a fundamental correctness about Descartes' position on self-affirmation, "I think, therefore I am," and I identify with this. There is something basically incontrovertible about the judgment, "I am a thinking self." There is something ridiculous in the image of a subject who goes around claiming, "I am not a thinker." The former seems coherent, reasonable, incontrovertible, and foundational. The latter is incoherent.

Second Strategic Judgment: the Notion of Being

If we are knowers in the sense of the self-affirmation of the knower described above, then we can implement this potential in all of the fields that are open to us. I suggested the simple judgment, "This is a computer" as a start. But this could be expanded in any direction, provided that knowledge comes by way of acts of reflective insight that grasp the sufficiency of the evidence for the inferring of the judgment. We can affirm all our commonsense judgments of facts; all the judgments posited in our own area of expertise, all theoretical judgments based on measurement or definition, all responsible value judgments that inform our life.

Is there any limit or unity to the content of all of these correct judgments? Where are we heading when we continue to affirm correct judgments? Philosophers coined the term "being," perhaps since the time of Parmenides. The history of philosophy tells the story of how this poor word has been used and abused, discarded and recovered, expanded and contracted, defined and divided. I am now in a position to present a somewhat new definition: being is the content of the totality of correct judgments. Let me explain.

Previously, I noted that the desire to know is unrestricted. There is nothing in the universe about which we cannot ask questions. We intend and desire knowledge about everything. Unfortunately, we cannot attain knowledge of everything about everything. Our time, our abilities, and our lifespan, not to mention the nature of human understanding, preclude a full grasp of everything about everything. Yet the principle remains that nothing is of itself, by itself, excluded entirely from being an objective of the desire to know.

As I understand the term, "everything" is a simple English equivalent for the technical philosophical term "being." Thus, we can also define being as the objective of the pure, detached, unrestricted desire to know. The definition is all-inclusive. It includes the known and the unknown; the possible and the real; the perfect and the imperfect; the actual and the potential; sense and nonsense; the regular and the irregular; the past, the present, and the future; the finite and the infinite; the temporal and the eternal; the concrete and the abstract; the personal and the impersonal; and so on forever and ever.

It is impossible to give a direct, normal definition of being because it is a unique notion. Normal procedures of definition specify what a thing is and what it is not. If we define a human person as a rational animal, then we are excluding inanimate things and irrational animals. But the trouble with defining being is that we cannot exclude anything from its scope. We must, then, use an indirect method by defining being as the objective of the desire to know. This includes everything that is known and everything that is to be known. It is a heuristic definition that anticipates the general lines of everything to be known. It is a very effective strategy that places the desire to know first and the known second. The advantage of this procedure is that we have a personal familiarity with the desire to know, and the intention of knowing gives us an indirect handle on the meaning of that difficult term "being." We can ask questions about anything; thus, we intend knowledge of everything. As a result, we can define being as the objective of the desire to know.

I have given a detailed account of the process of knowing. We can use this account to define the known; knowing is knowing being. Being is not a concept, because a concept includes the essential and excludes the nonessential. It is a notion in that it is an indirect way of specifying the objective of knowing. Being is not to be thought of as the most abstract of concepts, being qua being, of which the later Scholastics spoke. It is not separate and apart from the knowledge of common sense and science but, on the contrary, underlies, penetrates, and constitutes such knowing.

Third Strategic Judgment: Subjectivity and Objectivity

I suggested as the third strategic judgment the simple affirmation, "I am not this computer." This does not sound very difficult, and in light of our familiarity in making good judgments, it is not problematic; however, it is of crucial importance. Again, I am focusing on judgments as the expression of truth and judgments as the basis for our notion of subjectivity and objectivity. I chose the particular judgment, "This is a computer," but any other simple judgment could have been chosen. I can extend this judgment to most of the things that I know, and presume that each of these things that I affirm are not only distinct from myself, but also distinct from one another.

The first point of significance here is that we have moved from monism to pluralism. Implicitly, this statement affirms the real distinction between various objects of judgment and the self, and it also affirms that objects are distinct from one another. We have a universe of distinct persons and a universe of distinct objects of knowing. The Eleatic position in affirming that being is one and there is no becoming is implicitly rejected in the light of the affirmation of the existence of distinct real things and persons.

The second point of significance is that we reach a certain closure. The three judgments are interrelated and form a set of judgments. If the judgments are true, then we have succeeded in giving an implicit definition of the subject and an implicit definition of the object. The self of the first judgment is now really distinct from the object of the second judgment. We can give a meaning to subject and object that derives from judgments and not from an imaginative picture of in here and out there. In the next chapter, I will explore in detail the notion of subject and object, subjectivity and objectivity. But the essential groundwork has now been completed.

Conclusion

I have been making the transition from considering the activities of knowing from a neutral psychological point of view, to implementing that structure seriously and strategically, affirming it in all of its implications, and stating clearly what those implications are. We have made three strategically important judgments: (1) "I am a knower," as defined throughout this text; (2) "This is a computer," which is one particular instantiation of all that is to be known through the structure of knowing; and (3) "I am not this computer," which sets up a real distinction between myself and the computer, and hence, an implicit definition of subject and object. The full significance of these judgments comes when we put the three together in an interrelated and contrasting set, which amounts to a foundationally grounded epistemology. We have actually answered the question, "Why is doing that knowing?" And we have an implicit definition of subject and object. The subject performs the operations of questioning, understanding, and judging; the object is what is known when these operations are performed correctly. The subject is distinct from the object; subjectivity is different from objectivity. We are poised to elaborate on this in the next chapter.

11

From Subjectivity to Objectivity

The notion of subjectivity and objectivity is a many-sided one. Authentic knowing involves a series of different mental activities, unfolding on four levels of consciousness, and things can go wrong at either or all levels. In what follows, I will distinguish between a principal notion of objectivity and three partial notions of objectivity, namely, absolute, normative, and experiential. This chapter is conceived as a reply to the many difficulties that are raised against the possibility of objective knowledge. Throughout this book, I have stressed judgments as the only way to truth and reality. I now exploit this principle in order to establish the true meaning of subjectivity and objectivity in terms of explicit, clear judgments, rather than some vague imaginative thinking about in here and out there.

Subjectivity and Objectivity as Commonly Conceived

Sometimes, subjectivity and objectivity are conceived as opposed and mutually exclusive: the subjective is viewed with suspicion and presumed to be a bad influence, whereas, the objective is lauded as the real thing. They are opposed because of the imaginative schema of the subjective as in here and the objective as out there. This is so common as to be almost universal. The path to objectivity in this schema is to ignore, eliminate, or suppress all subjective elements, which interfere with the objectivity of results. In this case, what is called "subjective" lumps together everything—good and bad—that goes on in the mind, such as prejudice, bias, and self-interest, as well as questions, hypotheses, ideas, judgments, and values. Knowledge becomes so objective, so logical, and so controlled by rules and methods that it can do without human minds, by eliminating the subjective.

In this context, the critical problem is inevitably presented in terms of a bridge between the subjective in here and the objective out there. Descartes, Hume, and Kant all seem to have thought in terms of the in here and the out there, and their theories of knowledge unfolded against the background of these unquestioned, imaginative assumptions. But this imaginative presentation poses insuperable problems when we question how we know that what we know is true. How do we know that the subjective really attains the objective? In this imaginative context it could only be by means of a kind of super-knowing, by which we would compare the subjective and the objective to see if they really correspond. But this does not seem to be humanly possible. And so skepticism about knowing objective reality ensues.

Many of the misunderstandings identified in chapter 9 are versions of misunderstandings about subjectivity and objectivity. The senses are not a basis for distinguishing objective and subjective. Animal sensing provides an animal criterion of the real in the sense of real survival, real food, real enemies, and real dangers. But only humans can use the word "real" and know that it is the content of a true judgment. Materialists are quite happy thinking of the objective as imaginative lumps of inert matter and energy that can be sensed. But imagination is not the basis for distinguishing the objective from the subjective. Many situations are imaginable but not real; other situations are real but not directly imaginable. Imagination is indispensable but can also be a hindrance in the process of correct understanding and judging. Intuition does not put us in contact with reality; intuition cannot distinguish subjective and objective except on the basis of an imaginative in here and out there. It is judgments that attain the real, not intuitions.

Is there, then, an alternative way of viewing the notions of subjectivity and objectivity, that is, to view them as complementary rather than opposed? I think there is. The examination of the subjective aspects of knowing helps us to distinguish between the proper role of imagination to facilitate understanding, and the imperious force of imagination, which foists on us false problems and false solutions. We can discriminate between subjective factors such as bias, prejudice, and self-interest, which interfere, distort, and poison results on the one hand, and subjective factors such as commitment, honesty, ideas, hypotheses, and judgments, which are essential for correct human knowing on the other. My examination of subjectivity has been precisely in order to attain genuine objectivity. Objectivity is to be found not by eliminating subjectivity but by implementing an authentic subjectivity. We need to discriminate between various subjective elements, some of which are distorting and unauthentic, but many of which are essential to the proper unfolding of the process of correct knowing.

Similarly, developments in the objective pole help us to be more conscious of the subjective pole. It is the precision and accuracy of scientific method that has helped us to identity "theory verified in instances," thus, paralleling the very structure of human knowing in experiencing, understanding, and judging. The clash between science and common sense calls forth the distinction between description and explanation. It is the clash between classical science and statistical science that has provoked the need to identify inverse insights, which are insights into nonsystematic divergence from ideal frequencies. The struggle in science between the imaginable and the intelligible has helped us to distinguish between verifiable and nonverifiable images. Science has also worked on the distinction between hypothesis and verification and this has helped in discriminating between understanding and judging, between second and third-level cognitional activities. Intelligence and the intelligible are correlatives; they develop together. Genuine objectivity helps us to attain authentic subjectivity.

The so-called bridge between the subjective and the objective is a construction of the imagination and has to be abandoned. The transition from subjective to objective in my account is a matter of a shift of focus from the activities to the content, from the knower to the known. Anything that we say about subjectivity or objectivity must be based on judgments that are affirmed on the basis of sufficient evidence and the link between the evidence and the conclusions.

My motto is: "Genuine objectivity is the fruit of authentic subjectivity."[1] I hope that this examination of human knowing has been authentic, that is, attentive, intelligent, reasonable, and responsible. I have tried to face up to the data of consciousness, to sort it out, to identify the different activities, to relate the different movements, and to verify the conclusions by reference back to the data of consciousness. I have critically examined questions or conceivable objections about this approach. I have not been relying on authority or tradition or political correctness. Authentic subjectivity is the springboard for genuine objectivity. It has taken a long time to prepare the way for this step, because the shift from subjectivity to objectivity is often misunderstood. I will attempt to clean the slate and try to rehabilitate the terms "subjective" and "objective," not in terms of the imagination where they are opposed, but in terms of judgment where they complement one another.

1. Lonergan, *Method in Theology,* 292.

The Principal Notion of Objectivity

The principal notion of objectivity resides in a context of correct judgments, not in a single judgment. The single judgment, "I am a knower," is not in itself sufficient to establish the principal notion of objectivity. On its own, the judgment is consistent with a monist philosophy or with solipsism. A monist claims, "I am a knower," but considers that everything is one and that knowers are identical with the one; thus, there is still no objectivity. A solipsist claims, "I am a knower," but there is nothing else; this too does not establish the principal notion of objectivity.

Objectivity arises by combining the judgment, "I am a knower," with a context of other judgments such as, "This is a computer," and, "I am not this computer." These three interrelated, true judgments introduce verifiable distinctions between knowers and objects known, and hence, between subjects and objects. The principal notion of objectivity lies in these distinctions. The more correct judgments that we make, the more differentiated our principal notion of objectivity becomes.

Note that objectivity does not rest on the validity of a single judgment. It is not a judgment that something is out there as opposed to in here. It is not a judgment apart from the context of judgments. The context of judgments implicitly defines our notion of objectivity for us. The three judgments form a set by which we can implicitly distinguish subject and object. Not any random three judgments will do. The first judgment must be the judgment of self-affirmation. The second judgment can be any true judgment about anything in the universe. The third judgment must be a negative judgment that distinguishes the subject from the object. Then, we have implicitly affirmed a subject who is distinct from an object, and simultaneously, an object that is distinct from the subject.

The validity of this notion of objectivity rests on the validity of the particular judgments in question. If the three judgments are true—namely, I am a knower, this is a computer, and I am not this computer—then, implicitly, we have validated our notion of objectivity. If these judgments are not correct, then our notion of objectivity collapses.

This is what might be called an economical notion. It is the bare minimum of what can be justified by judgments and is not dominated by imagination. It leaves open further questions that could be answered by further judgments. It is an example of implicit definition. The principal notion of objectivity adds nothing new to the three judgments; it does not add a fourth judgment. This notion of objectivity rests on distinctions between knower and known, and not on a distinction between in here and out there.

The subject is doing the knowing; the object is the content of the known. The two are correlative; one is defined in terms of the other.

Further judgments can be added to the objective pole. We can affirm all of the true discoveries of technology, engineering, physics, quantum physics, particle physics, astronomy, medicine, and the like. It all adds to a differentiated notion of the objective world. But we can also expand our understanding and judgments about the subjective pole. There is so much more to be clarified about understanding, about the role of the senses in bringing relevant images to mind, and about the affective dimension and its ambivalent influences on the process of knowing. The knower can also be known; understanding can also be understood. We can distinguish between the self as subject and the self as object.

It might help to appeal to the image of triangulation. If a single ship on the surface is trying to locate the exact position of a submarine, the ship may find the direction of the submarine without knowing the depth or distance. But if three ships each have a reading on the direction of the submarine, the three readings can be put together in order to get an exact position of the submarine. Three unrelated readings are not enough; they must be coordinated readings to make a useful triangulation. In searching for objectivity, neither sensation nor imagination provide a valid reading. One single judgment is not enough either. Three coordinated judgments are needed to establish genuine objectivity.

Lonergan similarly invokes a military metaphor of breakthrough, encirclement, and confinement.[2] The judgment of self-affirmation is the breakthrough; it is a judgment, an example of the actually verified. It is a first strategic affirmation that is not open to basic revision, for which enormous amounts of evidence exists, and where contrary judgments are incoherent. Encirclement represents the affirmation that "this is a computer," and all other true affirmations that we can posit about the universe. The more true judgments we have, the more refined our notion of being and beings becomes. The third negative judgment that "I am not this computer" is represented by confinement, the consolidation, the closure. The issue is closed, objectivity is reached, and the war is won.

Immanence and Transcendence

The principal notion of objectivity solves the problem of immanence and transcendence. By immanence, I mean confined to or imprisoned in the subjective. By transcendence, I simply mean being able to go beyond the

2. Lonergan, *Insight*, 508–9.

self to an objective reality. The principal notion of objectivity as explained above solves the problem of transcendence. The problem of immanence and transcendence can be seen as a legacy of Kant. Kant held that we know by intuition (see chapter 9). In sensitivity, according to Kant, we have sensible intuitions of sense data; hence, at the level of sensing we transcend ourselves as sensing to that which is sensed. However, at the level of understanding there is no intellectual intuition of the intelligible. Hence, we cannot transcend ourselves to know the intelligible, or what he called the noumenon, the thing-in-itself. If we cannot know causes, relations, necessities, equalities, and the like, then we cannot know the real world. We cannot transcend our knowing to the known, we are imprisoned in immanence. We assume that the noumenon exists, but strictly speaking we cannot know that it exists. It is not easy to reply to this position of Kant, because the real problem is that he is answering the wrong question, the one posed by the imagination. He has left a heritage of immanentism and a challenge to come up with a better account of human knowing of objective reality. My approach to immanence and transcendence would be as follows.

Knowing is intentional and intends an object or a content; it is transitive. Questions aim at the known unknown; they give a direction to inquiry, set the criteria for a correct answer, and suggest ways in which questions might be answered. There is a purpose underlining the question that seeks an answer. It is the content that is intended; the activity of knowing is for the sake of the content. We do not indulge in the activities of knowing for personal amusement but in order to grasp the content.

All the activities of our knowing intend objects or contents other than themselves. In all our knowing there is an activity and a content. The content is different from the activity. It is distinct from the activity. There is always a subject pole and an object pole in knowing. This intentionality is present in the desire to know but unfolds in specific ways at each of the levels of consciousness. At the level of sensing, there is an intention of the sensible; sensing senses the sensible. At the level of understanding there is an intention toward the intelligible, which may be the possibly relevant hypothesis, or a possible definition or explanation. At the level of reflection there is an intention toward truth or correct understanding. The intention is not satisfied until such verification is attained. The intention of value asks about the worth of new inventions or discoveries and passes a judgment of value on them. The intention keeps the flow of questions moving until all relevant questions have been asked and answered in a satisfactory manner. The subject and object poles on these various levels is illustrated in the following table:

	Subjective Pole	Objective Pole	
One Knowing	Intent of Knowing ⟶ Content of Knowing		One Known
Evaluated	Judging Value ⟶ Value, Good		a good
Verified	Judging Truth ⟶ True, Real, Exists		is
Theory	Understanding ⟶ Intelligible, Idea		computer
In Instances	Experiencing ⟶ Sensible, Visible, Data		This
	Desire to Know ⟶ Being		

Table 2: Critical Realism and Objectivity

There is a kind of self-transcendence at the level of experience. There is a real distinction between the subject doing the sensing, hearing or seeing, and the object that is sensed, heard, or seen. We are responsible for the seeing but not for the seen. The content of sensing is given: we did not invent it, create it, or make it come to be; it is simply given. The sensing is different from the sensed, and we already have a rudimentary self-transcendence in that we attain to what is distinct from our act of knowing. We do not invent the data of sense that verifies our classical laws. There is an element of submission to the reality of what is given.

There is a kind of self-transcendence at the level of understanding. We intend the intelligible, namely, the relations, definitions, and causes that make sense of the data of sensible experience. There is a real distinction between the subject performing the activities of understanding and the objects or terms that are finally understood. This is not an intuition. It is not a simple, direct, intellectual seeing; rather it is a three-fold activity of asking questions for intelligence, developing ideas from images, and constructing concepts.

There is a further level of self-transcendence when it comes to critical reflection. We intend the truth, the actually verified. This is the objective pole of the knowing process. It is the terminus of all the activities. It is quite independent from the knowing subject. The activities of knowing depend on the subject, but the conditions for the truth of the judgment in itself do not depend on the subject.

Similarly, there is self-transcendence in judgments of value. The question intends the good, the valuable, or the usefulness of an action.

Deliberative understanding searches for evidence for and against possible judgments, works out arguments for possible judgments, and finally issues in a judgment of value: this is the best thing to do in these circumstances. The goodness is actually verified. The goodness is not created by the knowing but is discovered by the knowing. The conditions for the goodness of the thing do not depend on the knowing but are independent of the knowing. We do not make something good by our judgments.[3]

Our diagram (Table 2) illustrates the intentionalities at the different levels. It also shows the proportionality between the knowing and the known. The knowing is one, encapsulated in the left hand column as, theories verified and evaluated in instances. The known is one, instantiated in the simple judgment of value, this is a good computer. All is summed up in the last line; the desire to know is a desire to know being, that is, everything.

As we have seen, there are many versions of realism. There is the real of materialism as the sensible, the material, and only material. There is the real of the imagination as out there as opposed to in here. There is the real as the obvious, simple, incontrovertible, and common sense. There is the real as direct contact through intuition. The examination of the human process of knowing shows that all of these notions do not stand up to examination. Rather, the real is the verified: what is sensed by experience, what is questioned by the intelligence, what is formulated in concepts, what is criticized by reflective understanding, and what is affirmed in a correct judgment. Judgments should be seen as embodying the results of previous activities of sensing and understanding and not as leaving them behind.

Moreover, the notions of intentionality and self-transcendence are not enough to attain objective reality. For that, one judgment is not enough. To establish the subject as knowing, the object known, and the real distinction between them, three interdependent judgments are necessary that implicitly define the subject, the object, and the distinction between them. Once we have the three strategic foundational judgments, we can seek knowledge in every direction, further developing our knowledge of objects and our knowledge of subjects and of the process that links knowing to the known.

Absolute Objectivity

The term "objectivity" is used in many contexts with a range of meaning. Hence, I will distinguish between absolute objectivity, normative

---

3. There is a further level of self-transcendence when it comes to moral decisions and actions in conformity with judgments of truth and value, but that subject is beyond the scope of my project.

objectivity, and experiential objectivity, which approximately correspond to the three levels of judgment, understanding, and experience. Knowing unfolds through a series of interrelated activities and an appropriate notion of objectivity is called for in each case. There is a good way and a bad way of performing these activities. In this section, I am concerned with the objectivity of true judgments.

At the level of judging, we encounter a partial notion of objectivity, which I call "absolute objectivity." For example, imagine that an acquaintance sends a somewhat offensive email. He might immediately regret it. He might try to delete it. He might immediately send another email rescinding, apologizing, or asserting the polar opposite of the first email. But what has been done cannot be undone. Whatever he might try to do, it will be forever true, that at that time, in that place, he sent the offensive email. Nothing can change that fact. An almighty deity could annihilate the universe, make time go backward, or recreate dinosaurs, but even an almighty deity could not change the fact, that at that time, in that place, he sent that email. This truth does not depend on how many people read it, on how many people agree with it, on how many people know about it, or on how many people believe his denials that he sent it. If he sent it, he sent it, and nothing can change the absoluteness of that simple factual truth.

The absoluteness belongs to the element of truth and not to the material content of the judgment. The material content of a proposition changes according to whether it is contingent or necessary, probable or certain, particular or general, descriptive or explanatory, or scientific or philosophic. But any of these propositions can be either true or false. The absoluteness belongs to this truth value and not to the content of the proposition. If something is *de facto* true, then there is a certain absoluteness to that truth. Truth has this quality of absoluteness, even if it is a contingent, trivial, transient truth.

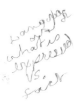

The basic reason for this is that the truth of a proposition does not depend on the knower, but it depends on the conditions being fulfilled and the conditions entailing the conclusion. When Einstein discovered that energy equals mass multiplied by the square of the speed of light, he was not bringing a new reality into being. It has always been that way; as far as we know it will always be that way. It would have continued like that even if Einstein had not discovered the equation. To the extent that that relation of energy to mass is true, it is absolutely true. Philosophers have searched for the absolute, but they have often searched in the wrong places. On my account, the absolute is the actually verified; if something is true, the conditions that make it true are independent of the knowing subject. The conditions need not necessarily be fulfilled, but in the actual case of $E=mc^2$, they happen to be fulfilled, and so the conditioned becomes the actually verified. To the extent that it is true, it is absolutely true.

In this text, I have focused on the subjective activities that finally produce true judgments. However, we must note that the conditions for the truth of a judgment are not subjective. What we know by judgment is what is. We do not make it to be by our knowing; by our knowing we know that it is and, perhaps, why it is. There is a fundamental detachability of the grounds of judgment from the knowing subject. In knowing, we know what is true, but we do not make it to be true by our knowing.

This is the source of the logical principles of identity and contradiction. These principles state that a thing is what it is, and the same thing cannot both be and not be at the same time, in the same respect. If something is true for today, it can become untrue tomorrow; for instance, it may be raining today, but it may not be raining tomorrow. From the point of view of description, a statement may be true, but from the point of view of explanation the same statement may be false. The principles assert that from the same point of view, at the same time and in all respects, something cannot simultaneously be true and untrue. This is the ground for the absolute notion of objectivity. If it is true that it is raining here and now, then that limited statement in relation to this place and time will always be true, and the negation of that judgment will always be false. If there is a correct judgment, then within the limits of time and space of the judgment, it will always be true and can never be truly negated. The principles of identity and contradiction are not conclusions of logic, nor are they only principles of logic. They are the conditions for the possibility of thinking and knowing. They are immanent in knowing; it is only by examining the process of knowing that we discover the principles of identity and contradiction. Knowing is impossible without these principles. They cannot be proved, they cannot be demonstrated; they are the conditions for the possibility of any thinking and demonstration. They are what thinking, understanding, and knowing are all about.

Both universal and particular judgments, if true, are absolutely true. The two statements, "It is raining," and, "Water is H_2O," if they are true and to the extent that they are true, are absolutely true. Both certain and probable judgments share in this absoluteness of a correct judgment. "It will probably rain," and, "It will certainly rain," if true, share equally in the absolute notion of objectivity. Both descriptive judgments and explanatory judgments can express the absolute notion of truth. From a descriptive point of view, it is absolutely true that the sun rises in the east and sets in the west. From an explanatory point of view, it is absolutely true that the earth rotates on its axis, and so the sun appears to rise in the east and set in the west.

This is extremely important in our answer to relativists, skeptics, and others who think that truth is only found in certain, permanent, immutable statements. Truth is very nuanced; there is the truth of probability statements, of universal statements, of contingent statements, and of scientific and philosophic statements. But to the extent that they are true, they are true.

By way of contrast, we can compare this with the attitude of those who say, "What is true for me need not be true for you." This is clearly the opposite position to this absolute notion of truth and accepts a totally relativist position. A limited relativism is inevitable in human discourse. Not everybody will agree with everyone about everything. People differ according to their tastes, priorities, age, contexts, perspectives, and cultures. Changes in the context introduce changes in the meaning, and consequently, changes in the truth value of a statement. But there is a limit to relativism; the same statement with the same meaning cannot be both true and not true at the same time and in the same respect. In many clear-cut examples there is no room for relativity or ambiguity. If the Seattle Seahawks defeated the Denver Broncos in the Super Bowl of 2014, then there is an absoluteness to the truth of that statement, such that it is eternally and absolutely true. Any denial of that truth must be a falsehood. It is true not only to me and to you but to all people of all time and place.

There is a widespread notion in our contemporary culture that we create or construct our own truths. But we can discriminate between areas where our knowing constitutes truth and areas where we discover the truth. Humans constitute truth when they create meaning through cultures, languages, symbols, social institutions, countries, laws of taxation, public order, and so forth. We make a country exist by drawing borders on a map, officially recognizing that country's existence, naming it, accepting it into international bodies, and holding it to account for law and order. We construct the meaning of money by defining its value, printing it, taking responsibility for it, maintaining its value, and trusting the government and financial institutions that back it. We grant meaning to particular languages by using them, accepting them, learning them, defining the meaning of words in dictionaries, and developing the rules of grammar. To that limited extent we constitute the truths of the human world in which we live in terms of language, symbols, laws, conventions, countries, and the like.

However, in the fields of common sense, scientific knowledge of the natural world, and philosophy, we discover the truth rather than create or construct it. There is an element of creativity in our knowing of these things in the sense that we construct hypotheses in order to verify or deny them. But it is the evidence that has the last word. This knowing is not creative in the sense that we determine what is to be true or false. Copernicus, Newton, and

Einstein were not imposing their own ideas on reality. They were discovering which of their ideas could be verified in the actual working of the universe. The solar system is heliocentric and not geocentric. There are three laws of motion that are immanent and operative in all examples of motion in the universe. Simultaneity is not the same for all observers of the same phenomenon. If some Kantian told them they were imposing a priori categories of understanding on the data of sensibility, they would not have been amused.

Is the notion of quarks an imposition on the data of particle physics or a discovery of what is really out there? Did quarks exist before they were discovered? This is a tricky question. If we answer in the affirmative, then we imply that quarks are little marbles that have always existed and we have just come along and put a name on them. If we answer in the negative, then we imply that in knowing them we are also making them exist for the first time. We get out of this dilemma by recognizing that our knowing develops. Over time, we get a more and more accurate understanding of subatomic particles, events, and forces. What is potentially intelligible is becoming actually intelligible. There is a multitude of data that is being uncovered by particle accelerators and the like. But it is only data. It has to be understood, terms have to be defined, and hypotheses have to formed and verified in the reflective act of understanding that grasps the link between the hypothesis and its fulfilling conditions.

In a sense, the quark has always existed, meaning that experiments do not create quarks, but rather lay bare the data that is the foundation for the affirmation of the existence of quarks. In another sense, the quark never existed before, meaning that the term is new, the hypothesis is new, and the verification is recent. Our knowledge of the existence of the quark is recent but there is no reason to think that our knowledge made the quark come into existence. The same data has always existed but it is only now that we have instruments to measure and verify it.

Normative Objectivity

Normative objectivity implies excluding influences that are detrimental to the proper unfolding of the process of knowing such as the subjectivity of bias, prejudice, wishful thinking, self-interest, obscurantism, and the like. The ground for normative objectivity is the proper unfolding of the pure, detached, unrestricted desire to know. It is this desire to know that throws up the further questions that reveal shortcomings in our conclusions. This is the foundation for intellectual probity, which reveals undue influences in the process of knowing. The desire is the foundation for the openness that is prepared to ask any question, face any possibility, look at all the data, and follow every clue wherever they may lead. I have objectivized this obligation in terms of the transcendental precepts to be attentive, intelligent, reasonable, and responsible.

This aspect of the notion of objectivity is fairly obvious. If we need an objectively minded referee for a sporting event, we do not pick him or her from the supporters of either side. If we want to conduct an investigation into possible misbehavior on the part of the police, we do not usually choose a policeman to conduct the inquiry; we choose someone who has no vested interest in the outcome. If we want to investigate the connection between tobacco and lung cancer, we do not choose someone from the tobacco industry to perform the research. It is very human to be influenced by self-interest or the interests of family, class, religion, race, or neighborhood. So we normally try to eliminate these influences from the start.

Contemporary philosophy is very conscious of the subtle influences that can interfere with the objectivity of knowing in this sense. Particularly the work of the three "masters of suspicion" comes to mind here, that of Freud, Marx, and Nietzsche.

Freud revealed some of the influences that the unconscious can exercise on the conscious mind and twist our motivations, our interests, and the direction of our actions. There are many processes of repression, sublimation, resentment, transference, defense mechanisms, needs for self-esteem, and the like that can distort the process of knowing and vitiate the objectivity of our conclusions. It is often concluded that these unconscious forces are always operating, and hence, we cannot be sure of the objectivity of our knowing.

Marx uncovered many of the social factors that influence our knowledge. The ideology of class tends to structure and color everything that we know in terms of class interests. There is no such thing as objective knowledge for Marx, only ideologies of different classes defending their own interests. We are not independent thinkers but are subject to class interests, which determine our values, our attitudes, and our understanding and knowledge. These class interests determine how we are brought up, what we are be expected to do, and how we understand our world.[4]

Nietzsche claims that we use masks to cover up our craving for power and manipulation of others. Moral norms and religious precepts are invented by the psyche to serve these hidden needs. God is merely an invention of an immature psyche that is still unable to take responsibility for existence and death. He claims that we can no longer take statements at their face

---

4. See Berger and Luckmann, *The Social Construction of Reality.*

value, but rather, must ask in what way the speaker benefits from his or her position, and who is exercising power over whom in this instance.

However, if the lust for power fundamentally corrupts the knowing process, then is this particular claim also corrupt? If social conditions fundamentally undermine the validity of our knowing, how can one have a theory of the ideological determinants of consciousness? Taken in their full sense, these positions are self-defeating. Further, the assertions can be turned back on the accusers. Nietzsche claims that religious people have invented God as a Father figure, because they will not take responsibility for the world. But what about his own Superman? As Copleston remarks, "In fine, Superman is all that ailing, lonely, tormented, neglected Herr Professor Dr. Friedrich Nietzsche would like to be."[5]

In my view, these influences do not totally undermine the process of knowing. Rather, we can be objective in the sense of controlling these influences, revealing them, making them explicit, and allowing the pure desire to know unfold in its own proper way. Normativity here means the obligation to be honest, to be detached, and to ask further questions. Social influences do tend to bias our knowing, but these influences can be brought to light and, to some extent, excluded. They need not undermine the project of objective knowing.

It is precisely in the name of preserving this ideal of objective knowing that logic, method, and methodologies have been developed. Logic is needed to check the internal coherence of any set of conclusions; it includes sets of rules concerning definition of terms, division of concepts, deductions, arguments, inference, and so on. These are formulated and made explicit in order to help us check our thought processes and conclusions. But these rules come from man, not from God. They are devices that we formulate in order to help ourselves be objective. Logic is the making explicit of procedures that we use spontaneously but can utilized improperly. People with no training in logic can recognize fallacies, appeal to evidence, and argue for and against a position. But it can help to make these processes explicit. Thinking comes first and logic comes second; logic is itself the result of human knowing.

The methodologies of the social sciences are formulated to exclude bias on the part of the survey designer, the researchers, the interviewers, the compilers, and the interpreters of the data; they are the result of insight and judgment. These methodologies are designed to be a help in excluding the grosser forms of bias and prejudice; nevertheless, they can also be ideologically in favor of positivism, mechanism, atheism, or secularism. They too can atrophy, become detached from reality, and become little gods. There is

5. Copleston, *A History of Philosophy,* 414.

nothing that can replace the pure, detached desire to know as the ground, source, and motive of all our knowing.

Experiential Objectivity

In experiential objectivity, objectivity is considered at the level of experience, in the sense of facing up to the data as given, rather than as screened or imagined or distorted. The data are the given, but even at this level there are ways that we can ignore aspects of the data, pick out things that we like, screen away things we are not prepared to face, or supply by wishful thinking what is not even there.

The data itself is pre-intellectual and pre-conceptual, the given as given. In itself it precedes questions and thinking. The categories of true and false, or real and unreal, do not apply until questioning transforms the data into hypotheses and judgments. But even at the level of sense our faculties can play tricks on us. We can be in denial when a doctor makes a diagnosis of a terminal illness; we go looking for a doctor who will give a more pleasing diagnosis. Conspiracy theorists will twist data, ignore data, or line up everything in support of their already established conspiracy. We can avoid data: we have serious chest pain, but refuse to visit the doctor. Memories can be repressed: traumatic incidents are forgotten and happier narratives constructed to cover over the gaps. A witness might tell half the story but leave out the other half. There are many ways in which data can be twisted at the level of experiencing.

Data can be either data of sense or data of consciousness. Both are equally given as experience, namely, that into which we inquire. The massive bias of contemporary culture is to privilege the data of sense and to ignore or deny the data of consciousness. Denying the existence and availability of the data of consciousness results in the loss of mind, a distrust of the process of knowing, and a view of knowledge that can do without knowers.

Conclusion

When I examined the sources of misunderstanding, I identified the deep source of misunderstanding in the unquestioned imaginative assumptions about what is real. I identified the predominance of extroverted consciousness, which leads to sense and imagination as the criterion of the real; what is real is what is out there now real. I identified intuition as another source of misunderstanding understanding: it is an illusion that we know by an intellectual seeing, a direct contact with the object, a simple, single, immediate touching of the object. Such misunderstanding pervades all discussions about subjectivity and objectivity.

However, I have clearly shown that human knowledge belongs to judgment and only to judgment. Judgment is the culmination of a process whereby we ask questions about what we have experienced in order to understand; our understanding is then subject to critical review by a process of reflective understanding in order to show that the criteria of truth are satisfied. Only then as reasonable adults can we affirm a judgment. Further, we usually ask about the possible applications of the discovery, or what is the best thing to do with the innovation. Thus, we embark on considering alternatives, and comparing and contrasting values, which culminates in a deliberative insight and a judgment of value.

I have tackled the difficult topics of subjectivity and objectivity in light of judgments of truth, and I have established a foundation that can be expanded in any direction. Operating in terms of judgments makes it an easy matter to tackle the skeptical, relativist, or Kantian objections regarding our knowing of what is objectively real. This is accomplished through the process of self-appropriation, through identifying unquestioned, imaginative assumptions, and through identifying the judgments that establish a critical theory of objectivity.

12

Mind Recovered

This final chapter is an exercise in integration and expansion. Where precisely have we arrived, where do we stand, and what use is this for the future? The approach, the method, and the style of this text is not typical of what one expects in a contemporary philosophical text. The conclusions are mostly countercultural; they challenge many of the positions of contemporary schools of philosophy and much of the political correctness that pervades our culture. I have arrived at the strange position that philosophy is based on facts—not the facts of the external world, but the facts of how the human mind actually works. I have made the outrageous claim that philosophy can be verifiable. This chapter highlights some of the principal arguments and conclusions of the text and explores their implications for the role of philosophy in the healing of our contemporary culture.

Being at Home in a Philosophy of Interiority

The journey involved in following this text is not just long and difficult, it is also included the stage by stage ascending of a mountain. It has involved moving from common-sense descriptions, to theoretical thinking, to understanding understanding, and in the end, to the higher viewpoint represented by a philosophy of philosophy, or a philosophy of interiority. By interiority I mean, not anything vague and mystical, but a position arrived at on the basis of our understanding of understanding. Interiority is not just a new theory: it is a new method, a new philosophical paradigm, a comprehensive philosophical viewpoint. From this viewpoint we are able to define and relate common sense and theory, description and explanation, classical and statistical, truth and value, the relations of the sciences to one another, lower viewpoints and higher viewpoints, and understanding misunderstanding.

Interiority represents a Copernican Revolution in the sense that instead of starting with objectivity (metaphysics, the data of sense, and science), we start with subjectivity (an epistemology based on the data of consciousness). We start by describing the act of understanding and in the end reach a critical realist objectivity as the ultimate goal. The central discovery along that vector is the conviction that the real is known in judgment and only in the affirmation of a correct judgment on the basis of the sufficiency of the evidence for the conclusion. On these grounds, one is justified in talking of the recovery of the mind, as I have offered a rediscovery of the unlimited power of the human mind to ask questions, and have outlined the activities needed to reach a critical realist knowledge of truth and value.

This suggests that the role of philosophy might be considered in a new light. It is not an abstract, irrelevant, speculative, disputed set of topics. It is not just for learning by rote, nor for absorbing the myriad thoughts and writings of philosophers throughout history; it is not about being clever, obscure, inspiring, original, or interesting. It is about the intellectual development of the aspiring philosopher—to help the seeker to discover the power of his or her own mind, to reach for intellectual maturity, and to be at home in critical thinking where correct judgment is the criterion of the real. It is personal rather than impersonal, engaging rather than detached, of relevance to life and love, and an integral part of the overall development of the human person seeking truth and value and love. It is not apart from the culture but should be a critic of the culture and a force for healing in society. The philosopher-king might have gone out of fashion, but the role of philosophy is to grasp the unity in the human person, in history, in dialectic, and the universe; it is a worldview that encompasses everything and excludes nothing. The method of self-appropriation helps to rediscover the infinite capacity of the human mind to unrestricted questioning and an ever fuller, deeper, and more comprehensive objective knowing of the universe of being.

Each successive higher viewpoint unifies and organizes data at a higher level of generality. A philosophy of science should understand the relationship between the sciences on the basis of some rational principle, but need not have a detailed knowledge of each and every empirical science. A philosophy of interiority will confer an understanding and organization of the whole of human life, the universe of being, the totality of all there is; however, it will not necessarily have a detailed knowledge of any specific discipline. The philosopher can be called the complete generalist. The advantage of generality is an overall unity and organization by which we can see how all the parts fit into the whole, how the parts are related within a whole. The disadvantage is that it tends to lose touch with the specificity of the concrete; it does not give specific answers to particular questions. It indicates where and how the answers are to be found but leaves that work to the specialists in the appropriate field. Specialists need generalists, as much as generalists need specialists. At some stage the work of the specialists must be integrated into the context of the discipline involved. At some stage the organizing framework of the generalist must incorporate and integrate the work of the particular disciplines. Every advance in knowledge is a contribution to that specific discipline and also to our understanding of the whole. Generality and specificity are complementary poles in the advancement of understanding.

Reaching a philosophy of interiority involves an arduous climb through many levels of understanding. Being at home in interiority involves multiple intellectual habits of implementing, applying, propagating, and explaining the principles of a critical realist position. The categories of systematic theoretical thinking need to be transposed into the categories of interiority. Lonergan showed how the categories of an Aristotelian/Thomist epistemology can be transposed into terms of psychology and self-appropriation. He also indicated how that needs to be done in transforming the systematic, theoretical Scholastic theology of the Middle Ages into the language of psychology, spirituality, and interiority. Neither task is complete. The same transposition needs to be achieved in the empirical sciences. The empirical sciences would benefit enormously if they better understood their own method as theory verified in instances, and if they understood the difference between verifiable and unverifiable images. They would benefit if they understood the difference between classical and statistical methods and that they are complementary and not mutually exclusive, and if they understood the role of philosophical presuppositions, which sometimes help and sometimes are a hindrance to correct scientific understanding. They would benefit if they understood that the real is to be found not in some imaginative out there, but in the truth of correct equations, laws, and judgments. Although this generation is familiar with the notions of subjectivity and consciousness, there is much to be done to complete the turn to the subject, and to be at home in a subjectivity that leads to genuine objectivity.

Method and Methods

In a philosophy of interiority emphasis shifts from formal logic to method. Questioning, experiencing, understanding, and judging truth and value is the basic method that I have uncovered and exploited in this text. This basic method applies to all areas of human knowing—practical, theoretical, ethical, skill, expertise, manufacturing, economics, and so on. Wherever questions for understanding are asked they can be dealt with in terms of a normative pattern of recurrent and related operations yielding cumulative and progressive results.[1] There emerges a sequence of intellectual activities culminating in a judgment; there is a right way and a wrong way of performing these activities, and if we reach correct conclusions that opens the way to further fruitful questions yielding further positive results. It is a basic universal method applicable to different areas, in different ways, yet not uniformly, but flexibly and creatively. Is there any discipline under heaven that can dispense with correct understanding? Is there any area of human knowing where the precepts of being attentive, intelligent, reasonable, and responsible do not apply? This study has focused on applying this method to the human mind itself, to the data of consciousness as well as the data of sense. There is a huge prejudice against studying mental activities and this has to be overcome; I have shown how fruitful this study can be.

There is a relation between this generalized notion of method and the specific methods developed in any particular specialized discipline. Methods are not to be understood as blindly following rules so that one will automatically arrive at results. Particular methods are intelligent, reasonable, and responsible in their specific sphere. I would formulate the relation between universal method and specific methods as the former underlying, penetrating, and transforming the latter. A universal method underlies particular methods in the sense that it is always there, and it is taken for granted even though attention is focused on more particular elements. It penetrates particular methods because there is always a structure to knowing; it is always a question or desire looking for a solution, form, law, or explanation in concrete data or in images. There is always the process of emergence of the solution and a checking to ensure that the solution is the correct one. A generalized method can transform a debate or discussion or science in that it presents a criterion of the real as the truly verified and often removes imaginative blocks imposed by false assumptions. There is a generalized methodology but it is related to the most specific, detailed, varied methods in the above terms.

Method will take on a different configuration in various areas; we can distinguish between a classical method, statistical method, genetic method, and dialectical method. Classical method is looking for direct understanding in areas where the abstract converges on the concrete; in this approach, positive understanding is to be achieved and that law, equation, or system can be applied extensively. Statistical method is employed where data diverges nonsystematically from the norm. Probabilities, averages, rates, and frequencies give us knowledge, formulas, and propositions; however, they contain a certain lack of expected intelligibility. They are not as satisfying

---

1. Lonergan, *Method in Theology*, 4.

as direct insights; our world is not uniformly intelligible. Genetic method is needed to understand living things, which have to be grasped as a linked sequence of stages which emerge successively. Living things are born, grow, reproduce and die; they need to be understood not as static entities but as dynamic. They are self-organizing and self-moving. Finally, there is the phenomenon of conflict, misunderstanding, and disagreement to be grasped somewhat imperfectly in a dialectical method.

Implementing a generalized method could result in a reoriented empirical science. The method of science can be expressed as theory verified in instances, thus paralleling the activities of experiencing understanding and verifying. A critical realism provides a framework of thinking where (1) what is real is what is verified, (2) images are different from ideas, (3) there are verifiable images of description and constructed pedagogical images of theory, and (4) there are classical and statistical methods that are complementary. Determinism, indeterminism, reductionism, and materialism are philosophical positions often assumed explicitly or implicitly by scientists. These assumptions effect the kind of questions that the scientist asks and the kind of research and experiments that are conducted. They effect the interpretation of results and what is considered important or not. They effect who will get funding and which projects will be undertaken. They effect the direction the science moves in, the kind of projects undertaken, and what results will be found.

The position of critical realism would suggest the fruitful questions to ask, the correct method to use for verification, and the right way of fitting new discoveries into a correct worldview. If philosophy is about the whole and the sciences are about the various parts, then surely the two disciplines are complementary rather than opposed. It is the philosopher who asks about human knowing, method, judgment, truth, value, and develops a coherent worldview. It is the scientist who specializes in a certain area of this diverse universe and develops laws and ideas appropriate to that area. The scientist can, of course, indulge in philosophical speculation but must remember that that is not his or her particular area of expertise. The relation of the sciences to one another and scientific method itself are not questions that are proper to any particular scientific discipline; but they are proper to philosophy.

A critical realist philosophy and method could result in a reoriented human science. The human sciences particularly need a correct philosophy of the human person as a framework for their contribution to further understanding of the human person and society. Behaviorism, materialism, reductionism, and the like propose unhelpful questions, block the really fruitful questions, usually emphasize quantitative data as opposed to qualitative and interpretive research, and interpret all results in terms of their assumed philosophy. The human sciences must recognize that the human person is one integrated being who performs many interrelated activities, such as feeling, questioning, understanding, judging truth and value, deciding and acting, and relating to the ultimate. The human person grows through a sequence of stages, struggles within him/herself between progress and decline, and is free and responsible. The human person is part of the universe, and can only be correctly understood as such, having emerged after many billions of years, and as far as we know, is the greatest thing the universe has produced. The human person is social: emerging from a family, living in a society, dependent on global conditions, living on one planet with seven billion other equal human persons. Christian Smith is an example of a sociologist working from a framework of critical realism.[2]

Can a critical realist philosophy play a role in healing contemporary culture or the culture of any given society? Culture is the beliefs, truths, and values that inform a given way of life. It is a rather nebulous reality, especially in a pluralist society where one might argue that there are many cultures and subcultures in place. But the actual culture is always a mixture of true and false, good and bad, values and disvalues, good practices and bad. It is a complex reality with many faces and tentacles. It usually expresses itself in a set of beliefs and values that are politically correct, namely, acceptable to the majority. Critical realism suggests that there is a correct way to find truth and value, that truth and value are everywhere and can be criticized and evaluated. There is a huge role for a sound pedagogy and philosophy to inform the educational system of any society. Putting aside the rather exaggerated system of Plato, it remains that philosophy has a critical role in the informing the educational system for the healing of the entire culture. This is of course a huge topic that cannot be embarked upon here. In my own experience of teaching philosophy for over 35 years, an education by way of self-appropriation and critical realism confers on the student a certain confident maturity and basic foundations. They have a personal grasp of their own minds, decisions, and feelings; implement a method of approaching all problems; are unperturbed by assaults on reason and value; and can defend their own position and specialize in any area. They do not know the answers to all questions, but they do know how and where to find them.

Dialectic Remains to be Overcome

The problem of dialectic will not just go away. Human knowing involves a tension of opposites. The principles in conflict can variously be identified

2. See, for example, Smith's *What Is a Person?*

as the following: sensing as opposed to understanding, imagination as opposed to intelligence, an animal criterion of the real as opposed to a critical criterion of the real, knowing as confrontation or knowing as identity and difference, and knowing on the model of seeing as opposed to knowing as a discursive series of activities. This is the root of the fundamental differences in philosophical positions. Philosophy remains divided into schools, which are in conflict and deep disagreement over fundamentals; philosophy thus shows no sign of convergence or dialogue or coming together. What some consider as progress others evaluate as decline.

In a way, the problem can never be overcome, as human knowing will always remain as a unique sequence of questioning, experiencing, understanding, and judging. Sensation, the imagination, the animal criterion of the real, and knowing as touching or seeing will always be in place in the child before the emergence of intelligence. On the one hand, understanding depends on and will build on experiencing; on the other hand, sensation and imagination will always impose its imaginative presupposition of what human knowing is like. The tension in human knowing is intrinsic to the nature of human knowing. It is tension that can be overcome but never eliminated.

It can be overcome by being recognized as a problem, by being made explicit, by becoming a topic for discussion. Attention could be shifted from the content of philosophical propositions to the method of reaching the affirmation of propositions. The elements of the problem could be laid out and identified, with clear examples and illustrations. Collaborative discussion and research could be accomplished on the most fundamental of all problems, namely, the root cause of philosophical disagreement and conflict. What are the root causes that interfere with the spontaneous procedures of intelligence? My answer is given in this text. But then, not everyone will agree with this solution.

Conclusion

This text has been an exercise in communication and is conspicuously lacking in scholarship and erudition. It has presented a view on human knowing, which is difficult because it calls for self-reflection and self-appropriation. It is easier to deal with theories, concepts, definitions, and divisions than it is to attend to one's own mind and pin down the buzzing confusion or sort out imagining from intelligence, the beginning from the end. However, it is worth doing. I have tried to treat every thinker in the history of philosophy as making some contribution to the clarification of the goal of philosophy, even if only by way of illustrating wrong paths. At least I have tackled a deep and serious topic, and if I have fallen short or made mistakes, even these will be an indirect contribution to the progress of philosophy.

I can only end with an acknowledgement of my debt to Lonergan. This has been a text on the human mind and not a text on Lonergan, and so I did not make many references to him or his work. He saved me from a neo-Scholasticism in decline in 1962. More detail and depth can be found in Lonergan's *Insight*. That is indeed a difficult book, but he has a habit of hitting the nail on the head, penetrating to the heart of the matter, and saying it like it is. It is said that philosophers rarely change their minds. *Insight* changed mine, and it might anyone who takes up the disciplined work of reading it.

Bibliography

Arendt, Hannah. *The Life of the Mind: Part One Thinking. Part Two Willing.* London: Harvest, 1971.

Aristotle. *Aristotle's Categories and Propositions.* Translated by Hippocrates Apostle. Des Moines: Peripatetic, 1980.

———. *Aristotle's Metaphysics.* Translated by Hippocrates Apostle. Des Moines: Peripatetic, 1979.

———. *Aristotle's on the Soul (De Anima).* Translated by Hippocrates Apostle. Des Moines: Peripatetic, 1981.

———. *The Ethics of Aristotle: The Nicomachean Ethics.* Translated by J. A. K. Thomson. London: Penguin, 1953.

Augustine. *Confessions.* Modern English Version. Grand Rapids: Spire, 2008.

Bacon, Francis, *The New Organon,* Edited by Lisa Jardine and Michael Silverthorne. Cambridge: Cambridge University Press, 2000.

Barden, Garrett. *After Principles.* Notre Dame: University of Notre Dame Press, 1990.

Barden, Garrett, and Philp McShane. *Towards Self Meaning.* Dublin: Gill and Macmillan, 1969.

Berger, Peter, and Thomas Luckmann. *The Social Construction of Reality: A Treatise in the Sociology of Knowledge.* New York: Doubleday, 1966.

Betti, Arianna. *Against Facts.* Cambridge, MA: MIT Press, 2015.

Beveridge, William. *The Art of Scientific Investigation.* London: Heinemann, 1950.

Blackmore, Susan. *Consciousness: A Very Short Introduction.* London: Oxford University Press, 2005.

Born, Max. *The Born-Einstein Letters: Friendship, Politics and Physics in Uncertain Times.* New York: Macmillan, 2005.

Braine, David. *Language and Human Understanding: The Roots of Creativity in Speech and Thought.* Washington, DC: Catholic University of America Press, 2014.

Brockman, John, ed. *Thinking: The New Science of Decision-Making, Problem-Solving, and Prediction.* New York: Harper Perennial, 2013.

Burtt, Edwin Arthur. *The Metaphysical Foundations of Modern Physical Science.* London: Routledge, 1980.

Butler, Christopher. *Postmodernism: A Very Short Introduction.* Oxford: Oxford University Press, 2002.

Butterfield, Herbert. *The Origins of Modern Science.* New York: Free, 1965.

Byrne, Patrick. *The Ethics of Discernment: Lonergan's Foundations for Ethics*. Toronto: University of Toronto Press, 2016.

Chalmers, Alan F. *What Is This Thing Called Science? An Assessment of the Nature and Status of Science and Its Methods*. Philadelphia: Open University Press, 1988.

Chaudhuri, Haridas. *The Evolution of Integral Consciousness*. Chennai: Theosophical, 1977.

Chesterton, G. K. *Saint Thomas Aquinas: "The Dumb Ox."* Nashville: Sam Torode, 2011.

Clayton, Philip, and Paul Davies, eds. *The Re-Emergence of Emergence: The Emergentist Hypothesis from Science to Religion*. Oxford: Oxford University Press, 2006.

Conn, Walter E. *Conscience: Development and Self-Transcendence*. Birmingham, AL: Religious Education, 1981.

———. *The Desiring Self: Rooting Pastoral Counseling and Spiritual Direction in Self-Transcendence*. New York: Paulist, 1998.

Copleston, Frederick. *A History of Philosophy: Modern Philosophy*. Vol. 7. New York: Image, 1994.

Cronin, Brian. *Foundations of Philosophy: Lonergan's Cognitional Theory and Epistemology*. Nairobi: Consolata Institute of Philosophy Press, 1999.

———. *Value Ethics: A Lonergan Perspective*. Nairobi: Consolata Institute of Philosophy Press, 2006.

Crowe, Frederick. *Appropriating the Lonergan Idea*. Washington, DC: Catholic University of America Press, 1989.

———. *Lonergan*. Collegeville: Liturgical, 1992.

———. *The Lonergan Enterprise*. Washington, DC: Cowley, 1984.

———. *Old Things and New: A Strategy for Education*. Atlanta: Scholars, 1985.

Damasio, Antonio. *The Feeling of What Happens: Body and Emotion in the Making of Consciousness*. Orlando: Harvest, 1999.

Danaher, William. *Insight in Chemistry*. New York: University Press of America, 1988.

de Mello, Anthony. *Sadhana, A Way to God: Christian Exercises in Eastern Form*. New York: Doubleday, 1978.

Dennett, Daniel. *Consciousness Explained*. New York: Back Bay, 1991.

Descartes, René. *Discourse on Method and the Meditations*. Translated by F. E. Sutcliffe. New York: Penguin, 1970.

———. *Principles of Philosophy*, Translated by V. R. Miller and R. P. Millar. Dordrecht: Kluwer Academic, 1991.

Dewey, John. *How We Think*. Lexington: Renaissance Classics, 2012.

Dimnet, Ernest. *The Art of Thinking*. New York: Simon and Schuster, 1928.

Doyle, Arthur Conan. *The Complete Sherlock Holmes*. Vol. 1. New York: Doubleday, 1906.

Dreyfus, Hubert, and Taylor Charles, *Retrieving Realism*. Cambridge, MA: Harvard University Press, 2015.

Eddington, Arthur. *The Nature of the Physical World*. Cambridge: Cambridge University Press, 1928.

Felt, James. *Human Knowing: A Prelude to Metaphysics*. Notre Dame: University of Notre Dame Press, 2005.

Flanagan, Joseph. *Quest for Self-Knowledge: An Essay in Lonergan's Philosophy*. Toronto: University of Toronto Press, 1997.

Flanagan, Owen. *The Really Hard Problem: Meaning in a Material World*. Cambridge, MA: MIT Press, 2009.

Fletcher, John. *Situation Ethics: The New Morality.* Westminster: Knox, 1966.

Foster, Jack. *How to Get Ideas.* San Francisco: Berrett-Koehler, 2007.

Gardner, Howard. *Extraordinary Minds: Portraits of Exceptional Individuals and an Examination of Our Own Extraordinariness.* New York: Basic, 1997.

———. *Multiple Intelligences: New Horizons.* New York: Basic, 2006.

Garrett, Eric A. *Why Do We Go to the Zoo? Communication, Animals, and the Cultural-Historical Experience of Zoos.* Madison, NJ: Fairleigh Dickinson University Press, 2014.

Giorgi, Amedeo. *The Descriptive Phenomenological Method in Psychology: A Modified Husserlian Approach.* Pittsburgh: Duquesne University Press, 2009.

Goleman, Daniel. *Emotional Intelligence: Why It Can Matter More than IQ.* London: Bloomsbury, 1996.

Gredt, Joseph. *Elementa Philosophiae Aristotelico-Thomisticae.* Vol 2. Friburg: Herder, 1938.

Gregson, Vernon. *Lonergan, Spirituality, and the Meeting of Religions.* Lanham, MD: University Press of America, 1985.

Griffiths, Paul. *Intellectual Appetite: A Theological Grammar.* Washington, DC: Catholic University of America Press, 2009.

Hadamard, Jacques. *The Mathematician's Mind: The Psychology of Invention in the Mathematical Field.* Princeton: Princeton University Press, 1973.

Hartmann, Nicolai. *Moral Values: Volume 2 of Ethics.* New Brunswick, NJ: Transaction, 2002.

Hebb, Donald O. *Essay on Mind.* New York: Psychology, 1980.

Hegel, G. W. F. *The Phenomenology of Spirit.* Translated by A.V. Miller. Oxford: Oxford University Press, 1977.

Heidegger, Martin. *Being and Time.* Translated by Joan Stambaugh. Albany: State University of New York Press, 2010.

Helminiak, Daniel. *The Human Core of Spirituality: Mind as Psyche and Spirit.* New York: State University of New York Press, 1996.

Hildebrand, Dietrich, von. *Ethics.* Chicago: Franciscan Herald, 1953.

Hirshfield, Alan. *Eureka Man: The Life and Legacy of Archimedes.* New York: Walker, 2009.

Hirst, R. J. "Primary and Secondary Qualities." In *The Encyclopaedia of Philosophy,* edited by Paul Edwards, 6:455–57. London: Collier Macmillan, 1967.

Hoenen, Peter. *Reality and Judgment according to St. Thomas.* Chicago: Regnery, 1952.

Holland, John. *Emergence: From Chaos to Order.* New York: Basic, 1998.

Hume, David. *An Enquiry Concerning Human Understanding.* Edited by Eric Steinberg. Indianapolis: Hackett, 1977.

———. *A Treatise of Human Nature. Book One: Of the Understanding.* Edited by D. Macnabb. London: Fontana, 1962.

Husserl, Edmund. *Analyses Concerning Passive and Active Synthesis: Lectures on Transcendental Logic.* Translated by Anthony Steinbock. Dordrecht: Kluwer, 2001.

———. *Cartesian Meditations: An Introduction to Phenomenology.* Translated by Dorion Cairns. The Hague: Nijhoff, 1970.

———. *The Crisis of European Sciences and Transcendental Phenomenology: An Introduction to Phenomenological Philosophy,* Translated by David Carr. Evanston, IL: Northwestern University Press, 1970.

————. *Ideas Pertaining to a Pure Phenomenology and to a Phenomenological Philosophy: First Book: General Introduction to a Pure Phenomenology.* Translated by F. Kersten. The Hague: Nijhoff, 1983.

————. *Phenomenology and the Crisis of Philosophy: Philosophy as Rigorous Science and Philosophy and the Crisis of European Man.* Translated by Quentin Lauer. New York: Harper Torchbooks, 1965.

Hutchinson, Eliot. *How to Think Creatively.* New York: Abingdon, 1949.

Isaacson, Walter. *Einstein: His Life and Universe.* New York: Simon and Schuster, 2007.

Jaynes, Julian. *The Origin of Consciousness in the Breakdown of the Bicameral Mind.* Boston: Houghton Mifflin, 1976.

Kahneman, Daniel. *Thinking, Fast and Slow.* New York: Farrar, Straus and Giroux, 2011.

Kant, Immanuel. *Critique of Pure Reason.* Translated by Norman Kemp Smith. New York: St. Martin's Press, 1965.

Keller, Helen. *The Story of My Life.* New York: Doubleday, 1954.

Köhler, Wolfgang. *The Mentality of Apes.* New York: Liveright, 1973.

Kuhn, Thomas. *The Structure of Scientific Revolutions.* Chicago: University of Chicago Press, 1962.

Kukla, André, and Joel Walmsley. *Mind: A Historical and Philosophical Introduction to the Major Theories.* Indianapolis: Hackett, 2006.

Lawrence, Frederick. "The Fragility of Consciousness: Lonergan and the Postmodern Concern for the Other." In *Communication and Lonergan: Common Ground for Forging the New Age,* edited by Thomas Farrell and Paul Soukup, 173–211. Kansas City: Sheed and Ward, 1993.

Levinas, Emmanuel. *The Theory of Intuition in Husserl's Phenomenology.* Translated by André Orianne. 2nd ed. Evanston, IL: Northwestern University Press, 1995.

Liddy, Richard. *Startling Strangeness: Reading Lonergan's Insight.* New York: University Press of America, 2007.

Locke, John. *An Essay concerning Human Understanding.* Lexington: WLC, 2009.

Lonergan, Bernard. *Collection.* Edited by Frederick E. Crowe and Robert Doran. Collected Works of Bernard Lonergan 4. Toronto: University of Toronto Press, 1988.

————. *Insight: A Study of Human Understanding.* Edited by Frederick E. Crowe and Robert Doran. Collected works of Bernard Lonergan 3. Toronto: University of Toronto Press, 1992.

————. *Method in Theology.* New York: Herder and Herder, 1972.

————. *Philosophical and Theological Papers 1958–1964.* Edited by Robert C. Croken, Frederick E. Crowe, and Robert Doran. Collected Works of Bernard Lonergan 6. Toronto: University of Toronto Press, 1996.

————. *A Second Collection.* Edited by William F. J. Ryan and Bernard J. Tyrell. Philadelphia: Westminster, 1975.

————. *A Third Collection: Papers by Bernard J.F. Lonergan, SJ.* Edited by Frederick E. Crowe. New York: Paulist, 1958.

————. *Topics in Education.* Collected Works of Bernard Lonergan 10. Toronto: University of Toronto Press, 1993.

————. *Understanding and Being.* Edited by Elizabeth A. Morelli and Mark D. Morelli. Collected Works of Bernard Lonergan 5. Toronto: University of Toronto Press, 1990.

————. *Verbum: Word and Idea in Aquinas.* Edited by Frederick Crowe and Robert Doran. Collected Works of Bernard Lonergan 2. Toronto: University of Toronto Press, 1997.

MacIntyre, Alasdair. *After Virtue: A Study in Moral Theory.* Notre Dame: University of Notre Dame Press, 1981.

Manen, Max, van. *Phenomenology of Practice: Meaning-Giving Methods in Phenomenological Research and Writing.* Walnut Creek, CA: Left Coast, 2014.

Maslow, Abraham. *Religions, Values, and Peak-Experiences.* New York: Viking, 1970.

Mathews, William. *Lonergan's Quest; A Study of Desire in the Authoring of Insight.* Toronto: University of Toronto Press, 2005.

McCarthy, Michael H. *The Crisis of Philosophy.* New York: State University of New York Press, 1990.

McDowell, John. *Mind and World.* Cambridge, MA: Harvard University Press, 1996.

McPartland, Thomas. "Consciousness and Normative Subjectivity: Lonergan's Unique Foundational Enterprise." *Method: Journal of Lonergan Studies* 13, no. 2 (1995) 111–30.

McGilchrist, Iain. *The Master and His Emissary: The Divided Brain and the Making of the Western World.* New Haven: Yale University Press, 2009.

Merleau-Ponty, Maurice. *Phenomenology of Perception.* Translated by Donald Landes. London: Routledge, 2012.

———. *The Primacy of Perception and Other Essays on Phenomenological Psychology, the Philosophy of Art, History and Politics.* Edited by James M. Edie. Translated by John Wild. Evanston, IL: Northwestern University Press, 1964.

Merriam-Webster's Collegiate Dictionary. 10th ed. Springfield, MA: Merriam-Webster, 1997.

Mill, John Stuart. *A System of Logic: Ratiocinative and Inductive.* London: Longmans, Green, Reader, and Dyer, 1872.

Morelli, Mark, *Self-Possession: Being at Home in Conscious Performance.* Boston: Lonergan Institute, 2015.

Morowitz, Harold. *The Emergence of Everything: How the World Became Complex.* Oxford University Press, 2002.

Mullahy, Patrick, ed. *A Study of Interpersonal Relations: New Contributions to Psychiatry.* New York: Science House, 1967.

Murray, Edward. *Imaginative Thinking and Human Existence.* Pittsburgh: Duquesne University Press, 1986.

Nagel, Thomas. *Mind and Cosmos: Why the Materialist Neo-Darwinian Conception of Nature Is Almost Certainly False.* Oxford: Oxford University Press, 2012.

Newton, Isaac. *The Principia: Mathematical Principles of Natural Philosophy.* Translated by Bernard Cohen and Anne Whitman. Berkeley: University of California Press, 1999.

Nietzsche, Friedrich. *Beyond Good and Evil: Prelude to a Philosophy of the Future.* Translated by Walter Kaufman. New York: Vintage, 1966.

O'Shea, Donal. *The Poincaré Conjecture: In Search of the Shape of the Universe.* New York: Walker, 2007.

Phillips, John. *The Origins of Intellect: Piaget's Theory.* San Francisco: Freeman, 1975.

Pinker, Stephen. *How the Mind Works.* London: Norton, 1997.

Pittsburgh Symphony Orchestra. *BeethovenFest: The Revolutionary.* Program. Heinz Hall, Pittsburgh, PA, December 5, 2014.

Plato. *The Meno.* In *Plato: Complete Works,* edited by John M. Cooper, 879–97. Indianapolis: Hackett, 1997.

————. *Theatetetus.* In *Plato: Complete Works,* edited by John M. Cooper, 157–234. Indianapolis: Hackett, 1997.

Poincaré, Henri. *Science and Hypothesis.* New York: Dover, 1952.

Polya, George. *How to Solve It: A New Aspect of Mathematical Method.* Princeton: Princeton University Press, 1945.

Popper, Karl. *The Logic of Scientific Discovery.* New York: Routledge, 2002.

Potter, Vincent. *On Understanding Understanding: A Philosophy of Knowledge.* New York: Fordham University Press, 1994.

Robinson, Marilynne. *Absence of Mind: The Dispelling of Inwardness from the Modern Myth of the Self.* New Haven: Yale University Press, 2010.

Renić, Dalibor. *Ethical and Epistemic Normativity: Lonergan and Virtue Epistemology.* Milwaukee: Marquette University Press, 2012.

Root-Bernstein, Robert, and Michèle M. Root-Bernstein. *Sparks of Genius: The Thirteen Thinking Tools of the World's Most Creative People.* Boston: Houghton Mifflin, 1999.

Rorty, Richard. *Philosophy and the Mirror of Nature.* Princeton: Princeton University Press, 1979.

Rothenberg, Albert. *Creativity and Madness: New Findings and Old Stereotypes.* Baltimore: Johns Hopkins University Press, 1990.

Rothenberg, Albert, and Carl R. Hausman, eds. *The Creativity Question.* Durham, NC: Duke University Press, 1976.

Ryle, Gilbert. *The Concept of Mind.* Chicago: University of Chicago Press, 2000.

Sala, Giovanni B. *Lonergan and Kant: Five Essays on Human Knowledge.* Toronto: University of Toronto Press, 1994.

Schear, Joseph, ed. *Mind, Reason, and Being-In-The-World: The McDowell-Dreyfus Debate.* London: Routledge, 2013.

Scheler, Max. *On Feeling, Knowing, and Valuing.* Edited by Harold Bershady. Chicago: University of Chicago Press, 1992.

Schwitzgebel, Eric. *Perplexities of Consciousness.* Cambridge, MA: MIT Press, 2011.

Searle, John. *Mind: A Brief Introduction.* London: Oxford University Press, 2004.

————. *The Mystery of Consciousness.* New York: New York Review, 1997.

————. *The Rediscovery of the Mind.* Cambridge, MA: MIT Press, 1998.

————. *Seeing Things as They Are: A Theory of Perception.* Oxford: Oxford University Press, 2015

Sellers, Wilfred. *Empiriciam and the Philosophy of Mind.* Cambridge, MA: Harvard University Press, 1997.

Smith, Christian, *What Is a Person? Rethinking Humanity, Social Life, and the Moral Good from the Person Up.* Chicago: University of Chicago Press, 2010.

Smith, Jonathan, Paul Flowers, and Michael Larkin. *Interpretative Phenomenological Analysis: Theory, Method and Research.* Los Angeles: Sage, 2009.

Snell, Bruno. *The Discovery of Mind.* New York: Harper & Row, 1960.

Snell, R. J. *Through a Glass Darkly: Bernard Lonergan and Richard Rorty on Knowing without a God's-eye View.* Milwaukee: Marquette University Press, 2006.

Sokolowski, Robert. *Introduction to Phenomenology.* New York: Cambridge University Press, 2000.

Sparrow, Tom. *The End of Phenomenology: Metaphysics and the New Realism.* Edinburgh: Edinburgh University Press, 2014.

Sternberg, Robert, and Janet Davidson, eds. *The Nature of Insight.* Cambridge, MA: MIT Press, 1995.

Strevens, Michael. *Depth: An Account of Scientific Explanation*. Cambridge, MA: Harvard University Press, 2011.

———. *Tychomancy: Inferring Probability from Causal Structure*. Cambridge, MA: Harvard University Press, 2013.

Taylor, Charles. "Retrieving Realism." In *Mind, Reason, and Being-in-the-World: The McDowell-Dreyfus Debate*, edited by Joseph Schear, 61–90. London: Routledge, 2013.

Thompson, David. *Daniel Dennett: Contemporary American Thinkers*. London: Continuum, 2009.

Toulmin, Stephen. *Human Understanding: The Collective Use and Evolution of Concepts*. Princeton: Princeton University Press, 1972.

Vaughan, Michael. *The Thinking Effect: Rethinking Thinking to Create Great Leaders and the New Value Worker*. Boston: Brealey, 2013.

Vertin, Michael. "Lonergan on Consciousness: Is There a Fifth Level?" *Method: Journal of Lonergan Studies* 12, no. 1 (1994) 1–36.

Wallas, Graham. *The Art of Thought*. Kent, UK: Solis, 2014.

Watson, James. *DNA: The Secret of Life*. London: Arrow, 2004.

Watson, Peter. *Ideas: A History of Thought and Invention, from Fire to Freud*. New York: Harper Perennial, 2005.

Webb, Eugene. *Philosophers of Consciousness: Polanyi, Lonergan, Voegelin, Ricoeur, Girard, Kierkegaard*. Seattle: University of Washington Press, 1988.

Wilber, Ken. *A Brief History of Everything*. Dublin: Gill and Macmillan, 1996.

Wilson, Edward O. *Consilience: The Unity of Knowledge*. London: Abacus, 1998.

Young, John Webb. *A Technique for Producing Ideas*. New York: Walking Lion, 1960.

Index

Note: Page number in bold type face indicate a substantial discussion.